N I L

Episodes in the literary conquest of

New York

NIL

void during the nineteenth century

ROBERT MARTIN ADAMS

Oxford University Press 1966

809
A

Contents

NIL

Opening

solitude, récif, étoile . . .
MALLARMÉ, *"Salut"*

Nothing is closer to the supreme commonplace of our commonplace age than its preoccupation with Nothing [1] — that is, with the elected experience and deliberate exploitation of Nothing, which may be un-self-conscious non-experience in one sense, but in another is willful submission of oneself to non-experience as an active form of experience. Experiments which have captured the imagination of the time deal with weightlessness, silence, interruption of the sense-continuum. A popular comedian bears, by choice, the first name of Zero. A popular comic strip portrays an owl lecturing to an alligator and an infant rabbit on a new type of mathematics, called Aftermath, in which zero is the only number permitted; all problems have the same solution — zero — and consequently the discipline consists of discovering new problems to lead to the inevitable answer.[2] A musical composition has been played — and in some halls enthusiastically encored — which consists of 4 minutes and 33 seconds of unbroken silence rendered by a skilled pianist, and in evening dress, seated at an operational Steinway. String quartets are convoked to render — *allegro con fuoco* — wholly inaudible compositions. The philosopher who speaks most closely to the contemporary condition is Jean-Paul Sartre,

1. Nothing in the sense of void will be distinguished from the "there's nothing worse than" usage by a capital letter.
2. *Pogo*, 20 March 1965.

3

whose preoccupation with Nothingness and the pressures it brings to bear on men is too well known to need documenting. Kenneth Burke makes man's capacity for negation one of only four elements in his essential definition of humanity.[3] Freud sees negation as an essential screen behind which repressed material can rise to consciousness;[4] this psychological mechanism give another content to the assertion in Hegel's *Phenomenology* that the force of negation and negativity, the pressure of nay-saying, is that which not only defines the self but enables it to rise to self-consciousness and true freedom. More a fad than a serious philosophy, at least in the West, Zen Buddhism invites one to perceive objects out of all intellectual context, as unique, immediate, unverbalizable presences; its highest objective is to liberate the mind completely from bondage to things, so that it may seek its proper freedom in the realm of Nothing, i.e. traditional Buddhist Nirvana. Beats, if there are any left, take as their ideal an exhausted, alienated, and deranged sensibility, existing as it were in an artificial self-created void. The mystique is not easily summarized, but it seems to be permissible for the fully beat to create out of their condition, but better if they wish to and cannot — the blocked artist being, in effect, more authentic to his metaphysical void than the fulfilled one. A major playwright of our time, Samuel Beckett, deals at a first approximation with no topic other than Nothing. The topic finds voice in the slow, meaningless dialogue of his characters, in their anguished immobility, in the long waits and empty pauses between their sparse and despairing words. Paralyzed on a throne, constipated and incapable of movement, crouched in garbage cans or funeral urns, they are frozen from the first moment of the "action" into immobility. The end of

3. "Definition of Man," *Hudson Review*, XVI, 4 (Winter 1963–64), 491–514.
4. "Negation" in *General Psychological Theory* (Collier's, 1963), p. 213.

all their actions, represented and representing, is Nothing; and the plays themselves are tissues of delay, behind which, more palpable than any stage-figure, looms the urgent pressure of emptiness. Moravia and Musil and Borges are at one with Beckett in their fascinated contemplation of inner void. So too in a medium as popular as the movies. Michelangelo Antonioni's *L'Avventura* allowed the camera to follow for nearly an hour the motions of various characters spreading out over an island in search of a girl whom they never found. The texture of the island itself was beautifully scrutinized, but in terms of audience-expectation what the camera discovered was precisely Nothing. Even more pointedly, the same director's *L'Eclisse*, after investigating the non-relationship of a boy and girl, concluded with the image of a street-lamp blazing silent and immobile in gathering darkness for no less than five unbroken minutes. Nothing happened, nothing was seen or heard; the light glared into the camera for five minutes and then the movie stopped. The poetry of Wallace Stevens deals almost entirely with the confrontation of a naked object; given a momentary mythical context (a coiffure of style, a chapeau of philosophic system), it acquires a tremulous mode of significant existence which only a slight shift in perspective can cause it immediately to lose. Then we revert to a welter of unrelated somethings, an ocean of accident, scarcely distinguishable from Nothing. A recurrent concern of André Gide was a rupture in the chain of circumstance, the performance of an act with no cause and no purpose, an act with Nothing behind and before it, an *acte gratuit*. One of the best known passages in Hemingway describes the thoughts of a tired waiter left alone to minister to an old man who is drinking relentlessly in the hope or despair of escaping from "Nothing."

> What did he fear? It was not fear or dread. It was a nothing that he knew too well. It was all a nothing and a man was

nothing too. It was only that and light was all it needed and a certain cleanness and order. Some lived in it and never felt it but he knew it was all nada y pues nada y nada y pues nada. Our nada who art in nada, nada be thy name thy kingdom nada thy will be nada in nada as it is in nada. Give us this nada our daily nada and nada us our nada as we nada our nadas and nada us not into nada but deliver us from nada; pues nada. Hail nothing full of nothing, nothing is with thee.[5]

This swift summary is evidently designed merely to remind the reader of things he has already seen and appreciated; it could be extended indefinitely. The basic point needs no arguing. In art, in literature, in science, in our culture as a whole, we are a void-haunted, void-fascinated age. A proper study would probably proceed immediately to ask, "Where do we go from here? After the void, what?" I have preferred to address the tamer and more tractable problem, "By what stages did we get this way?" There is nothing, to be sure, more familiar than the stock Darwin-Marx-Freud-World-War-I answer to this question. With the disappearance of God, the rise of science, machine civilizations, and mass cultures, the cynical and destructive study of ideologies, and the shattering impact of international conflicts, we have enough social fact — even without the hackneyed, all-purpose atom bomb — to explain much more than a vogue for the void. This sort of explanation has been piled up again and again; depending on the explainer's sharpness of nose and keenness of prepossession, it traces the roots of the modern canker back to the Industrial Revolution, the Puritan Revolt, Martin Luther, William of Occam, Adam, Eve, the serpent, or the apple. With such a diagnostic approach the present study is largely unconcerned. Taking for granted that a steadily increasing interest in Nothing must have deep-

5. "A Clean, Well-Lighted Place."

seated yet all-too-discoverable causes, I have undertaken to look at the process by which this curious topic got domesticated, primarily in literature, during the nineteenth century. People do not usually, it seems, set out with clenched teeth to write about Nothing — or if they do, what they come up with is labored, ingenious trifling, like Fielding's "Essay on Nothing," or the Earl of Rochester's metaphysical japing on the same theme. The game is simply to wreathe the forms of rhetorical magnification and expansion around an absence of subject — an agreeable, if limited, exercise for exhibiting the author's powers of verbal invention. But such displays have little in common with modern, "serious" uses of void. The inventors or victims of modern vacancy usually start on a specific, positive topic, and then, gradually or abruptly, the awareness of Nothing impinges on them; they are led to or fall into the yawning void. But their passivity can be overstated, and is if we imply that an artist necessarily persists in the topic or recurs to it without actively soliciting or exploiting it.

If we find void turning up over and over again in the imaginative work of an age, we are equally wrong in supposing it there without reason or without rationale. Its occurrence may be due to circumstances outside the artist; its persistence can be explained only as it serves or is made to serve some principle of temperament, answer to some chord of artistic or philosophic need. Whatever the reason for which a theme pops up, it will be retained and reiterated only because it can somehow be turned to account. So it has been my purpose in this essay to explore some early-middle turnings-to-account of a most unpromising theme — one which seems at first glance refractory to any sort of artistic treatment whatever. Yet by trying it out, first in one context, then in another, the imaginative writers of the nineteenth century learned to command its keyboard, pedals, and stops; they asserted their control over its reverberations, and made possible the harmonies with which today — for better or worse — our ears and minds are occupied.

Philosophically, mathematically, and scientifically, there have been degrees of void and qualities of Nothing, to which a student of the topic must grant at least a bob of respectful attention. Pascal, for instance, distinguishes mere void, i.e. empty space, such as one can produce by exhausting the contents of a chamber, from absolute non-being, which, as he reminds us, includes the abolition of space and time.[6] Kant makes a quadruple distinction between varieties of non-being: (1) empty concepts without objects, i.e. *ens rationis*; (2) empty objects of concepts, i.e. *nihil privativum*; (3) empty intuitions without objects, i.e. *ens imaginarium*; and (4) empty objects without any concepts, i.e. *nihil negativum*. (1) and (3) are actions of the percipient with a deficiency of the object; (2) and (4) are objects with a deficiency of the percipient. *Nihil privativum* might be figured as an object with a non- in front of it — nonentity or non-sense; *nihil negativum* as a logical contradiction which actually does away with itself, a rational impossibility. In

6. Pascal's *Expériences sur le vide* (and associated letters in defense of it) had the general scope of domesticating empty space among the phenomena of nature, in contravention to the ancient adage that nature abhors a vacuum. This wheeze, which no doubt antedates even Plutarch, had flourished in the shelter of a larger philosophic presumption that nature is a plenum, to predicate a void within which would be to deny Providence. Pascal, taking Torricelli's experiments as a point of departure, concluded that what had passed for instinctive, sympathetic hostility to void on the part of the natural world was simply a consequence of air pressure. In the process he had to dispose (and with exquisite economy did dispose) of the usual verbal flimflam and empty rhetoric on the part of his unscientific antagonist, who happened to be a Jesuit father. The cool power of his destructive logic is wonderfully impressive. Yet one cannot help feeling a conflict in Pascal between his readiness to recognize void in the physical world and his sense of void as a radical evil in a moral and psychological context. The instability one senses as a result of this contrast probably has its sources in the perilous imbalances of the fideist argument.

the history of mathematics it appears that zero, which was so unimportant in classical times that Roman numerals have no symbol for it, became increasingly significant as a concept with the advent of algebra, where its various peculiar characteristics make possible the form of the linear equation. The differential calculus was developed during the eighteenth century, and refined in the nineteenth, as a means of bridging that gap which Zeno's paradox represents as infinitely elastic, between zero and the other ordinals; philosophers as well as mathematicians have been exercised by it, but their labors are too terrifying even to contemplate. As for physics (to pass over the last decade's ventures in acclimating man to interstellar space), the multiplication of artificial voids in the late nineteenth century paved the way for all sorts of practical and now-familiar developments in the form of vacuum tubes, light bulbs, X-rays, and technical gadgets galore.

But, however interesting and useful in themselves, these versions and practical applications of controlled Nothing did not open up any world behind the oval mirror of the zero-sign. To this day they have not provided space and depth for the imagination to make itself free. For the purposes of the imagination, zero and infinity are alike outside the human dimension; they are not representable, we are not even in proportion to them. To suggest them, we gesture vaguely with makeshift concepts like "very small" and "very big." Even today we cannot be really at home in interstellar space, any more than we can really imagine the dimensions revealed by the electron microscope; yet these dimensions really are just very big and very small. Void and infinity, existing outside of all series, are even harder to reconcile with human dimensions, human conceptions, humanly proportioned representation. It is probably idle to pretend that they have been or ever will be areas within which the literary imagination can hope to move freely — no question, therefore,

of "absorbing them" or "being absorbed" by them. Nothing is
not a subject-matter to be learned. With infinity (and, by
easy extension, eternity) a certain posture is almost prescribed;
one stands on the shores of these great expanses, exalted or de-
pressed by one's insignificance, and allows the contemplative
mind to voyage out, ever further out, to the limit of its conceiv-
ing, where the mind faints from sheer duration — and then,
with the despairing reflection that one has scarcely started to
conceive the first tiny fraction of this mental journey, which
must be multiplied by infinite infinities before — but there is
no "before" or "after," and so one relapses perforce into the
finite.

The notion of Nothing, on the other hand, opens up in various ways, under many different circumstances, and invites us to
a variety of responses. It has a cosmic locus, whether amid the
stars or within the heart; it has numerous possible emotional
colorings; it invites to various perspectives; it may be allowed to
exist within the universe of the work-of-art either as beginning
or end, either intermittently or persistently; its function there
may be suggested by metaphors like test, proof, mirror, window,
baseline, backlight, and so forth — for all of which it will be our
business to try to provide meanings.

The nineteenth century, for purposes of this study, does not
include Yeats, Eliot, Kafka, Joyce, Valéry, Rilke, Gide, Georg,
Hesse, Proust, Conrad, or Thomas Mann (these figures and
their immediate followers represent the middle phase of a development only the early stages of which are my concern). On
the other hand, it does include James, Bradley, Maeterlinck,
Verhaeren, and D'Annunzio. Clearly it is neither a straight nor
a sharp line which I have drawn through the twilight years
1900–1915; but period definitions are nothing if not provisional
and not much even then. To prevent my reader from getting
bored (for I confess to an image of him as an active, impatient,

cantankerous fellow, with mind and temperament of his own),
I have preferred to end some discussions with a metaphor
rather than a QED, to shove my companion-antagonist off in
search of his own truth rather than nail him to the floorboards
of mine. As much as possible, I have tried to write always with a
specific text in front of me, and under a sense that the real generalizations about this topic remain to be made. In quoting, I
have cited from the most readily available editions, wherever
they were not patently insufficient. Prose passages are given in
English translation (my own unless otherwise indicated) eked
out with words from the original wherever a specific paucity of
English vocabulary might blur understanding. (We have, for
instance, no word which corresponds precisely to French "néant": "void," "vacancy," and "non-being" won't do, "nought"
means "zero" which doesn't fit, and "nothing" is too expansive,
indefinite, and unpsychological.) Poetry is cited in the original
and translated, as literally as possible, into English prose at the
foot of the page. Only a sketchy effort has been made to record
intellectual obligations and critical differences. No ladder was
deliberately disdained that seemed to lead upwards, but in dealing with so diffuse a topic I no doubt, through ignorance, neglected many. Let the wiser reader exult and use them to build
higher.

II

The idea that there exists, or can be conceived, a void — a place
where the textures of sense-impression which we rely on to feed
our inner, creaturely appetite for sensation suddenly cease to
exist — such a notion is of course very old and perhaps universal. It is one of those notions which are formed by subtraction,[7]

7. Kant's *nihil privativum* is clearly this sort of simple subtraction — a concept is given, then taken away with a negation; *nihil negativum* is a more

which are dependent upon abstraction from a given something rather than upon direct experience. Weightless, motionless, blind, deaf, senseless, and hung out in the infinite void, we should still have, as long as we were alive, the sense of ourselves, of our cycles and organs and potential for experience. Experience, within the definition of the word, cannot be of Nothing. In fact, like those other absolutes infinity and eternity, void cannot even be fully conceived — a finite mind formed by experience being able to propose to itself only imperfectly a state in which it does not exist, a state which is the negation of experience. At least, if we can conceive of Nothing, it must be boundless, eternal, and seen from no particular point of either space or time, since any of these limitations would immediately make it something. This is no easy exercise. But in daily life, the subtraction which yields Nothing is much easier and more common. A room full of furniture, books, plants, odors, echoes, shadows, and air will be said to contain "Nothing" when the source of a mysterious noise is what we are seeking. A child enters the house after three hours of furious activity; his mother asks, "What were you doing?" and of course he answers, "Nothing." After an hour of opening and shutting his mouth, a politician is judged to have said "Nothing." The notion that Nothing is a very small positive quantity — much less than one expected, but still a minimal thing — finds an ancient support in etymology. French "rien" is said to be derived from Latin "rem," the accusative singular form of the word for "thing," and indeed Old French frequently uses "rien" in a positive sense:

"Justice amez sor tote rien," says the *Chronique des ducs de Normandie:* "Love justice above every other thing." Spanish "nada" and Italian "niente" are derived from participial forms

---

violent and far-reaching subtraction, like a negative multiplication, by which a concept is exploded out of the very possibility of existing.

of Latin "nasci," meaning "to be born"; in all its forms, Nothing is at root a veritable thing.

Nothing is frequently what we do not know or cannot imagine, a word to express our ignorance. What exists beyond the farthest galaxy? Very probably another galaxy — which is simply a way of saying that the question is improperly stated. But an answer just as meaningful and probably more frequently heard would be one word, "Nothing." "Nothing" is what is either too small or too large and impalpable for our senses to perceive, and we shall find the word clustering around the notions of death, infinite space, and eternity, as well as about the exceedingly minute and the empty.

In the natural, unstrained speech of everyday, Nothing can be as little as a high ratio of expectation to experience. When one anticipates a great deal and experiences very little, the trajectory of one's disappointment is, vulgarly, Nothing. Thus it has been said that the disappearance of God from the cosmos leaves man in a soulless, mechanized void. Doubtless this has been a frequent sensation, but it depends on a certain level of expectation. If outer space is not filled with moral schemes and benevolent intentions, it can be fairly described as containing a lot of carbon molecules responsive in the main to Newton's three laws of motion; and this is either a ghastly aching void or a tidy, busy little cosmos, depending on the eye with which one regards it. One man's void is another man's plenum. The conviction of irrelevance, of being beside the whole point of some immense indifferent process taking place around one produces a sense of inner cancellation which is one kind of void; contemplative fixation, particularly on a point within oneself, leads to another kind of inner emptying. There is an ominous and preparatory Nothing, as a sudden hush before the storm; there is a Nothing of completion, the void which follows on a cycle fully worked out. It is the clear intent of many tragic actions to

clear the moral atmosphere by reducing their viewers to this
pure simplicity, all passion spent. A kind of blank, impersonal
Nothing lies at the heart of the erotic experience, which no
doubt contributes to the ancient pun on "dying" as the word
for sexual climax as well as to the ancient psychic connection
between death and love. There is an immense spectrum of
comic Nothings, from the astounded silence of a double-take to
the pratfall of an anti-climax or the vaudeville of a deliberate
hiatus in MS. There is philosophic Nothing — the mind poised,
confronting with all its perceptions and non-perceptions the object or non-object and registering, precisely, Nothing. There is
vindictive Nothing, arrogant Nothing ("we Nothing-
knowers"), perverse Nothing, joyous Nothing, deep and shallow Nothings, significant and insignificant, obvious and intricate Nothings, exterior and interior Nothings, labyrinthine
and bald Nothings, anxious, anguished Nothing, ravishing and
ecstatic Nothings, multifarious and Protean Nothing. We shall
never come to the end of the list, for clearly there are as many
varieties of Nothing as of things, people, and attitudes. In fact
void itself is for the artist a projection, a coloring. It is not an
experience, nor even the absence of one, but a repertoire of potential effects, a palette — or so at least it will be the business of
this study to consider it. What this procedure loses in sharpness
of outline, it may hope to redeem in a perception of permuta-
tions and iridescent thematic combinations which would otherwise be invisible.

There is, no question about it, something perverse about
viewing the nineteenth century, of all centuries — an age team-
ing with vast physical and psychic activity, with social, domestic, and intellectual texture — in terms of its attitudes toward
Nothing. It is like reading a photograph from the negative, or a
print from the plate. Yet the idea is frequent enough in art that
reversing familiar images may yield fresh perceptions of them.

Though any interest in Nothing projected back from the twentieth century carries built-in dangers of anachronism, seeing things for a moment in a new light may enable us to see them better in a familiar one. Aerial photographs taken at dawn or sunset, when the sun's rays strike the land obliquely, are best at bringing out the land's contours. But this is too limited and defensive a defense of the present proceedings. I think the nineteenth century no longer opens fully (if it ever did) to the old key-concepts of social reform, religious questioning, and scientific growth. Its ideals were tremendous, but they were at once easier to grasp and more limited in appeal and influence than the terrors and hauntings of the age. The further we recede from this colossal manic-depressive time, the more it appears to us an age of ricochet and revulsion, an era of deep psychic disease and downright fright. Alternative forms wrong our understanding here, as in most matters of motivation, for the question is less one of *either-or* than of *both-and* — as soldiers advancing upon an enemy frequently find themselves running *toward* and *away from* and *with* all at the same time. For all this, the things men fear are often better evidence of their mental intention than the things they say they desire, especially when one deals with philosophical idealists and optimists. This is no categorical novelty in discussions of the nineteenth century, which can scarcely be considered at all without distinguishing the shaggy façades of such as Browning and Ruskin from the cringing innocents under the skin. But these are hackneyed themes, as is the old overpaid account of rationalization and ideology. The great game of stretching appearances to cover realities is one at which the nineteenth century was so surpassingly good that in effect the nightmare of Nothing comes mostly to those who, for a multiplicity of possible reasons, seek or invite it. A certain sort of mind, at once bold and uneasy, comes to the fore, perhaps a streak of vindictive egotism. Some stock figures disappear without a trace, others are radically transformed; the shift in focus produces a shift in actors, as well as in the action of an age.

To see a whole century primarily in terms of a peculiar topic and a special temper may be, ultimately, to falsify the total reality. But the perspective, though designedly narrow, need not be uncritical. Above all, it need imply no provincial complacency about the sins of the nineteenth century. All centuries are afraid of something, and the historian of our own, when he seeks a perspective, may find it in our very readiness to take void for a purpose. Nietzsche supposed that we were being driven to that option by an even deeper void within ourselves, but he flattered. The modern dilemma is as desperate as all that only if one happens to be Nietzsche. Our future historian may see the vogue for void simply as a sort of chafed and irritated bid for cheap distinction. All the limited goals can be, have been, and will be criticized; void is an ultimate without responsibilities. Our metaphysical niceness is curiously out of character. Hedda Gabler, frigid perhaps but no prude, won't get off the mythical train imaged for her by Judge Brack — the train which is carrying her, beside her learned dolt of a husband, ineluctably down the boring road to smash — because someone might pass a remark on her ankles. Our fear of being committed to the prudent and possible, going no deeper in many instances than that instinctive refusal of someone else's possible advantage, may be for the future historian as good a key to our times as the nineteenth century's fear of Nothing is to its.

Meanwhile, let us see how good that is.

Sénancour, Novalis, DeQuincey:

Equivocal Romantics

After wandering through the wilderness of this world in search of something, one may reach Nothing as a terminus; so seen, it may be figured as an elevation or a collapse. Beyond the collapse is sometimes found an enchanted landscape, an inverted Everything; this side of it, reluctant yet no less fascinated agents often prolong the vaudevilles of psychic mobility.

His grave in Paris bears neither name nor date, but only a passionate brevity: *Eternité, deviens mon asile!* That epitaph is a plunge into the void almost voluptuous in its abandon; yet it has been remembered as a more ambitious memorial would not have been. A man so anonymous *in extremis* must clearly have had a taste for Nothing; yet he also lived in dread of it, and the paradox fills his work and history. If annihilation proved his refuge from life, yet a recurrent motif of that life was attempted escape from annihilation. The novel by which he is remembered describes a search for asylum, if asylum can include refuge from the self and its demands; yet it is also, and not just automatically, an act of self-definition, self-exploration, self-affirmation. It celebrates and exemplifies the strenuous, vigilant integrity of the mind, yet it affirms simultaneously the futility and incapacity of the mind. Its passionate austerities, gloomy exhilarations, and exalted moral soliloquies have made *Oberman* (1802) and its author Etienne Pivert de Sénancour the objects of a small yet persistent cult.

In form, *Oberman* is a straitened epistolary novel — straitened in presenting merely a half-correspondence, the letters of a single persona, of whom "Oberman" is either the name or the pseudonym, but who is certainly modeled directly on Sénancour himself. (The name not only reflects a Germanic inspiration — though evidently without benefit of the German language — but also a persistent impulse to exaltation and hauteur; no doubt by way of a common relation to Jean Paul, Oberman, it seems, is bound by ties of kinship to the Ubermensch.) Oberman's letters cover a period of some ten years; either a happy accident or a deliberate design of the author's allows him to begin in the year I of the Revolutionary calendar, as with the dawn of a new era. The friend to whom he writes, and from whom we hear only in a muffled, offstage way, is one of those colorless, anonymous recipients of letters, reasonable and domestic and timid, who serve in epistolary novels to set off the dramatic adventures of their correspondents. Average as a Greek chorus, Oberman's pen-pal has just enough character to move from Lyons to Bordeaux, from one bourgeois, commercial town to another.[1] Meanwhile Oberman, like Alceste, renounces his lawsuit in Paris, forsakes his business interests, and moves to the mountainous wilds of Switzerland, where he explores, in a series of extended soliloquies, the consequences of a quarrel with "the world" which grows steadily deeper and less mediable.

The novel — if in fact it qualifies for that title — contains little in the way of external action or social circumstance. Oberman is essentially a soliloquizer; by the end of the book he has acquired a residence, Imenstrom, and a friend, Fonsalbe, whose watery names may or may not be symbolic. He has also achieved

1. Very likely this friend appears, under another hat, as editor of letters which Oberman, according to the myth, had no notion of publishing. His prudence, sense of editorial proportion, and leaden literal-mindedness would be altogether, and rather comically, in character.

a single active resolution, to write a truthful book, which may or may not be the volume to hand. There is a meager suggestion of romantic interest in the sister of Fonsalbe, Madame Del————, who makes a small figure in the later letters; but she is not very vigorously present, and, given the temperament of Oberman, seems more like a threat than a promise. In many of its parts the book is veiled and excerpted autobiography, rearranged and idealized; it hints only vaguely at an unhappy marriage, says nothing of two resulting children, suggests the ruin of a sizable fortune though not the Revolution which caused it, but does not really attempt consecutive, substantial narration.

The romance of *Oberman* is an inner one, is psychic; but what the hero cannot quite make clear is whether he is describing an adventure or a condition. In rejecting society and its daily business, Oberman is merely discarding makework — "those uneasy distractions which wear away our time on earth, confuse our life with the shadows which precede and those which follow it, and leave it no other advantage than that of being a less placid void [*néant*]" (p. 73). Behind such a judgment lies the respectable weight of generations of contemplative thought; Oberman stands squarely in an ancient ascetic tradition in electing to withdraw from the hurlyburly of life in order to savor its essence. Ordinarily, however, ascetic withdrawal has some sort of religious coloring; and just here Oberman's eighteenth-century background asserts itself. With dry irony, with cool politeness, with Voltairean *désinvolture*, he makes clear that he has no faith at all. In a long, straight-faced letter, he develops a fantastic numerological theory to its conclusion that numbers are the root of morality — and then darts its satiric point at his orthodox correspondent:

> If you find a certain insubstantiality in these ideas, put it out of your mind, redouble your faith; this is just what the first light of the first centuries [after Christ] declared. Ten

is justice and beatitude resulting from the creature which is seven and the Trinity which is three. Eleven is sin because it transgresses ten which is justice. You see here the high point of the sublime, beyond this peak we must fall silent, and Saint Augustine himself knew nothing more (p. 222).

His account of what happens to the fire in the fireplace when it goes out is equally ironic: "it goes off into another world to be rewarded in eternity if it warmed your feet and punished forever if it scorched your slippers" (p. 182). Oberman is skeptical, not only of theology and its proofs for God's existence, but of contemporary churches; and he does not hesitate to say so:

All the religions pronounce anathema on one another because none of them bears the mark of the divine. I appreciate that yours does, but the rest of the world cannot see it because it is hidden, and I am like the rest of the world, I have trouble seeing what is invisible (p. 229).

But though God and church have both evaporated (the latter, on all evidence, more missed than the former), Oberman is not a theology-haunted man, and he is neither defiant nor nostalgic about God. Outside a single major section of the book, his thoughts do not recur to religious topics, and in fact when they do arise, he is sooner tired of them than his correspondent. "Go look at your jasmines," he writes, not without a touch of contempt, "leave my doubts and my proofs alone." And when in his own thoughts he takes most careful account of his condition, God scarcely figures in the balance-sheets at all, nor is his absence remarked.

God, then, is gone, leaving neither vacancy nor regret; moreover, Oberman explicitly denies that he is seeking

in an outlandish order of things for objects which are desirable only because their imagined existence, being changeable at will, would be clothed in my eyes with specious

> shapes and a pure, unmixed beauty even more fantastic than they are (pp. 40–41).

In other words, he is not looking for an ideal world or a private fantasy; he seeks only "the life of people who are good, my peace in the peace of all." There is nothing supernatural, nothing even idealized about this ideal; it is downright bourgeois.

> To tell the truth nothing which exists has — so far, at least — earned my full affection, and an inexpressible void [*vide*] is the constant custom of my thirsty soul. But everything I desire could exist, the whole earth could answer to my heart's desire, without anything being changed in nature or in man himself, except the passing accidents of the social structure (p. 42).

Not only does Oberman protest thus, in the abstract, that his ambitions are practical, social, and of this world; he gives repeated evidence, in specific contexts, of a sensitive social conscience. He pities the poor, the old, the drab, and the outcast. He does not want to be thought particularly virtuous, he prefers to be a simple, everyday *"homme de bien,"* and the spectacle which most horrifies him is that of social injustice in its humble, practical forms. He protests, he pities; but the stench of humanity is in his nostrils, and he does not get any closer to the problem than he has to. For in fact, what is wrong with the world is not something which a little social engineering would clear up. Oberman himself is afflicted, alienated from the world and his attempt to express, if not to explain, this sense of aloneness occasions some of the most moving passages of the book:

> I am alone; the energies of my heart are communicated to no-one, they boil within it, they wait for expression; and here I am in the world, wandering, lonely in the middle of the crowd which means nothing to me; like a man struck with an

ancient deafness, whose avid eye fixes itself on all those silent
beings who pass and perform in front of him. He sees everything, and everything is denied him; he guesses at the sounds
he loves, seeks for them, and does not hear them; in the midst
of the world's noise he hears a universal silence; amid a world
of living beings, he is an absentee (pp. 100–101).

Insensibly, he is led by his solitude, his disgust, his despair, to
contradict categorically what he had said before about wanting
only a little adjustment of the social structure:

> When the resistance, when the inertia of a dead, brutal,
> hideous power shackles, swathes, grips us, and holds us deep
> in doubts, disgusts, childishness, and follies either imbecile
> or cruel; when one knows nothing and possesses nothing
> [rien]; when everything passes before us like the weird fig-
> ures of a hateful and ridiculous dream — who will deny our
> hearts the need of another order, another nature (p. 110)?

Thus the wheel of Oberman's thought turns, and not for the
last time, full circle.

Sénancour's is a long book, and diagnoses of the hero's condition vary from letter to letter and mood to mood; there is little
clear progression, but rather that sort of steady back-and-forth
oscillation described by Proust in picturing the water-lilies of
the Vivonne. Now Oberman finds it is the world which has become so thin a tissue of illusions, so meager a diet of perceptions that man is hard put to survive in it:

> I shall live as if at random . . . happy . . . if I can retain
> in my isolation, and within the bounds of an accidental ne-
> cessity, this hungry innocent heart, to which nothing will be
> given; if I can teach it to feed itself in its destitution, to
> repose in the void, to remain calm in this odious silence, to
> survive within a voiceless Nature (pp. 46–7).

But again, persistently, it is the mind which is at fault; degenerating into monotonous self-disgust, it refuses to take even the first primitive steps to health:

> Void becomes tedious [*fastidieux*] in the end; it degenerates into a gloomy habit; and, sunk in our lofty indolence, we allow the fire of life to dwindle away in a trail of sad smoke for lack of breath to revive it (p. 204).

Yet at last it is the conjunction of these inner and outer voids that brings the psychic desolation of Oberman most passionately before us:

> Every cause is invisible, every purpose delusive; every shape changes, every space of time comes to an end; and the torment of the insatiable heart is the blind movement of a meteor wandering in the void and soon to be lost there. Nothing is possessed as it is conceived, nothing is conceived as it exists. We perceive relations, not essences; we never enjoy the things themselves, only their images. Thus Nature, which appears elusive without and impenetrable within us, is everywhere shadowy. "I feel" is the only word for the man who wants nothing but truth. And that which constitutes the certainty of my being is also its torment (p. 274).

Most of Oberman's moral lectures bear directly on his own condition, and their eloquent formulas gain dramatic point from his anguished inability to implement them:

> It is easy to escape from it [*la fatalité*]; it is high time; it is necessary: and scarcely is that word spoken, when the impulse fails, energy flags, and I find myself plunged again in the sleep which is annihilating my life (p. 206).

Somber passages of this sort are not infrequent, but characteristically the book is neither miasmic nor moping; the cold wind of a sharp and questioning intelligence blows through it, and intellectual energy supplies the dominant chord. Quite apart

from formal philosophic doctrines, Oberman makes his peculiar
vigor in despair felt through such devices as a mountain-storm
scene, the twisted angularities of which are both perilous and
exhilarating (pp. 417–22), or the brief description of a birch-
tree: "It was at that time that I particularly remarked the birch,
a solitary tree, which already tinged my thought with sadness
and which since I never encounter without pleasure" (p. 72).
Sadness, solitude, and joy are twisted here into a single knot.

When one deals with Sénancour at all (and well-known his-
tories of the French novel have managed to dodge him), it is
frequent enough to set him down among the neo-Wertherian at-
titudinizers of the early century, whose tears and torments rose
from no source deeper than self-pity and a sense of the fashionable. Beyond question, much of Oberman's melancholy is morbid; he says so himself. But what makes it dramatically interesting is the sharpness of his struggle against it. A major weapon in
that struggle is disdain. Oberman has a convincing talent for
sensing the theatrical and the cheap in ideas. He makes short
work of the familiar bet (what have you got to lose compared
with what you have to gain?) as a grounds for faith, and has no
patience with the pseudo-superior who affect to disdain money
or the pseudo-humble who praise the unspoiled life of the poor;
he loathes the pieties. Rather, his virtues are those of energy,
integrity, self-knowledge:

> in each particular moment of his life what concerns every
> man above all is to be what he must be [*doit être*] (p. 25).
> . . . Energy in suffering is better than apathy in pleasure.
> . . . What you fear is vain, what you desire is vain. One
> thing alone is good for you: to be what nature has chosen
> (p. 116).

"Nature" in this context is human nature and one's individual
nature, as well as old Mother Nature; her injunctions point to-

ward an enlightened and skeptical epicureanism, which Oberman is learned enough to bolster with references to Aristippus
the Cyrenaic. He does not, to be sure, present himself as the
consistent exponent of this or any other philosophic system.
Like most men, in many of his circumstances and attitudes he
draws freely upon stoicism; his early thinking particularly is
tinged with Rousseauistic meliorism, and he retained an abiding
sense of nature's purifying powers. His was also an *anima
naturaliter christiana* if we understand by this a post-Christian,
not a pre-Christian disposition, and give a somewhat ironic
emphasis to the word *naturaliter*. This temperamental philosophic eclecticism responds nicely to the inner needs and outer
skepticism which he asserts explicitly: "I no longer pretend to
use my life, I seek only to fill it up" (p. 45). Life is a void to be
given content, or rather two voids — that of outward nature,
which provides man with no direction or purpose in the form of
happiness, that of inward nature which remains apathetic and
impenetrable in the absence of motivation. Oberman tries
rather vigorously to make analysis do duty for will; in seeking to
penetrate the secret of his inner void, he experiments with the
spontaneous and unforeseen, he reflects acutely on the ways in
which cultivation renders the heart sterile, and on one occasion
he describes at near-Proustian length his dreams and the process
of his going to sleep. Always, the secret of the mind's motion
escapes from its questioning, while the questioning becomes insensibly a substitute for action in which the mind might have
revealed itself. Sénancour/Oberman is a motionless pilgrim, his
immobility an ever-deepening probe into his own rootless-
ness.

Standing, as it were, at the portal of the nineteenth century,
Oberman is a prophetic evidence of omnipresent Nothing. M.
Merlant defines the arc of Sénancour's career as a failure in the
search for happiness followed by a partial success in the substi-

tute pursuit of truth.[2] This is right as far as it goes; but it does not try to account for the thinness of experience one senses in *Oberman,* the rarefied quality of the book's atmosphere. Sénancour's pessimism has something of Schopenhauer's pride and energy; in the immediate presence of Nirvana behind the veil of circumstance, he is reminiscent of that later, lonelier Swiss Buddhist, Amiel. But he is neither as blustering as the one nor as despondent as the other; the flavor of *Oberman* is dry and invigorating — he has something of that disabused tone for which Stendhal was seeking when he said philosophy should be written as by a banker who has made his fortune. Sénancour had done even better — he had lost one.

We shall hear a good deal later in the century of submitting oneself to void as a hardening process which tempers the soul to a necessary acerbity; Sénancour, at the opening of the century, gives us to wonder if the contrary process may not also be operative. A certain hardness of surface and temper is evidently prerequisite to discovering one sort of void. The rationalism of Sénancour was an engine in the hands of his instinctive hauteur; and it led him ever further up the heights, toward the rarefied atmosphere of Nothing. He seems like a philosopher, not because he thinks deeply but because he sets his eye high, viewing life from a persistent elevation. He is an experimenter, with himself for a laboratory; the hardness of his mind and the loftiness of his vision both contribute to this sense of a self above and behind the self. The void upon which he enters, under these circumstances, though cruelly testing, is in the end exultant.

The "hardness of mind" here invoked to account for an aspect of Sénancour is a slippery, undefined concept, of which we must urge the reader to be properly suspicious; still, the no-

2. *Sénancour* (Paris, 1907), p. 56.

tion may be given a certain scope by a mere naming of some later enthusiasts for an elevated Nothing. Leopardi's cosmic voids found expression in a strict style and a bitter rejection of the romantic softness of his day. So did Nietzsche's. Ibsen defined his style of mind in opposition to the enthusiastic gigantism of Wergeland, Poe made hard-shelled use of rational forms and illiberal ideas against the soft-minded frogponders of his time, and Mallarmé purged his poetry enthusiastically of Baudelairisms, i.e. too-facile, too-romantic exploitations of his own personality. These are plainly leads to be followed up elsewhere. Meanwhile, a contrast of Sénancour with Novalis may set before us the difference between void as exaltation and void as collapse, between the mountain peak and the abyss.

Both are, in the first place, authors with major temperamental similarities; both are introspective contemplatives, readers in the book of themselves, who hope to acquire by self-searching the key to an understanding of the cosmos; both pursued passionately the gleams of a fitful and evanescent insight. Neither one is a systematic philosopher, yet both are on the track of inward illumination. If anything, one would think Novalis's avid, open death wish more likely to bring him into the immediate presence of void; "suicide," he declared roundly, "is an eminently philosophic act," and no poet ever solicited non-being with more hungry anticipation. Yet, curiously, a reading of the "Hymnen an die Nacht" (1800) seems at first to yield no sense of the void, nor even very much of the terminology. The experience which Novalis describes under night-imagery is surpassingly sensual and ecstatic; it is a surrender of self and a discovery of self, the annihilation of the world and its reconstitution. As the world of sense falls away, serving no further function than to limit the expansion of the ego by reflecting it back on itself, the inner world recedes into infinite dimensions and perspectives:

Abwärts wend'ich mich
Zu der heiligen, unaussprechlichen
Geheimnissvollen Nacht —
Fernab liegt die Welt,
Wie versenkt in eine tiefe Gruft,
Wie wüst und einsam ihre Stelle! [3]

Though essentially inward, Night is more than darkness, more than subjectivity; it is the creative unconscious, it is death and a world beyond death, thus an experience rich in joyous suggestions of erotic surrender; here the lover will be at last and forever reunited with his beloved:

Du kommst, Geliebte —
Die Nacht ist da.
Entzückt ist meine Seele —
Vorüber ist der irdische Weg
Und du bist weider Mein.
Ich schaue dir ins tiefe dunkle Auge
Sehe nichts als Liebe und Seligkeit
Wir sinken auf der Nacht Altar
Aufs weiche Lager —
Die Hülle fällt
Und angezundet von dem warmen Druck
Entglüht des süssen Opfers
Reine Glut. [4]

The world of Night, to which the poet's ultimate allegiance is given, does not altogether replace the world of garish day,

3. I turn away to the holy inexpressible mysterious Night. Far off lies the world, as if sunk in a deep abyss; how desolate and solitary its place!
4. You come, beloved; the Night is here. My soul is bewitched, the earthly path is ended, and you are mine again. I look deep in your dark eyes, seeing only love and felicity. We sink before the altar of Night, onto its soft bed; the body falls away, and, kindled in warm embrace, the pure passion glows of a sweet sacrifice.

but instead supports and enriches it with gleams from beyond the veil. Addressing the world of Light, the poet says,

> Sie trägt dich mutterlich
> Und ihr verdankst du
> All deine Herrlichkeit.[5]

The transcendence of the dark world is taken for granted because the things the conscious mind can know are mere shadows and appearances; only the death-devoted, imagination-intoxicated ego is creative and ultimate. Thus Novalis plunges into this strange, illimitable ocean of the beyond, not as into destruction or self-annihilation, but with ecstasy and orgiastic delight. Death is almost entirely fulfillment, hardly at all negation. Evil is a mere illusion, like the world in which it occurs; neither Doctor Pangloss nor Mary Baker Eddy (and German idealism has streaks of both characters) could be more emphatic on this score. The "philosophic suicide" which Novalis advocated, and in effect practiced, was therefore an act of supreme confidence. It involved living in this world as if one's only intent were to die, making death a part of one's daily life. One might continue to inhabit the flesh for a while, and to incarnate one's intuitions in meager human words — but one would live only provisionally, while maintaining behind all one's human values an infinite, ironic reservation.

He envisaged a "cancellation of the distinction between life and death," [6] and thanks to congenital tuberculosis, the timely death of an adored fiancée at fifteen, generous philosophical borrowings from Fichte, and a special gift of abstract imagination, this confusion was effectively accomplished. The world became a dream, and his dream a world. Under these circumstances Nothing (in the full sense of cosmic emptiness) was difficult

5. She bears you like a mother, and you owe to her all your magnificence.
6. *Novalis Schriften*, ed. Heilborn (Berlin, 1901), II, 73.

and should in strict theory have been impossible for him to discover. For even if the nullity of the sensible world be assumed, the omnipotent imagination, the energetic will, the creative ego should be capable of filling quickly any temporary void. If, seeking the *"Unbedingte,"* he found mere *"Dinge"* everywhere, his own philosophy might have assured him that it was only because he was creating them. Faith, for Novalis, is at the root of ordinary perception — how much more at the root of the visionary process by which the poetic-religious imagination is forever re-creating and reconstituting the world.

In this process, it is but natural that the perspectives are shortened and the outer world, the world of not-void (of history, for example, and ethical generalization) tends to sink from sight. Though it is infinite and opulent, the visionary world of Novalis looms before us immediate and continually present, a smothering rush of perceptions; experience goes on and on, the mind passing through it like a train through a tunnel, without panoramas or sweeping overviews. It is a little like the recessing frameworks of which Keats was so fond, as one vision opens endlessly into another. Immediacy counting for so much, it is not altogether surprising to find Novalis melding the pattern of one violent sensual absorption with another, and persistently thinking of sexual love as a covert form of eating.

Of course this whole procedure of achieving an opulent, transfigured world via annihilation of self rests on an inexplicable mystery. How the death of the soul gives rise to ecstatic bliss, how Nothing is in effect transfigured into Everything, is no matter for sober prose to investigate. Still, sinking first into and then through the self is evidently an approach to a sort of Nothing, a way of visionary insight which Keats and Rossetti and Richard Wagner — to name no others, and to propose three very diverse figures indeed — are at one in following. The Nothing they find seems to be defined in adjectives like soft, dark, inner, passive, and enveloping; it is seen, characteristically, from the inside out; the critical, discriminating mind being laid asleep, Nothing absorbs and confuses the operations of soul and sense; indeed, the experience is so transcendent, that the full resources of the language must be strained merely to suggest it. Whether a Nothing so busy and positive is still Nothing is a question that will occupy us in future.

But if there is a void above and a void below, a void within and a void without, he who is intent on escaping void has need of a certain imaginative mobility. Here we are not likely to make any startling discoveries, for the exercise of psychic mobility is so much a literary norm that its ordinary manifestations are hardly noticeable. Does not every writer start in the presence of a yawning void, his blank sheet of paper (through which his mind's eye passes down the infinitely receding white archways of the quire) — to fill which he must invoke the teeming phantoms of his imagination? The material with which he fills it may be thick with recognizable thingly circumstance or thin, streaming, and patently fantastic — so far as single-minded students of Nothing are concerned, the presence of one stuffing or another makes, of itself, little difference. Social observation, it is conceivable, exhausts its given materials more quickly than imaginative enthusiasm — leaving a poet like Byron, for example, up against the brute fact of inner emptiness (see below, pp. 200–201), while poets of greater mobility can perhaps postpone this recognition for longer. Conceivably too, in the face of a particular threat, freely flowing fantasy may be mobilized more dexterously than stiff social fact to avert that motionless, distinct cessation which is proper void. But these distinctions are nugatory as well as vague. Anyone who wants vigorously to avoid dealing with Nothing can always make something serve as a pretext for not doing so, whatever his imaginative commitments. The topic cannot be crept up on or slipped into imperceptibly from some nearby outpost; one does not diffuse or diminish the texture of imaginative experience till it becomes imaginative non-experience. Actually, Nothing lends itself very poorly indeed to fantastic adornment. This point (if it were not perfectly obvious) could be documented at tedious length out of fantasiasts like Jean-Paul, Lautréamont, and Rimbaud. Derange the senses, loosen all bonds with the here and now, suffer spirit to skylark at liberty through the meadows of metaphor — and it will always find some new trick of language or thought to divert it. Behind the iridescent evocations of imagination, no doubt, one often senses the presence of a latent void, but it is a temporary and fleeting presence. Only in an occasional and special figure, of whom Thomas deQuincey may stand as the example, do psychic alarums become so gymnastic and their exercise so pointed that we are justified in pausing a moment to look at the psychic menace which helped evoke them.

DeQuincey is a surpassingly mobile writer of prose — the fact needs no emphasis; he writes as on a palimpsest, overlaying one set of thoughts with another, quick to transform one ostensible theme into a second, infinitely schematic and almost totally planless. Thus a disquisition on mail coaches turns into a tone poem on sudden death; a catalogue of excruciatingly physical symptoms opens into a moral essay; and an extended description of a specific childhood experience turns into a recurring opium-tinged fantasy. It is a world irregularly gaited and splotchily textured which deQuincey sets before us. At one moment the prose is flat and ecclesiastical, at another, whirling, and luminous with exotic images. Now it toils through a luxuriance of undramatic digressions, now it gallops through telescoped landscapes to an impassioned apostrophe. Within this lightning-lit, restive cosmos, blank Nothing rarely occurs. DeQuincey works hard at a special cross-purpose prose — dallying, when one expects him to get on with a story, and plunging forward when one thinks he must be at a stand. Thus Nothing takes its place in a stream of other visions, no one of which is ultimate; solitude, silence, infinity, and the abysm itself are merely arches thrown up for a moment while deQuincey passes through them. As in the famous vision of Piranesi climbing endless flights of stairs, he presents emptiness through a series of infinitely-recessed stages, one more instance of which is the pseudo-system itself of deQuincey's elaborately outlined rhapsody.

It is neither religious nor psychic void which presses most closely upon deQuincey. If he thinks of death as a void, it is a void of which man has already known the depths, of which he receives constant reminders in the course of his life, and which, even in physical corruption, is not ultimate:

> The solitude, therefore, which in this world appalls or fascinates a child's heart, is but the echo of a far deeper solitude through which already he has passed, and of another solitude, deeper still, through which he *has* to pass: reflex of one solitude — prefiguration of another.[7]

Though void is part of process, and one passes freely into it, one does not so freely get out, as the opium-eater, haunted by the sense of falling, could not escape from his dreams even by waking up. The nightmare here is a real waking nightmare, not to be handled by paradox or put off to a remote perspective by being associated with the sparse poles of the scientific universe. It does not use as backdrop the rocks and waves of reverberant nature; it is psychological hollowness, either of ultimate loneliness within one's skull, or of a wanderer among the disembodied, depersonalized faces of the city. Indeed, when human features are abstracted from human personality and set to

7. DeQuincey, *Works*, I, 189.

mocking the functions of nature itself, the misery of the opium-
eater is at its height:

> Hitherto the human face had often mixed in my dreams, but
> not despotically, nor with any special power of tormenting.
> But now that which I have called the tyranny of the human
> face began to unfold itself. . . . Now it was that upon the
> rocking waters of the ocean the human face began to appear;
> the sea appeared paved with innumerable faces, upturned to
> the heavens; faces deploring, wrathful, despairing, surged
> upwards by thousands, by myriads, by generations, by cen-
> turies. . . .[8]

This appalling elasticity of space, time, and every natural appearance of the outside world marks the great imaginative
achievement of the *Opium-Eater* (1822). There are no ulti-
mates; the sense of being a diminished wanderer between
towering precipices of architecture and emotion, down long halls
of time, leads to no resolution. There is nothing to anticipate.
One wakes from nightmares to daydreams, and though the
stream of consciousness and the stream of events both remain
full, yet the intermittent confusion and separation of them allows images to take meaning from whichever context they will:

> No loneliness can be like that which weighs upon the heart
> in the centre of faces never ending, without voice or utterance
> for him; eyes innumerable, that have "no speculation" in
> their orbs which *he* can understand; and hurrying figures of
> men and women weaving to and fro, with no apparent pur-
> poses intelligible to a stranger, seeming like a mask of maniacs,
> or, oftentimes, like a pageant of phantoms. The great length
> of the streets in many quarters of London; the continual
> opening of transient glimpses into other vistas equally far
> stretching, going off at right angles to the one which you are
> traversing; and the murky atmosphere which, settling upon

8. DeQuincey, *Works*, I, 117.

the remoter end of every long avenue, wraps its termination
in gloom and uncertainty, — all these are circumstances aiding
that sense of vastness and illimitable proportions which forever brood over the aspect of London in its interior.[9]

As deQuincey, like Piranesi, is out of all proportion to the size
of his urban architecture, so also is he out of proportion to his
own writings; they always tower, in their plans, far larger and
more intricate than he has power to build them, and the
perspective which they invoke, whether of the boundless desert
outside man or the infinite abyss within him, are always such as
to dwarf the little child-actor who is deQuincey the personage.
    Yet though he is infinitesimally small, deQuincey is irresisti-
bly persistent and resourceful; though he has only the phantasm
of a plan, and proceeds only indirectly by sidewise methods of
digression and analogy, yet the effect of his strange beetle-like
activity is somehow to fill up a previously hollow void of experience. A recent analyst points shrewdly to deQuincey's odd habit
of filling up his rooms with books and papers, stuffing and
cramming them to the absolute limit, and then moving out
— as a paradigm of his literary and spiritual activity.[10] His writings never raise the structure they set out to raise, but in the
course of his furrowings and burrowings, a series of secret
springs are tapped, the stir of his doing unleashes a flood of hidden waters, and as the toppling, jerrybuilt structure of his
thought collapses, there is a gush of redemptive emotion from
beneath. An image fascinating to deQuincey is the tarn, a lake
in reverse, which, being fed by subterranean springs, is literally
bottomless. As in "Kubla Khan," the model is that of a dome
built over a subterranean spring bubbling forth beyond the control of conscious intention. The image of disaster in the vertical
venture of climbing or building being redeemed by an action of

9. Works, II, 208–9.
10. J. Hillis Miller, The Disappearance of God, p. 41.

cradling from below or outside simply dramatizes this pattern. In fact, all deQuincey's prose has about it a sense of teetery high-wire work, of dangerous equilibrium, to which deQuincey himself calls repeated attention. He insists on his own consecutive logicality, yet is perpetually threatening to wander out of control, he is on the verge of falling, he stumbles, he falls, he is lost, lost forever, and yet he is unexpectedly caught, redeemed. His prose is like a substitute cosmos, an alternate existence. If it contains little and only impermanent void, the reason may be that the prose is itself an act of ingenious recurrent warfare against void.

DeQuincey is in effect a more subtle, less heroic player of the same game as Whitman — an ingenious, strenuous joker with an india-rubber ego which he is forever stretching to cover a multitude of circumstances or a sequence of logical-illogical inferences. Logic, or a sort of logic, spread much too thin, holds the extended front line; behind are drawn up sundry mobile detachments of the spirit, of the imagination. And hence all those incantatory mobilizations, those midnight assemblages and headlong charges of spiritual reinforcement, that hustle of vast nocturnal enterprise, which is characteristic of the deQuincey strategy. In these maneuvers many of his troops are assigned to make feints, demonstrations, and diversions; many others are set to reconnoitering the battlefields of long ago; and in the spiral of developing war, the same engagement must be fought many times over. Perhaps for these reasons, one's final feeling is that the whole conflict will never be allowed to surpass the stage where purple passages will redeem it.

II

Mirrors and Windows:

Poe, Gogol

Skaters over the brittle ice of ideology, the meager membrane of civilization, may break through into local areas of void repeatedly and with vaudeville effect, or into ultimate void, figured as blind unconsciousness or infinity, climactically and to an effect neither tragic nor comic but macabre.

The tug of Nothing against limited, prudential arrangements of practical existence is inherent in the topic; but what it is allowed to amount to in a work of art is very much up to the artist. A first step in seizing the elusive and prickly spirit of Poe is to distinguish that element of his mind which is ideological and *philosophe*, which asserts pugnacious dominion over the practical world, from that which is called "morbid" and "decadent" because it is impelled toward a darkness one major aspect of which is Nothingness. Any such sweeping division is, naturally, only provisional. A mind is diseased as a whole, and the neurotic rationalist will immediately turn his rationalism to the service of his neurosis; in part, this is the story of Poe. Yet, if only as surface, the technical, rationalist element of his mind makes itself variously evident. There is, for instance, the façade of universal erudition — an erudition which displays itself, above all, in reference to actual *philosophes* of the late eighteenth century, Marmontel, Condorcet, and so forth. The same psychic element is apparent in the repeated triumph of the reasoning mind over puzzling or hostile circumstance. By sheer power of rationality Dupin and Legrand, French heroes of intellection,

decipher the cunning signs left by the criminal mind or the no
less conspiratorial universe. Other heroes attack persistently the
sacred riddles and ciphers of the self. Even a story overshad-
owed by obsession and morbidity, like "Berenice," is distinguished by the victim's effort to control, analyze, explain, and
denominate the disease into which his mind is sinking. Montresor, the coldly rational French narrator of "The Cask of
Amontillado," tricks and holds with contemptuous ease (despite his own warnings and pleadings) and finally buries alive
the drunken Fortunato, walling him up with a click of rational
bricks, and discovering in the process that under the drunkard is
a human being — as it were, a portion of himself. The narrator
of "The Pit and the Pendulum," given almost no sense data at
all, yet reasons so well with the little he can scrape up, that he
evades one inescapable threat after another, till rescued by enlightened French troops. In the act of sliding into the Maelstrom, the natural philosopher masquerading as a Norse seaman
discovers a physical law (false in real life, as it happens) which
in the action of the story preserves his existence. The lady
Ligeia has so powerful an intelligence that even after death it
survives, usurps, and finally metamorphoses the corpse of the
fair Rowena. This passion for testing mind against material circumstance manifests itself in many ways, most strikingly in the
fabrication of pseudo-scientific devices and procedures to overcome death. In this sense, death is the most challenging of a
series of riddles, conundrums, and mystifications, the other extreme of which is a mere mechanical gimmick like "Maelzel's
Chess Player." [1] Mesmerism, galvanism, thought-transfer, met-

1. Maelzel was in fact an exhibitor of automata (see Chapuis & Gélis, Le
Monde des Automates [Paris, 1928], Vol. II), but his chess-player was, as
Poe saw, a rudimentary fraud. Electronic brains, I am informed, are by now
(1965) pretty good at checkers, to the point of beating nine out of ten
players they face; but chess, though theoretically within the capacity of a
machine, is a much more intricate game to program.

amorphosis, and metempsychosis are all pseudo-logical demonstrations of the power of the mind to overcome the last enigma. Sometimes the elaborate precautions and devices which Poe calls into service have an almost comic aspect; a story like "Premature Burial" assembles so many accouterments and conveniences for life beneath the mold that the hero seems to be preparing for a camping trip in the grave.

But triumph in the grand endeavor is by no means assured; in many of the stories, a main point is the mind's defeat in its master endeavor to solve the problem of death. The ingenious, presumptuous man invites hatred, not only from other actors, but from the narrator. Prince Prospero, thinking to elude the Red Death, retires to the deep seclusion of one of his crenelated abbeys; but his arrogance only singles him out the more surely to come first under dominion of the plague. The teller of "The Black Cat" describes himself weeping and deploring the crime he commits even in the instant of committing it; when later he reveals himself as the murderer of his wife, it is the last act of a drama in which he personates both the passionate criminal and the rational prosecutor. In "The Tell-Tale Heart" and "The Imp of the Perverse," the ambitious calculations of the criminal mind are defeated by an unpredictable, almost hysterical, movement of the incorruptible heart. "The Fall of the House of Usher" is explicitly a collapse, a *ruina*, of a palace "in the monarch Thought's dominion"; the disappearance of its fragmented masonry into the sullen waters of the tarn is the disappearance of a mental as well as a physical structure. Elsewhere a catastrophe of thought is barely concealed; the maelstrom and the pit are images of nightmare engulfment from which the ingenious narrators are rescued only so that they can recite their stories — and down into which they will inevitably and forever be falling, if only in imagination. A. Gordon Pym penetrates almost to the antarctic pole, to the heart of a vision at once white and deathly, to a vast, ambiguous figure — only to collapse in the "exterior" catastrophe of the supposed author's supposed demise. The effect is magnificently inconclusive — as if Poe had painted himself into a narrative corner, accepted the "logical" consequences, and committed suicide then and there. This too is a logical pattern, the carefully created *cul de sac* with a suicide in the middle of it, yet its final logical step lies outside, reverses, and actually undermines the sequence of the story proper. A concluding footnote very properly describes the resulting situation as a "vacuum."

A remarkable number of Poe's stories deal with the experience of falling or drowning or being buried; even the man who rises above his troubles as far as the moon is named "Hans Pfaal," and for most Poe heroes, horizon is the very lip of the grave. To these images of void — the long fall through empty space, the long descent into the grave — Poe's mind clings in fascinated horror; when reason proves powerless, these are the vortices down which he is hurled. Ultimate disaster is threatened so often and so long, it is averted (if at all) by such acrobatic and hairbreadth maneuvers, that all human relations are eaten out by it, becoming artificial and rhetorical. The diagram of personality that Poe represents is of a defensive palisade poised at the brink of a precipice, furiously assaulted from in front and, as the earth crumbles underfoot, in perpetual danger of sliding into the black abyss behind. There is no redeeming counteraction, as with deQuincey. Apart from Poe's always-deplorable humor, probably the greatest obstacle to an appreciation of his fiction is the sense of bluff and façade which clings to it. But it seems probable that just this notion of personality as exoskeletal — thin, fragile, and under furious attack — made bluff and façade necessary, and rendered Poe of interest to Baudelaire, who was also obsessed with a sense of beleaguered personality. "Poe looks to me like a helot who wants to shame his master," Baudelaire wrote; [2] but there is an ambiguity about the observation which is not clearly intentional. Traditionally in Sparta it was the masters who, in order to teach children self-control, made drunk the helots. Whoever instigated the display and for whatever reason, the struggle for moral advantage and literary effect between high Poe and low Poe is amply documented in the stories, and is a source of their interest.

To be sure, it is a fragile paradox which makes an author's interest depend on the transparency which his fictions cast over a personal psychic dilemma. Yet with Poe we are committed to such a gambit of defense; and we can reinforce it by emphasizing a kind of voluptuous particularity, an unusual fullness of response and insight, as soon as it is a question in his work of the mind's lapse from sentience into insentience, or back. A classic instance of this process, lovingly described, is the opening of "The Pit and the Pendulum," a virtuoso passage which describes the muffled gropings of a mind in search of its first bearings as it rises through the strata of sleep, its gradual self-reconstruction from the chaos of unconsciousness. The slow, stunned movement of these pages, the anxious emphasis of the style, false in logic but true in character, are the very reverse of the glib, mechanical manner popularly associated with Poe, to his discredit. A mind's reluctant process to understanding, a slow overcoming of obstacles, a gradual, stubbornly contested defeat — these are topics where Poe instinctively knows his way, which he renders movingly.

Yet in the end we wrong Poe in taking him as a psychological writer, for he is largely unconcerned with ruminative introspection, the careful analysis of his own or anyone's inner life. Rather he is caught up in a battle with the consequences of experience, a battle so ferocious that he has no chance to look be-

2. Preface to *Nouvelles Histoires extraordinaires* in *Oeuvres complétes*, ed. Gautier and Dantec, Paris, 1918–   , Vol. X.

yond panic as an enemy in itself. He can even recognize that
there is no good reason for fear without diminishing his own
terror of it:

> I have indeed [says Roderick Usher] no abhorrence of danger,
> except in its absolute effect — in terror. In this unnerved, in
> this pitiable, condition I feel that the period will sooner or
> later arrive when I must abandon life and reason together, in
> some struggle with the grim phantasm, FEAR.

This peculiar halfway use of psychology — to bury the object
obscurely in a perceiver's response to it, and to use that response
as a given fact, a shield against the uncovering of deeper facts
— is very characteristic. Fascinated as he is with death and post-
mortem survival, Poe has no faith or interest in the immortal
soul; he is exercised by the corpse, not the spirit, and the idea of
a general resurrection scarcely enters into his calculations. There
is not, in fact, much religion of any sort in his writings, no
heaven to speak of, and not much more than the intimation of a
hell. Wormy circumstance, along with the mind's unaided
struggle to accommodate to it, is all. As for "love," that sticky
word, the point needs no laboring that hopeless adoration from
afar is the essence of Poe's version. But his passion for exteriors
takes many forms. An intense concern for decor and furnishing
is expressed in "Landor's Cottage" and "The Philosophy of
Furniture"; the swagger and prestidigitation of his criticism is a
showing-off of glossy surfaces, and so is the nostalgic pseudo-
aristocracy of his politics. Fear of "insides" may well be responsible for the abrupt truncation of certain stories which one
could describe as "romances of penetration." Arthur Gordon
Pym cuts off his narrative at the exact moment when he has
reached the heart of mystery, the center of adventure; "The
Domain of Arnheim," describing a vast project toward a second
and improved nature, takes us through a long series of choices

and preparations and approaches to the very door of Ellison's (read "Allan's son's") residence, and there dissolves the vision in vague splendor.

Creature of threadbare exteriors, threatened by void without and vertigo within, Poe always raises the cracked house of reason next to the tarn of death and despair; his narcissism finds expression not merely in the repetition of his own name and features under the guise of his heroes, but in the heroes' mirroring of themselves in the water. The reduplication of Usher's house in the still waters of the tarn foreshadows its fate, and the nameless narrator of "Eleanora" falls fatally in love only when the happy couple see themselves mirrored in the waters of the River of Silence. Dead waters not only return and distort one's image, invite to reflection, and so lead to hallucinated mental fixation, they may swallow up the person of the looker as well as his mind. Usher, the Maelstrom-sailor, Arthur Gordon Pym, the narrator of "MS Found in a Bottle," and the actors in "The Assignation" are all swallowed up or closely threatened with disappearance into black and fatal waters. Still another recurrent device of self-perception which turns into self-destruction is the double. The second wife turns out to be the first one metamorphosed or in disguise ("Morella," "Ligeia"); the dream of Bedloe turns out to be the life-history of Oldeb ("A Tale of the Ragged Mountains"); Montresor echoes word-for-word much of the language of Fortunato, as he buries him alive; and William Wilson is pursued through life by a second self which, in unmasking his criminal enterprises and thwarting all his conscious endeavors, forces him always to confront his real self and his real hatred of it.

Absorbed, through these various devices, in the contemplation of exteriors — *existing*, as it were, chiefly in the act of self-inspection — the Poe heroes sometimes crumble, self-fascinated, into the waters of the inner tarn, sometimes fall more spectacularly to pieces under pressure of forces from without. Mere contemplation may effectually detach fragments of the human anatomy, as the narrator of "Berenice" finally reduces the lady to her teeth; like an equivalent protagonist of Gogol's, the actor of "Lionizing" exists chiefly in and for his nose; while "Predicament," a foolish effort at humor, describes a lady who without any ill effects is decapitated by a large church clock. As for Toby Dammit of "Never Bet the Devil Your Head," it is obvious what happens to him; while General Smith, of "The Man That Was Used Up," is discovered to be a mere collection of prosthetic and cosmetic devices attached to a small nondescript bundle which is the general, so to speak, proper. "Loss of Breath" is another sort of deformation, a little hysterical, as usual in these stories, in which the hero's irritation with his physical misfortune is comically independent of its usual consequences.

The joke of these dismemberment-fables often consists of taking metaphorical language literally, of acting out in the physical world some piece of figurative speech at which the author has suddenly stopped and looked afresh. And this suggests another principle of Poe's art, which is to distort the surface of his world by selective focusing. "The Sphinx" is a parable on this habit; the vast and deadly monster in the distance turns out to be a tiny insect seen from very close. "The Purloined Letter" is another study which illustrates failure to see as a result of failure to focus. Often the sinister and terrible elements of Poe's world are in themselves neither sinister nor terrible; they are simply observed in a special obsessed perspective. An irritating cat, a lady's handsome set of teeth, the gleam in an old man's eye — it is the exacerbated sensibility of the narrator that catches on these details, focuses on them, and generates around them magnetic fields of hate and fear. It is as if there were a slipping clutch between the world of things and the world of the person. This makes for a sort of freedom; deQuincey's type of psychic mobilization takes place readily in Poe. But also there is a reverse of this procedure; the mind, so swift to rally to its own fears, is parodied as glib and self-assured in making up rules which have nothing to do with any specific facts. Poe's narrator, shrewd and knowing fellow that he is, populates the world with these off-balance, off-point generalizations: "there never yet was any person named Charles who was not an open, manly, honest, good-natured, and frank-hearted fellow" ("Thou Art the Man"); or "if you flog a boy left-handed, you might as well not flog him at all" ("Never Bet the Devil Your Head"); or "jokers are, ninety-nine times out of a hundred, large, corpulent, and oily men" ("Hop-Frog"). The generalizations are usually out of the way of the story; they have an odious, complacent tone about them, which Poe is evidently out to deride; and as they illustrate, they burlesque the mind's mobile tendency to slip into and out of focus on what it accepts as the real world.

Poe's juggling act uses these and similar instabilities. Whether his fiction ever transcends vaudeville is a larger question. For certain passages within certain stories it can be claimed that the rendering has depth and fullness and all the extensive virtues traditionally attributed to a literary rendering. Yet this is not the distinctive thing about Poe; and sooner or later the argument in his behalf has to become a defense of his flats and façades. This obviously cannot be a defense on the score that they impress or deceive us, but on the score that in seeing through or around them we are fulfilling Poe's authorial intention. His work refuses to take on density and opacity, partly because of his own verbal inadequacies, partly in response to editors and readers who were satisfied with cheap tricks, but also because, at bottom, Poe had no intention of creating an artistic surface where the reader could repose, untroubled. He was forever shaming and betraying and confessing himself out

of a feeling that his symbolic fall would echo in a void already
known to the reader. At the head of Poe's book should be written the accusing line familiar from another:

— Hypocrite lecteur, — mon semblable, — mon frère!

In this context, the elusive, inventive character of Poe's
Nothing becomes one of his major achievements. It is everywhere in his work, in the swoons and trances of his characters,
in the outer space through which they hurtle, at the end of
their explorations, into the omnivorous maw of Death. For Poe
the fabric of the universe is transitory and sheer; it came from
Nothing, it will return via a great vortex to Nothing, the cold
wind of Nothing can be felt even now blowing through its
sleazy texture. Though it does not have (and perhaps could not
have) lapidary solidity, Poe's Nothing does possess a remarkable
variety of colorings and literary shadings; it has been imaginatively apprehended.

But because it has made solidity impossible, in Poe as well as
his universe, Nothing has also invoked perforce a new definition
of the reader, who can no longer be a placid, substantial gentleman, sitting in an overstuffed library chair, to be tickled with
entertainment, edified with instruction. He becomes an antagonist, a collaborator, a fellow-victim. All his potential energies
and inertias are tapped — which implies a deliberate gamble on
Poe's part as to his positive content. This gamble is Poe's vul-
nerability; it is also a condition of an imaginative achievement
which is also, sometimes, his. He is a charlatan, but a disaster-
haunted charlatan, a medicine-man who is deathly sick of the
human fever. Behind his buffoonery lies something open and
empty which greater men than Poe will in the decades after his
death make intimate to us and a bond between us.

On every score, Gogol is no doubt a greater artist than Poe;
but in both may be felt the same special dualism, which is easy

to schematize: a violent subsurface energy distorts or destroys the surface arrangements, rational and limited, of the social narrative. This undercurrent is felt from the beginning in *Dead Souls* (1842); it moves and works even on seemingly inanimate things, which provide, perhaps, the best evidence of its intermittent, unpredictable working. For the universe of *Dead Souls* has a composition not very easy to describe with assurance; it can be, at moments, thick and fleshy, almost disgusting, while at other times it is airy, genteel, and a little bit evasive. On occasion it has no quality at all, it is perfectly blank and featureless, as if a hot iron had passed over a wax figure, obliterating its wrinkles and features; very often pieces get arbitrarily detached from the continuum and sail off into orbits of their own. There are all sorts of gaps and interstices, which are filled in a random, inconsistent way — frequently with Nothing, so that they are just inconclusively there. And it is Nothing which haunts the author's vision, Nothing which inspires his most agonizing vertigo.

The opening pages of the novel are justly famous. They describe the arrival of a gentleman with no characteristics in a town which has no name other than N:

> The gentleman in the carriage was not handsome but neither was he particularly bad-looking; he was neither too fat nor too thin; he could not be said to be old, but he was not too young either.[3]

Two peasants, watching him arrive, detach for purposes of conversation a single wheel from his carriage; idly, vacantly they set arbitrary limits to the powers of the wheel. It would get to Moscow, all right, but not to Kazan; and the conversation, having served its only purpose, to relieve the two peasants of their inner emptiness by making them for a moment critics of the

3. *Dead Souls* (Penguin), tr. David Magarshack, p. 17.

world, lapses and is never resumed. A young man walks by, wearing specific canvas trousers, a swallow-tail coat, and a very individual pin indeed. The wind almost blows off his cap, but instead blows him out of the story forever.

Thus specific bits and vivid meaningless fragments of cosmos fly between the reader and that featureless, indeterminate gentleman who happens to be the hero of the story; what wind blows them we do not yet know. But the wall of represented substance which forms the backdrop for Gogol's characters has oddities of its own. It is unexpectedly neutral; it bulges and clots to a thickness in unanticipated places. Chichikov is ushered almost immediately into a familiar, ordinary Russian room at an inn — "where for a couple of roubles a day travellers are given a quiet room with cockroaches peering out from every corner like prunes" (p. 18). And these cockroaches, scuttling behind the woodwork, transform themselves imaginatively into that quiet, inquisitive man next door, who is all the more present in his silent curiosity as his presence is remarked just once and then left vacant. Chichikov now makes his way to the inn's public room, which is just like every public room everywhere else, exactly the same in every detail — "the only difference being that a nymph in one of the pictures had such enormous breasts that the reader cannot possibly have seen anything like it before" (p. 19). It is the essence of Gogol's grotesque that one feature of a drab landscape can suddenly swell to such obscene proportions; just so, in the story "The Nose," his nose separates itself from Kovalev, swells to human dimensions, dresses itself up in a fine uniform, and goes off to pay house-calls.

Amid this palpitating, pneumatic, fragmented universe wander the characters of Gogol — among them, no less bemused than the others, the story's narrator. This is not a very steady-gaited narrator to begin with, and amid the perils and pitfalls of this peculiar cosmos, he reels, staggers, and teeters from difficulty to disaster. Right away he gets tangled up in Chichikov's scarf, which for an ordinarily competent narrator would be no obstacle at all:

> The gentleman took off his cap and unwrapped from his neck a woollen rainbow-colored scarf, such as wives are in the habit of knitting with their own hands for their husbands, furnishing them with suitable instructions on how they should wrap themselves up; who provides them for bachelors I'm afraid I cannot tell — goodness only knows — I have never worn such scarves myself (p. 19).

His narration is particularly apt to bog down on a worldly generalization (like those of Poe) such as a categorical distinction between fat and lean civil servants, which has nothing to do with his fable; for the moment, wrenching himself away from the scarf problem, he gives Chichikov dinner, allows him a short nap, and takes him on a tour of the town. It is a dreary little town; the depths of its dreariness are measured in the thoroughness with which Chichikov inspects some spindly trees and reads the playbill through from beginning to end, both sides, including the printer's label. And its officials are perfectly commonplace, including the governor who, like Chichikov, was neither fat nor thin. We do learn about him that "he wore the order of St. Anne round his neck and it was even rumored that he had been recommended for the order of St. Stanislav; he was, however, a good fellow and sometimes even did embroidery on tulle" (p. 22). Thus, agile and insecure as a clown on skates, our narrator slides from skewed *non sequitur* to vapid irrelevance; words are used in what the second part of the book will call the "haemorrhoidal" sense; and in tripping over his own verbal feet, the narrator announces the hollowness not only of his characters but of his whole narration.

He explains very seriously that he will introduce Selifan and Petrushka, the servants of Chichikov; for he is a methodical narrator, and even though these are only secondary, or even tertiary characters, still he will introduce them. So he tells us that Petrushka was always reading books and had a very distinctive disagreeable odor; while, as for Selifan — but this is going *too* far, nobody wants to meet such a low-class person. And so we are never introduced to Selifan. Similarly when Chichikov meets Manilov — who has no character at all, no interests, and isn't even middle-aged — we are told at length of the disorder of the ménage. The chairs are not all covered, one of the candelabras is splendid, the other grubby, the house is messy, and Manilov in fact a sloven. "His wife. . . . Still, they were perfectly happy with one another" (p. 35). Or again, a page or two later: "One might perhaps make the further observation that Mrs. Manilov. . . . But I must confess I'm very much afraid of talking about ladies, and, besides, it is time I returned to our heroes" (p. 36).

As the narrator tumbles into and climbs laboriously out of little holes and pockets of void, so the personages of the novel are haunted almost tragically by void and vacancy. Manilov is well-mannered inane emptiness in a cellophane wrapper; his life is composed entirely of yawns, good intentions, and great, goggling, watery daydreams. He is so meager mentally, he does not even know he is bored; and he sees the whole world in his own insipid image. Nozdryov is a contrasting character, frantic with emptiness; he rushes about, kicking at reality or provoking it to kick him, in order at least to escape momentarily the frightful emptiness of his existence. His mania is for betting, cheating, quarreling; he bets to lose, makes wild assertions to be contradicted, cheats to be caught, and quarrels in order to feel, beating on his face, the fists of inescapable, undeniable reality. One of the saddest and funniest scenes in the book is that in which

Nozdryov takes his brother-in-law and Chichikov on a tour of his property. They see two mares and a stallion, for which Nozdryov says he paid ten thousand roubles. The brother-in-law has doubts about this improbable price, and Nozdryov wants to bet on it, but nobody will bet with him. Then they look at some stalls in which there were once good horses. They inspect the fishpond and hear of fish so enormous that two men were hardly able to pull one out. They look at some dogs with excellent haunches.

> Then they went to have a look at a Crimean bitch which was blind and, according to Nozdryov, would soon be dead, but which two years ago had been a very good bitch. They inspected the bitch too, and, to be sure, the bitch was blind. Then they went to have a look at a water-mill, which had lost its 'flutterer' or iron ring on which the upper stone rests as it turns rapidly on its axle or 'flutters,' as the Russian peasants so wonderfully express it.
> 'We shall soon come to the smithy,' said Nozdryov.
> And, to be sure, on going a little farther they saw the smithy; they inspected the smithy too (pp. 82–3).

The vacancy of those terrible open empty fields, the gentlemen plodding bored through the mud, the landowner fretting and exploding in his vain rage for something worthy of notice — it is a remarkable episode in a remarkable book. Plyushkin the miser lives in an even more squalid and sinister wilderness; we are not surprised to find his character defined specifically in terms of void. Peasant revenues, paid to him in the form of goods, were "put away in the storehouses and got mouldy and full of gaping holes and in the end he himself became a kind of gaping hole in humankind" (p. 128).

Vapid, suspicious, blockish, frantic, grasping — the landowners encountered by Chichikov are at the roots of their characters so many responses to the void that surrounds, invades, and threatens to supplant them. Chichikov himself is, socially speaking, a perambulating hollow; his enterprise, the purchasing of dead souls, is the shell of a substantial enterprise. When he finally opens a mysterious box which has been teasing us for some time, we are given an elaborate account, not of its contents, but of the partitions which divide it. And, like other empty characters whom he meets, Chichikov is avid to fill himself up in the most direct way possible; he is a frantic eater. Gentlemen of the middling sort, it seems, are all fond of sucking pig with horseradish and sour cream, roast veal, sturgeon cheeks, fish and cabbage pie, sterlet soup, mushrooms, curd tarts, and a thousand other delicate dishes with which they try, on every opportunity, to give themselves some substance. *Dead Souls* is a romance overflowing with food; the author misses no opportunity to specify in loving detail all the dishes in the enormous meals which his characters devour. Petukh, talking to Platon in the second part of the novel, tries to tell him that life is never boring; and indeed, as he lives it, ennui is quite impossible:

> I wake up in the morning and there's the cook to see, dinner has to be ordered, then I have breakfast, and then I have to see my estate agent and then I go fishing and then it's dinner time. You have hardly time to take a nap after dinner when it's time to see the cook again and order supper. When is there time to be bored (p. 306)?

This monologue has a clear satiric point to make against Petukh (whose name means "cock" or "rooster"); but it leaves little room for complacency on the part of handsome, empty Platon, whose boredom admits of no relief at all. If Platon with his philosophical name "stands" in some sense for the life of the mind and Petukh for that of the gut, a point is reinforced here which can be traced, like a scarlet thread, throughout the mesh of *Dead Souls;* it is a deep suspicion and hatred of thought.

Chichikov returns late and tired from his adventures in the countryside, goes to his room at the inn, is greeted by the waiter, and lied to by Petrushka — all accepted routines:

> Ordering a very light supper, consisting only of sucking pig, he undressed immediately after it, and getting under the bedclothes fell fast asleep, fell into a sound sleep, into that wonderful sleep which only happy mortals enjoy who know nothing of haemorrhoids, or fleas, or strongly developed intellectual faculties (p. 141).

This is one sort of Gogolian by-blow at the philosophic mind. Or again, when he approaches Plyushkin's house, Chichikov passes through a grotesque and gaping forest, full of unlit chasms,

> yawning like the open mouth of some huge wild animal; it was plunged in shadow and in its dark depths could be dimly discerned: a narrow path disappearing in the distance, broken-down railings, a tumbledown summer-house, a decaying willow trunk, full of holes, and from behind the willow-tree a dense gray caragana thrust out its thick stubble of twigs and leaves, tangled and intertwined and withered from growing in this terrible thicket; and, finally, the young branch of a maple-tree, stretching sideways its green claw-like leaves, under one of which a shaft of sunlight suddenly transformed it, goodness only knows how, into a transparent, fiery leaf, gleaming wonderfully in that dense darkness (p. 122).

The wilderness as described is scarcely charming; on the contrary, everything about it suggests distortion, violence, savagery. Yet its effect, in juxtaposition with the miser's house, is unexpectedly beautiful, beyond the reach of either nature or art by itself,

> as only happens when they unite together, when nature's chisel puts its final touch to the often unintelligently heaped

up labor of man, relieves the heavy masses, destroys the all
too crudely palpable symmetry and the clumsily conceived
gaps through which the unconcealed plan reveals itself so
nakedly, and imparts a wonderful warmth to everything that
has been created by the cold and carefully measured neatness
and accuracy of human reason (p. 122).

Upon these principles, a bramble-patch would add beauty to
the Parthenon. But evidently Gogol is not talking simply about
forests and residences. . . .

Though by no means subtle indications of attitude, passages
like these are marginal; the book's real impatience with conscious mind explodes in the author's recurrent, intermittent
outbursts against his own story. Chichikov is a traveler, a bachelor, a rootless, insubstantial man on a kind of pilgrimage; he
drives into the book from nowhere, going only vaguely anywhere; and the author expresses or implies frequent impatience
to get him through with the masquerade. As early as the opening of Chapter 2, the reader is being assured that he will learn
about Chichikov's project "gradually and in good time, if only
he has the patience to read through this very long story, which
will assume greater and much vaster dimensions as it nears its
end, which crowns all" (p. 29). The digression at the end of
Chapter 5, on the peculiar, rushing, restless power of the Russian word calls one's attention to an energy which is not finding,
and cannot find, expression in the human comedy. Indeed, the
occasion for the digression is precisely a word that cannot be repeated, that is represented in the text of Dead Souls only by a
discreet nineteenth-century dash. But this screened and latent
energy erupts again at the opening of Chapter 7, in an apostrophe to the happy traveler. He is the one who has a family to
come home to. "Happy the family man who has a home of his
own, but woe to the bachelor!" The happy traveler, the married
man, is identified with the idealistic poet, the writer who "with-

out touching the earth has immersed himself completely in his own exalted images that are so far removed from it." All mankind is his loving family, they welcome him home and bathe him in love and affection. But the writer who picks a low topic from real life, the outsider, the bachelor, gets no such reward:

> without fellow feeling, without response, without sympathy, he is left standing alone in the middle of the road like a homeless wayfarer. Hard is his calling in life and bitterly he feels his solitude.
>
> And [the passage continues, modulating into unabashed first person singular] for a long time to come am I destined by the mysterious powers to walk hand in hand with my strange heroes, viewing life in all its immensity as it rushes past me, viewing it through laughter seen by the world and tears unseen and unknown by it. And the time is still far off when the terrible storm of inspiration will rise up in another stream out of a head encircled with a halo, inspiring sacred terror and, abashed and in trepidation, men will hear the majestic thunder of other words (p. 142). . . .

This passage, like similar outbursts in the last two chapters, is stirred by an image of the story itself as a journey, an adventure. Behind its pathos and rhetoric, intruding upon the artifice of the novel and whirling its paper-cutout characters into wild spirals, is the breath of a passion for the infinite and the limitless which finally translates itself into the mad gallop of those mythical horses, the wild careering of that supernatural troika beyond time, space, artifice, convention — out of this world. The novel simply goes out of control at the end, as it was threatening to do all along, peels off into a long climbing turn, and disappears among the thunderous stars.

Looking back, one senses how telling was that reversal, managed by Gogol's feeling at the start of Chapter 7, where the idealist was described as a domestic figure, the disagreeable real-ist as a bachelor. This exactly reverses the conventional posture of things as represented, for example, by Marchbanks and Morrell, in Shaw's *Candida*. For Gogol, the lofty and inspirational writer winds up taking what amounts to the short view of experience (ideals unify, comfort, soften life; they bring people together), while the embittered bachelor, who forces people to see what is directly under their noses, takes an ultimate perspective on it. He can perhaps do so because the Nothing of things offers him easy passage through them; but if he had a married man's confidence in the surface tension of life, the void might not be there at all. Perhaps in the storm of inspiration both ways — the way above and the way through — will be made one. But for the moment they are terribly opposite; and in their opposition the old heroic mode is irremediably fractured. The old-fashioned hero, like his own statue, imposes himself as a monumental shape or shell; the new ultimate is reached by a collapse of the ordinary, which collapses more radically, and enables us to see more deeply into the hollowness of things, as it is emptier. Such a psychic action accomplishes neither the cruel distancing of comedy nor the sympathetic release of tragedy but a wry and violent tension beyond which, for the moment, we need not look.

III

The Ordinary in Front of the Infinite:

Flaubert and Others

Nothing as Death may be used to cast back a remote and chilling light on or through human life; but more intricate and poignant effects rise from Flaubert's persistent vision of it as a principle of human life itself.

Death as personal annihilation is an ancient and available variety of Nothing, with traditional functions in artistic representation. It is a terminus (and in an art-work that carries with it the idea of a resolution); it is a distancing, suggesting an ultimate perspective or perhaps a last judgment; and its cold authenticity can be used to spook the complacent adjustments of a here-and-now to which readers are inevitably committed. Dr. Rank's calling card (in A *Doll's House*) suggests many of these functions in miniature. It acts as a mirror at the end of a dark hallway, flashing out of a blackness into which the character has already half-disappeared, and calling the audience's attention to the shallowness of that well-lit, comfortably heated room within which the Helmer ménage exists. The audience does not see into or through the card (which has been arranged to signal Dr. Rank's approaching death); it is given the X to look at and an instant to estimate the imaginative distance from which that symbol comes. Then we return to the domestic comedy in the foreground, but with a sense that its doings have been rendered translucent for an instant, and gossamer-thin. The same momentary glimpse into a cold, far perspective is used repeatedly by Maupassant to erode the social and creaturely satisfactions of what he sees as a superficial existence. George Duroy, the flashy, brassy hero of *Bel-Ami* (1885), has just fleshed himself in the good life when he steps from a warm drawing room into the cold night, to stroll home with a fellow employee, Norbert de Varenne. Talking idly, almost to himself, the old poet tells his young colleague what it means to live alone, face to face with the fact of death:

> Yes, she has ground me down, the bitch [*la goueuse*], she's completed softly and terribly the long process of ruining my existence, eating every second at it. And now I feel myself dying in everything I do. Every step I take brings me closer to her; every motion, every breath hastens her horrible work. Breathing, sleeping, drinking, eating, working, dreaming, whatever I do, it's all dying. Living is nothing but dying.[1]

Alone in this world, and skeptical of the next, he recommends domesticity to Georges Duroy, but almost mechanically; and the very simplicity of the panacea makes apparent that for some reason, the more impressive because unspecified, it does not apply to him:

> Loneliness now fills me with a horrible anguish: loneliness in one's room, by the fire of an evening. Then it seems to me that I am alone on the earth, horribly alone, but surrounded by vague dangers, unknown and terrible threats; and the wall which separates me from my unknown neighbor makes me as remote from him as from the stars I can see out my window. . . . It is so deep and so gloomy, the silence of the room where one lives alone. It is not just a physical silence, but a silence around the soul . . . (361).

This discourse does not have much effect on the brassy assurance of Bel-Ami; he barely murmurs to himself, "Gawd, can't be very cheerful in *his* house," when the odorous passage of a

1. *Contes* (ed. Pléiade), 358–9.

perfumed woman drives the whole topic from his wolfish head. But the reverberations of death are never stilled; detailed touches of episode pick them up again and again; and as they hollow out the sensual, unscrupulous animal Bel-Ami, they hollow out also the world within which he fits so glibly.

Thus the death or loneliness which Maupassant uses to haunt his characters has invariably a cosmic overtone, appeals to the icy chill of the stars or invokes the unthinkable distances of outer space.[2] It erodes the concerns of this world by introducing the far perspective of another one. Its ultimate development is a direct attack on the reader, and the reduction of literary character to a pretext. One sees this development at term in Tolstoi's "Death of Ivan Ilyich." In looking through Ivan Ilyich (featureless fellow that he is, generalized even in his name), the reader is to catch a reflection of his own existential condition from the mirror of ultimate void, to see his own essential loneliness as a human animal. That he may not get in the way of this vision, Ivan Ilyich is made as featureless as Manilov; and the effect of his death staring through him at us may be described as an action of primitive backlighting — more complicated versions of the same essential action will be on display later. But the reversed light of "Ivan Ilyich" could not be stronger, nor the fictional screen more transparent. The effect is something like that produced by overlighting in photography, an indiscriminate glare.

Flaubert, on the other hand, gives void a larger meaning, associates it more intricately with the business of this world, and does not hang his effects so directly on a cosmic perspective which eats out all human behavior. But his relation to Nothing

2. See, for example, the parallel meditations of Christiane Andermatt in *Mont-Oriol*, at the moments of falling in love with Paul Bretigny (I, vi) and of being deserted by him (II, vi). Astral distance comments on, and reduces to nothing, all illusions of human community.

is too elaborate and interesting to be summarized, it must be traced. We begin with a sense of something dead within the novelist himself, an impression widely recorded, of which Flaubert himself made frequent use. A passing portrait in *Charles DeMailly*, novel by the brothers Goncourt, makes this ancient buried death the key to his character:

> He is a man who has had something killed beneath him in his youth — an illusion, a dream, one can't tell. Deep within him grumble and yawn the rage and frustration of a vain attempt to storm some distant heaven.[3]

When Flaubert himself uses equivalent images to tell Louise Colet that he is incapable of a grand passion, he is to be suspected of defensive maneuvers; yet he recurs to them frequently, and with a monotony which is almost evidence of sincerity:

> The hand which I burned, the skin of which is wrinkled like that of a mummy, is less sensitive to cold and heat than the other. My soul is the same; it has passed through the fire; no wonder if it will not warm up under the rays of the sun.[4]

Another nearby letter ends with a metaphor of himself as an empty glass from which Louise or anyone else will be hard put to draw a drink of water (II, 16), and a dozen different images lead always to the same vision of a damaged life.

Ravaged by other flames, he protests; and so it may have been, and it does not militate strongly against this dramatic notion that the only conceivable incendiary, Mme. Schlesinger, seems to have had no particular sense of high temperature. There are inner flames. But not everyone who has suffered from them cultivates the aftereffects with Flaubert's tender loving care. Whatever inward chagrin his third decade may have

3. Section XXX; (Paris, 1913), p. 162.
4. *Corresp.*, ed. Louis Conrad (Paris, 1926–27), II, 12; 23 Feb. 1847.

suffered from love or ambition,[5] it can only have been his sense of all-but-universal nineteenth-century *bassesse* that amplified inner desolation into the cosmic pessimism of his middle years.

Flaubert's most acute sense of void derives neither from introspection (he is not the wandering outlaw of his own dark mind) nor from contemplation of ultimate distances (death, solitude, infinity), but from the middle ground of human experience and human history, seen in a special light. Instead of opposing death and domesticity in a clamorous contrast, he collapses them. This is the desert through which the artist voyages like a Bedouin, poised between the void of the waste sands and the void of heaven (possessing "ni base ni echo"), while his thoughts, like following eagles, spiral ever higher.[6] He is a priest of the cult of thirst. If circumstances do not favor such a figure with a ready-made desert, he will have to create one himself, and it is not hard to sense that Flaubert took some pains in that direction.

So far as he could arrange it, Flaubert was a man to whom Nothing was continually and deliberately happening. One notes how often his letters conclude with the almost-triumphant phrase, "absolument rien de nouveau." Alone at Croisset, he rose at noon, worked till 3 or 4 in the morning, saw no visitors, scarcely ventured forth into the sunlight, distinguishing neither one day from another nor day from night, and described his life to Ernest Feydeau as a "savage and extravagant existence which pleases me greatly, without an event, without a sound. It's the

5. He is saying to Louise Colet in 1847 that she should have met him six or eight years ago when he was unscarred (*Corresp.*, II, 13); that would have been in 1841, at the latest, when he was no more than twenty. But his passion for Mme. Schlesinger began at the precocious age of fifteen — and must thus be presumed not to have scarred him for the first five years, or six. Behind all this confusion of dates and vagueness of persons, one feels a certain doubt on the part of Flaubert himself as to what had happened to him, a readiness to attribute it to any handy circumstance.

6. *Corresp.*, IV, 39, letter to Louise Colet of 19 March 1854.

objective void [*néant*] entire" (*Corresp.*, IV, 286, letter of 19 Dec. 1858).

Confined to a sharp edge of consciousness by a literary theory which forbade him to write of his private life, further constricted by his hatred and contempt for the civilization around him, he cultivated that "néant objectif" which he called in another context "une vie *neutralisante*" (*Corresp.*, II, 445-6). The artificer's pride in creation sustained him in so many ways — against inner and outer voids, against the needs of his own personality (including the threat of death and annihilation), against society's lures, against the "natural" in its many aspects — that he inevitably came to dream of making Nothing itself his theme. Why should the perceptive reader need more support from the world of reference than the author?

> What seems fine to me, what I would like to do, is to write a book on nothing [*rien*], a book without any exterior support, which would sustain itself by the inner force of its style as the world, without being held up, rides through space, a book which would be almost devoid of subject, or at least in which the subject would be almost invisible, if that were possible (*Corresp.*, II, 345).

Two ideals run together here, in a pattern which is the more interesting because it is not strictly logical. The book about Nothing is to be without "attache extérieure," it declares independence of a world of flesh and blood; but it is to be a world in itself, is to have that magnitude and coherence which are its title to independence of conventional gravities. Biographically speaking, the man who aspired to write that book about Nothing is observed throughout his career to write books which are about more and more, which are documented with greater and greater particularity, till the last one, *Bouvard et Pécuchet*, is about little short of everything. Yet it is centrally about Noth-

ing too; about the exploration of everything, the discovery of
Nothing. The notion of Nothing has expanded, from little
patches and pockets of void in the early books, to an archaeo-
logical enclave in hollow *Salammbô*, to a perfect globe of complacency and folly in the last novel. But always it is a social phenomenon; by contrast with the awful emptiness of the social
animal, the emptiness of outer space is almost consoling, and
the *trou noir* of death is downright comfortable:

> This sense of my own weakness and emptiness [*néant*] com-
> forts me. I feel myself a mere speck of dust lost in space, yet
> I am part of that endless grandeur which envelopes me. I
> could never see why that should be cause for despair, since
> there could very well be nothing at all behind the black cur-
> tain (*Corresp.*, IV, 196, letter to Mlle. de Chantepie, June
> 1857).

Another passage declares, "The hypothesis of absolute void
contains nothing at all which terrifies me. I am ready to fling
myself into the great black hole with perfect calm" (*Corresp.*,
IV, 170, letter to Mlle. de Chantepie, 30 March 1857). Again
one suspects of *blague* these lectures on popular philosophy de-
livered to the soft, sympathetic ear of a bluestocking confidante
(Flaubert writing to a male contemporary was a much more
Rabelaisian and matter-of-fact fellow); but once again the
"pose" is maintained with remarkable consistency. Toward the
idea of death Flaubert did in fact turn the calm, antique "fixité
d'un visage pensif" (*Corresp.*, IV, 464, undated letter to
Mme. Roger des Genettes — 1861?); by contrast, the mere presence of a bourgeois drove him foaming and blaspheming from
the room. The infinity of death, like that of galactic space, had
about it an icy dignity, in the face of which style gained its ultimate meaning; but to be void of style was the real void, an
emptiness more awful because more crass and assured than any

authentic austerity. His real loathing, Flaubert told Louise Colet in a memorable letter, was for those who would

> invite humanity to be seated, monstrous in its obesity . . . and to be there, shifting about on its hams, drunk, blissful, its eyes shut, digesting its dinner, waiting for its supper, and squirming around on its crotch. Ah! I shan't die without having spat in its face with all the force I possess (*Corresp.*, IV, 33, letter of 2–3 March 1854).

Fat, empty, and bloated with self-conceit; this is humanity as it presses on Flaubert.[7] One of his choicer images for it is that of an old, drunken, slovenly whore returning late at night from a masked ball, comfortable in her carriage and protected by the gendarmes from bad boys who might hoot and jeer. The void which enraged Flaubert pushed up against him, cracking-fat as a sausage-skin, and was no less a void for that beastly presence of assured, unclean brawn. By contrast, cosmic void, as it gives man reason to doubt his own intellect and sense his own diminished proportions, has about it something aseptic and soothing. The fictions develop these feelings with a curious inevitability.

The mother of Charles Bovary, though forced by nature to work with cursed and cross-grained materials, had nothing less than Napoleonic ambitions for her son. Having bustled and threatened him through medical school, she found him a place

---

7. See, for a comparable image from the fiction, the picture of Homais and Bournisien, ancient antagonists, sleeping by the corpse of Emma: "They were opposite one another, bellies puffed out, faces swollen, expressions scowling, after so much disagreement finally at one in the same human weakness; and they budged no more than the cadaver beside them, which seemed to sleep" (*Madame Bovary*, ed. Garnier, p. 368). This scene in turn is probably based on one which Flaubert remembered, of sitting up by his sister's deathbed while her husband wheezed and the priest snored, and Flaubert himself looked up from reading Montaigne to reflect on mortality and the stars (*Corresp.*, II, 3, letter to Louise Colet, undated — early 1847?). The scene is beautifully commented by René Girard, *Mensonge romantique et vérité romanesque*, pp. 156–7.

to practice where the competition was safely moribund, and briskly pushed him into it.

> But it wasn't enough to have raised her son, to have had him taught medicine, and to have discovered Tostes for him to practice it; he needed a wife. She found him one: the widow of a bailiff from Dieppe, forty-five years old with an income of 1200 francs a year.
>
> Though she was ugly, dry as a stick, and speckled as springtime, Madame Dubuc had no lack of suitors to choose among. To gain her ends, Mother Bovary was obliged to outwit them all, and she even thwarted very cleverly the intrigues of a butcher who had the support of the clergy (I, i).

The marriage itself, the arrangements, the honeymoon, the settling-in of the happy couple, we pass over now, in the interval between one paragraph and the next; Charles is to know nothing of marriage, in this first experience of it, but the disenchantments. Flaubert's handling of the details is brusque and business-like. One sees him leaning number against number (45 years versus 1200 francs of income) and metaphor against metaphor ("sèche comme un cotret" versus "bourgeonnée comme un printemps"). And since this last balance occurs within a subordinate clause we have scarce time to sense its comic emptiness (analogous to Donne's mistress in "The Anagram," widow Dubuc has nothing of the spring but its spots and pimples), before we are embarked on the absorbing, ambitious strategy of outwitting the butcher.

Such a whirl of activity in a novel of sedate pace is exceptional. To be sure, Flaubert is covering preliminary ground here; the first Madame Bovary, aside from being the mere creation of Charles's mother, exists within the book chiefly as a setting for her successor. But the author is also building toward a positive effect. One could describe widow Dubuc as a repulsive tent of personal disabilities draped over the pole of her 1200 francs, to be invested by one of her several suitors. And this concurrence of suitors, though described with dry reserve, is presumed to "prove" the stability and worth of the structure being assaulted by *la mère* Bovary. The massing of priests behind the butcher suggests that both spirit and flesh are in agreement on the supreme value of widow Dubuc. What holds her up is the money; what engineers Charles into her embrace is his mother; and Flaubert's swift, hard sentences give the reader no more opportunity than Charles has himself to question this ferocious bit of social mechanics.

Once set up over him, the tent of widow Dubuc drips exasperations on Charles; they fall at irregular, relentless intervals for the rest of her fourteen months as Madame Bovary. She is querulous, plaintive, domineering; she wants of her husband "a tonic for her health and a little more love" — the conjunction of these beseechings implying awful things about their life in bed. If the marriage is achieved under the image of a construct, an arrangement, a contrivance hanging off the money, the widow within it is seen under the image of a knife. She is long of fang, sharp in speech, sharp in business practices, wears a dress like a sheath ("sa taille dure était engainée"), and when Charles's mother comes to visit, the two women chop him up like a couple of mincing knives between them.

It just happened — "il arriva" — at the beginning of spring that a notary who held some of Mme. Dubuc's funds absconded; in the investigation, the tentpole supporting Mme. Dubuc collapsed. She had no money; she had lied. Her house still stood but it was eaten up ("vermoulue") with mortgages; her interest in the boat was only half what she had said; the absconding notary had the rest. And in the rage and recriminations which follow, one finds Charles, her chief victim, taking her part against his own parents — independent at last, just in time to side with this deflated horror, whom his father, for the first time, is clear-sighted enough to call by her proper name — "une haridelle . . . dont les harnais ne valaient pas la peau" ("an old hag, whose harness wasn't even worth her skin"). She is deflated by accident; without warning, for no specified reason, she dies. "Quel étonnement!" says Flaubert, speaking through the mind of Charles, and summarizing, in that little pop of surprise and nothing more the full emptiness of his response. Later we shall see the bereaved husband learning to sentimentalize his loss ("She had loved him after all"). Still later the only memory which will remain of widow Dubuc is the icy coldness of her feet in bed. But for the moment, only that little pop of a sudden void, and nothing to fill it except the moment's surprise. Le père Rouault, recently bereaved, had howled like a dog; and when he thought of all the other fellows, with their snug little wives "à les tenir embrassées contre eux," he had been wild with grief and jealousy. But in Charles there is always less than meets the eye. His marriage had been hollow, his love for Heloïse (!) a pretense; the void within, responding to a sudden void without, echoed simply — pop! And thus Charles, that man of infinite emptiness, has presided over a first preliminary demonstration of the void in Flaubert. It is abrupt and climactic; it appears from inside, not outside, as a result of an accident or unforeseen development, at the end of a process of solidities; it is neither terrifying nor threatening, but cruelly comic. At the novel's end, when Charles ceases to live as abruptly as his first wife had done, the doctor makes a post-mortem, and finds — once more, as always — Nothing.

Pervading the novel, Nothing as it impinges on Emma is generally somber in its tonality. It is sensed behind the reverberant pomposity of Homais's verbiage and that of the agricultural orators, it is in the indifference of Abbé Bournisien to Emma's cry for spiritual help (pp. 122–3), it is summarized in the figure of Charles, besotted with domestic comfort, driveling endlessly by

the fireside while Emma shakes with impatience to get outdoors
where her lover is waiting (185–6). Void becomes vibrant and
predatory in a direct physical sense at that moment when
Emma, overwhelmed by Rodolphe's letter, rushes blindly up
into the attic and looks out over Yonville:

> The rays of light which mounted directly from below were
> drawing the weight of her body toward the void [*l'abîme*].
> It seemed to her that the ground of the square was shaking
> to and fro, rising along the walls, and that the floor was
> tilting at one end like the deck of a rolling ship. She held
> herself at the edge, almost hanging out, surrounded by an
> immense empty space. The blue of the sky flooded through
> her, the air rushed through her empty brain, she had only to
> let go, let herself be taken; and the buzzing [*ronflement*] of
> the lathe never stopped, like a furious voice which kept calling
> her (227–8).

The "ronflement" of the lathe echoes back to Charles, snoring
indifferently in the marriage-bed; heightened now to an angry
voice shouting in Emma's ear, it becomes the tumult of incho-
ate demands which are drawing her down; and the beauty of
the passage is the sense of her existence drawn very thin, almost
gauzy, under pressure, and fluttering for a moment over the
void which reaches up to take her as Rodolphe has now let her
drop.

By herself, feeling bored, Emma is merely a fashionable
young lady idling about empty fields near Tostes with her grey-
hound Djali, dreaming of Paris, pale passionate gentlemen, and
blue mountain-passes. She is committing the classic female fault
in mistaking what Flaubert somewhat coarsely calls the "cul"
for a more exalted principle; but she would never be driven to
arsenic-eating by this alone. What drives her frantic with despair and irritation is finding herself in the slack, fumbling grasp
of nerveless males. Her affair with Rodolphe was on the verge
of petering out from sheer ennui; what gave it fresh, though

OF VOID DURING THE NINETEENTH CENTURY

vindictive, point was Charles's inane botch of Hippolyte's leg. But her revulsion from the husband bats her back like a tennis-ball on emptiness again — back to Rodolphe, whose cynicism has been given a most ambiguous description:

> He had heard these things so many times over that they held no freshness for him. Emma was like all his other mistresses; and the charm of novelty falling away from her bit by bit like a garment left naked the eternal monotony of passion, which always assumes the same forms and the same language. He did not distinguish, this practiced man, a difference of senti-ments beneath equivalent expressions. Because libertine or venal lips had murmured to him the same phrases, he be-lieved only weakly in the sincerity of Emma's. One should discount, he considered, exaggerated speeches covering medio-cre sentiments; as if the fullness of the soul did not overflow sometimes in the emptiest metaphors, since nobody, ever, can give the exact measure of his needs or of his thoughts or of his sorrows, and since human speech is like a cracked kettle on which we beat out tunes to make bears dance, when our desire is to touch with passion the stars (211–12).

This passage has been taken, on a primitive level, as an apologia of Flaubert's for his novel. The author is saying, it would seem, that he cannot render a dialect for Emma which will show that she was really sincere; so if the reader does not want to seem gross like Rodolphe, he will believe in her clichés and plati-tudes. . . . But this much we do not want; no reader can possi-bly reverse his whole view of Emma so abruptly. In fact, she has no sensation to offer Rodolphe that he has not had a thousand times before; and her high romantic vein is just as radically used up for the reader. Inescapably, she is a bear-musician (and in-effectual at that) rather than a softener of the stars. But after we strip off novelty, strip off forms and language (ambiguously presented as the naked unchanging shapes of passion, but also to be discarded as exterior dress), we are allowed to glimpse what is hidden from Rodolphe, "la dissemblance des sentiments." Rodolphe cannot see this difference (which wholly subverts "l'éternelle monotonie de la passion"), he has been emptied of his power to do so by too much "pratique"; he not only fails to see passion, hidden by its forms, its language, even its novelty, but also the things behind passion which would soften the stars if they could be seen — "besoins, conceptions, douleurs." Flaubert is not apologizing for incapacity to render this buried instinctual life; he is merely reminding us that it is there, remote as the heavens, beneath frock-coat and crinoline, though neither of the actors on his stage can articulate it, and one cannot even perceive it.

In fact, the life of instinct, which is intimately involved with the spiritual ideals that make tender the stars, *has* been rendered in the novel. "Liberty," "hope," and "happiness," all used within a single line and without significant irony, are the words that define the days of Emma's youth, of her unspoiled sensuality, of her peasant existence (190). There is a nearby reference to "illusions," to be sure, but it cannot undercut Emma's remembered childhood joys — which, as they were not based on a philosopher's definition of error and a syllogistic deduction therefrom, are not really subject to error, being in fact nothing but what they seem to be.[8] Perhaps it is an illusion to think that one can "attendrir les étoiles" at all; but if one can (and the metaphor at least suggests a major effect of Flaubert's art), it will be with a truth of the heart. The truth of Emma's early years is woven richly through the story of her fury and frustration amid the white-collar bourgeoisie. There was a beehive outside her window at les Bertaux,

8. In fact the "abondance d'illusions" of this passage is dramatic; Emma, heartsore, is recalling pleasures no less, but also no more, illusory than her present mood of despair. "Illusions" is a word tinged by that mood.

and sometimes the bees, circling in the light, struck against the panes like bouncing balls of gold (190).

Days of furry gold balls, rebounding in the light, to contrast with the long drab journey of her middle-class life, from which the shattered and broken illusions drop steadily away, "like a traveller who leaves a bit of his money in each of the hotels along the way" (190). Or again there is the little vignette of Charles and Emma drinking curaçao in the kitchen at les Bertaux; having filled his, she pours a ladylike sip into her own glass:

> As it was almost empty, she leaned back to drink; and, her head thrown back, her lips pouting, her neck strained, she laughed at touching nothing, while the tip of her tongue, slipping between her fine teeth, licked daintily at the bottom of the glass (23).

Socially, this is a conventional girl (the tiny sip); sensually, an avid one (the strain to lick up the last drop of liqueur); but she is also, in the fullness of her commitment, a St. Theresa for the spoiling; and her young laughter at feeling Nothing in the inverted glass echoes many later tears.

Illusions, ideals, or instincts, Flaubert refers to them variously in his novels and correspondence, usually distinguishing among the three words as occasion demands. But they are alike in growing out of creaturely needs, conceptions, and griefs, and in perishing under the inevitable years; they largely make up the ruined poetic debris over which rises the portly fabric of a notary.[9] In these definitions of ourselves we escape the middle range of social being, where we are mere trained stereotypes — dancing bears — acting out a definition. And that Emma

9. For Maupassant the stars are an emblem of unreachable distance, hence of loneliness and death; for Flaubert they are not only an escape from bears and bear-music but capable of pronouncing sympathetic benediction on our most intimate impulses.

should have secret access to a mode of existence beyond that of
Charles or Rodolphe or Homais is necessary to the novel. The
benediction of the senses, actually pronounced in one passage
but implicit in a thousand others, acts to irradiate Emma's otherwise foolish and unredeemed idealisms. Her romantic dreams
are empty metaphors in which the fullness of her soul — and of
her sensuality — overflows. She is a prudential fool to confuse
the two, and a fool in a more ultimate sense; but as outsider she
is a sacred fool, existing in a *vrai* or *juste* to the reality of which
a sensitive and disinterested register like Justin bears just witness. She attracts the reader's sympathy by being vulnerable
where Homais and Rodolphe are invulnerable, exposed where
they would rather not exist at all. But their damnation, and that
of their common code, is defined by the reader's sense of
Homais as a wind-machine, Rodolphe as pleasure-mill.

It is no very subtle observation that, wherever Emma goes,
she finds Homais; in Charles, in prudent, practical Rodolphe,
and ultimately in timid Léon, within whom a poet perishes as
by process of nature. And this death, which is less climactic
(less cruel, less marked) than Rodolphe's two denials of Emma
— which is so much less of an "effect" than anything else in the
book — is in fact Flaubert's strongest touch. He had an old
conviction that "masterpieces are dumb [*bêtes*]; they have a
tranquil expression like big animals and mountains" (*Corresp.*,
II, 451). The finest example of this empty gigantic gape was the
end of Voltaire's greatest satire: "for me the ending of *Candide*
is proof positive of genius in the highest order. The claws of the
lion are marked on this quiet conclusion, as stupid as life itself"
(*Corresp.*, II, 398). His own novel is leonine in much the same
way, and the silent silting-over of Léon is one of the several
things that make it so.

Salammbô (1862), less interesting as a novel than *Madame
Bovary* (1857) (perhaps because more successfully "bête" or at

least because more simply a spectacle), is also less intricate and various in its handling of Nothing. Having chosen, as few other authors could conceivably have chosen, an entirely dead civilization to write about, Flaubert's problem was to make it present and substantial. Thus one vast void lies this side the novel proper; Flaubert noted it when he wrote to Feydeau, "Few people will guess how much sadness was required to undertake the resurrection of Carthage! It is a Thebaid into which disgust with modern life has driven me" (*Corresp.*, IV, 348, 29–30 Nov. 1859).

Not only the decision to resurrect Carthage but the choice of the mercenary war as a theme bespeaks Flaubert's despair with the modern world. It was a war of monstrous cruelties, even by ancient standards; and the mercenary, by definition, has given up on the usual motives for action — has died to himself as radically as the Roman who sold to another for five minae the right to butcher him in the public arena. Flaubert's Carthaginians are urban-maritime bourgeois, his mercenaries are ironically deprecated outlaw-artists in whom something has died. They wander in the desert among crucified lions, tormented by physical thirst without and spiritual-sensual thirst within, till in the final image Mathô their leader is literally picked apart by the whole civilization.

The book is full of high panoramas and ripe ordure, with an immense gamut of dimensions both vast and tiny, nerves very sensitive to, and inquisitive of, the feeling of things. For so weighty a book, its seeing eye is oddly mobile; one feels at every point an impulse to realize, a deliberate exercise of scrutiny and sometimes empathy. The surface over which this cold and complete eye plays is full of clefts and blanks, to be crammed with gobbets of tortured human flesh; Flaubert has a particular passion for displaying pieces of people mixed up with scraps of harness and broken clots of earth. Reducing human creatures to bloody rags excites all his ingenuity; and one sort of void which the book invokes is that shattering silence which follows a program of systematic extermination. But this is a limited exercise, and more interesting vacancies are invoked by Schahabarim, the eunuch priest of Tanit who presides over Salammbô like a Carthaginian Svengali

The lady herself, as ascetic priestess, suffers the familiar hot flushes of solitary yearning; Mathô, intoxicated by a brief vision, alternates romantic rage and romantic languor; but Schahabarim, invested by desires he cannot hope to satisfy, a priest without a religion, is unalterably alone in a world to which his own learned imaginings must give a shape. Lean, indirect, and cold to the touch, he trails his serpentine coils through the echoing corridors of Hamilcar's palace, and winds himself more intimately even than the family fetish around the simple consciousness of Hamilcar's daughter. But he can never possess her physically, she slips steadily away from his mental domination, and as the sacred serpent sickens and dies, his faith in Tanit herself vanishes. We leave him weakly gesturing obeisance to the Baal from whose service he is forever debarred by his disability.

So described, Schahabarim appears a theatrical mixture of mechanism, "heavy," and oppressive vapor; and that he is. His love and hatred for Salammbô, combined with doubts about his own faith, lead him to sacrifice his pupil's aristocratic chastity to heavy-thewed, mindless Mathô, and then to despise her for following his instructions. The superstitious verbiage which he flourishes about her head serves to humiliate and discipline his pupil, whom he rejoices to see suffering for a divinity that he cannot himself embrace. His cold influence over her is measured by her sufferings, but wanes when she has learned from Mathô the simple pleasures of male fervor. Then the python, which has been a sign of his influence over her, dies; and her indifference to its demise signals the end of his power. Yet he remains a lost and malignant presence; and the point is made that after all his wide-ranging experience in the schools, knowledge had become more and more questionable to him,

> until now there was growing up in his mind a private religion, without any distinct creed, and for that very reason full of dizzy yearnings. He no longer believed the earth was made like a pine-cone; he believed that it was round, and falling eternally through space at such a prodigious rate that its fall could not even be perceived (*Salammbô*, Paris, 1886, p. 201).

It is a nicely layered irony that ultimate despair should take the form of a fantasy which, under a modern perspective, is perfectly accurate.

Schahabarim is an insubstantial character to serve as fulcrum for the action of a book so brassy and external as *Salammbô*; but aside from the strangely intermitted figure of Hamilcar Barca, he is the only locus of intelligence within the book and within the civilization. His lost vocation, lost virility, and sense of cosmic emptiness frame a waste land deeper than the deserts of Carthage, a sickness of civilization more popularly associated with the 1920's than with the 1860's — or, for that matter, the third century B.C. Yet somehow this quality augments rather than minimizes the novel's impression of being a hollow masquerade.

The sequence of thought and feeling traced in these two books helps clarify that last troublesome heritage of the master, the uncompleted and posthumous *Bouvard et Pécuchet* (1881). One way to get at the problems of this thorny text is through its very incompleteness. We are given to understand, by Flaubert's scenario of the concluding pages, that when everything has fallen to pieces under their hands, his protagonists return, shamefacedly but with real inward pleasure, to their old trade of copyist. And the question has been asked, What do they copy and in what spirit do they copy it? The alternatives would seem to be that they copy blindly and uncritically whatever falls under their notice; or else that, having learned something from their long train of misadventures, they copy with critical sense and discrimination, not the best that has been said and thought in the world, but the worst. Fascinated with the "charmes atroces" of human stupidity, they may be supposed to copy some such florilegium of *panmuflisme* as Voltaire's *Sottisier* or its successor the *Dictionnaire des Idées Reçues*.

But it seems hard to imagine this twist without converting the two innocent *bonshommes* into sardonic and erudite Flauberts, and so minimizing the book's naïve comedy. If by constant study two middle-aged comic incompetents can acquire the intellectual acuteness of Flaubert, they cannot have been comic incompetents in the first place. There is a further difficulty of narrative convention; where or how in the fictional village of Chavignolles could they possibly lay hands on a text like the *Dictionnaire?* And finally, given their strange fictional immortality,[10] it seems in the nature of a ferocious punishment rather than a liberation for them to be set to copying a single book over and over — particularly the *Dictionnaire*, which appeals to an arrogance they are pathetically incapable of sharing.

A major element in the destiny of Bouvard and Pécuchet is evidently their simple decision to resume copying; and this is a liberation only if it means a laying down of intellectual burdens too heavy for them to carry. Despite many modifications of

10. They are given as forty-seven years old when the novel starts in 1839; it has been elaborately calculated that the events of the novel cannot take less than 30 years and may extend over as many as 38. Yet the two heroes are just as middle-aged at the end as they were at the beginning, like characters in a comic-strip — to which *Bouvard et Pécuchet* might profitably be compared.

tone which express Flaubert's increasing tolerance and even liking of his clowns, they are not fit at the end of the book to navigate in the ocean of ideas. Indeed, Flaubert's scenario shows them even less fit at the very end than in the episode where his death broke off the finished text. When they go back to copying, Bouvard and Pécuchet must be understood to abandon the life of the mind. They cease trying to conclude about anything; hence, whatever trite and stupid phrases swim into their ken, they copy cheerfully and uncritically. They know nothing, less than nothing; they also know the sum of everything, which is simply that nothing can be known. As René Girard says, thinking more generally of the later Flaubert novel and its impulse to become a list: "Between the various elements of the novel's universe no real working relationship is possible. . . . The inventory may be prolonged, but the sum of the items is always equal to zero" (*Mensonge romantique*, p. 156). So that even if they copy the *Dictionnaire des Idées Reçues*, one would expect them to do so in the spirit of happy, grubby children picking through the verbal litterpile of history. They do not hold up the well-worn pebbles of human inanity to scorn and vengeance; like Joyce in *Finnegans Wake*, they cherish a stupid idea as much as a clever one because in the last analysis all are equally foolish and equally sensible. Having learned the folly of trying to know anything, they find themselves in the *vrai*, and express this happy circumstance by recognizing themselves for what they are, copyists.

They are redeemed, then, in the end — liberated, at least partially, from the problem on which the pearls of their folly have been strung. And what is the distinction that redeems these absolute bourgeois from Flaubert's absolute scorn for their species? Their gloriously unpuncturable innocence, for one thing, as contrasted with the low cunning of their neighbors; the loftiness of their ambitions as contrasted with the comic ineptitude of their proceedings; and a kind of mild and naïve sensuality, as of two work-worn cabhorses released in their last years to the fresh fields. In other words, they are redeemed by their instincts, their ideals, and their creaturely needs — by anything at all except their practical intelligence. The villain who in the early part of the book crushed them — as Homais crushed Emma, as the notary in Léon buried the poet, as Schahabarim crushed Salammbô — was the rational mind. Reverting to copyists, Bouvard and Pécuchet die, as it were, to themselves, and voluntarily become mercenaries of the pen. Professor Lionel Trilling contrasts this fate with that of Bartleby the scrivener, in Melville's story, who deliberately perishes as a consequence of his alienation from the everyday world — and concludes that American despair is deeper than French. But the same facts will support an entirely different conclusion. Flaubert suggests not only that one can die as a mind without dying as a person, but that this process may be to one's advantage, practically and psychologically. Mental death is not an eccentric disaster by which a solitary man disappears down the whirlpool of his inner fixity, it is a beneficent, hygienic operation, like a prefrontal lobotomy, against which one can protest only in the name of an almost-forgotten ideal of humanity. But as a matter of social adjustment, there is nothing to be said against it. The snoring of Binet's lathe is the music of the spheres; it will go on forever, as Bouvard and Pécuchet, emblematically immortal, sit forever at their double desk, copying, copying, copying. The only pain anyone will feel is in the vanquished, vanished mind; but that pain is an undying worm, and its host will gain no consolation from lying down with kings and counsellors.

Bouvard and Pécuchet win their freedom from all culture, not by escaping or opposing, but by submitting to it. As they gain in wisdom by casting off knowledge, they increasingly let the culture carry them where it will. The ending of the novel was to have been "bête comme la vie," and one envisages that second volume which Flaubert never got around to writing as a flowing and formless tide of verbal garbage — not selected brilliants of folly in settings of ironic artistry, but a flood of worn and indiscriminate verbal junk. A specific locus of Nothing in this last novel as we have it is the style, which builds to no climaxes, stoops to no transitions, exercises little charm. Whether from a failure of inner energy or from conscious restraint, the jokes are often repetitive and foreseeable, the rhythms rough, the *coupe* of the sentences abrupt. In effect, the greatest French stylist of his day is observed here writing a ragged and graceless narration, not so broadly inept as the "Eumaeus" episode of *Ulysses*, but controlled like that episode by the idea of mental vapidity. Style, which in the earlier novels amounts almost to a separate personage, a distinct and lofty point of view, is here debased almost to the level of the two clowns. Presumably the gap between ideal and "real" has widened till satire itself, with its lofty perspective, is now impossible. Or, to rephrase it, the void at the center of human life has swelled out so far that bears and stars at the antipodes can no longer be held in focus, or be used to comment one another. The only style which will answer to a world without discrimination, without tension, and without luster is a Nothing style.

IV

Ironic Voyages

How far must one go to find Nothing? Does it redeem or destroy? Is the voyage even possible, or is motion itself an illusion?

Nothing may be discovered by staring through experience, centering on a point and plunging imaginatively past it or reflecting light back through it — after all, omphaloskepsis is a traditional path to Nirvana. But Nothing may also be the culmination of a voyage, usually conceived in comic or ironic light — a voyage, thus, more complicated even than the ordinary voyage-narration, which has its own special way of working on a reader. For such a story usually concludes with a homecoming and a contract or renewal of marriage, events which imply a happy ending and a comic mood. (All voyages are Ulysses' voyage, leading the hero safely back to Ithaca.) Yet the voyager, by definition, is an over-reacher, a scorner of safety, an adventurer afflicted with aspirations which draw him far out of the common round. Though dazzled by immense wealth or power, and sometimes momentarily in command of it, he often returns home with only spiritual rewards, of wisdom, patience, self-understanding. In all these respects the voyager acts, or may act, as tragic lightning-rod or scapegoat. His discovery is usually far off the point of his original aspiration — either he gets something different or his prize has unsuspected meanings, so that his original venture is seen, sooner or later, to be folly if not madness. Yet his error is often a door to discovery; he sails under the motto "I'd rather be lucky than good," and proves it true, thus suggesting again the comic blunderer. His hardships, on the other hand, require of him unusual, even heroic tenacity, however questionable the end to which he is bent. The voyage is an initiation, a rite of passage; the voyager departs innocent, shows himself resourceful, and returns, tempered with wisdom. Not too much, however; for if he is rendered so wise as not to resume his travels, we take it as a sort of defeat. His folly is his distinction; as readers we have nothing to learn from his prudence. Under another aspect, he is a tester of his own given condition (the more ordinary, as with Gulliver, the better); subjecting himself to strangeness and distance as to a process of chemical analysis, he emerges with a definition of himself and us which is strange but convincing because it is the fruit of more experience than we can place against it. He tests the laws in order to prove them, like a tragic hero; he survives, and is bound to survive, with the lawless impudence of the comic cork. He is a representative of our lawless, inordinate id-selves, which we like to see successful but not dangerously so, and which, after a round of strenuous trials, return and submit to the most wonderful fantasy of all — home, ego, prudence, our social selves as we have been (and known ourselves to be) ever since we picked up the story.

Since they are mostly undertaken with an objective in mind, or at least a rationale, literary voyages are naturally predisposed for under- or over-fulfillment; they would not make very good stories if the hero merely got what from the first we knew he was after. The contradiction works cheerfully in Xavier de Maistre's *Voyage autour de ma chambre* (1794), which is a tiny epyllion of the mobile mind. Precisely when his body is nailed down (our hero is confined to quarters for 42 days, as a result of a duel or suspected duel), his mind is liberated, his imagination unshackled, as if he were a character in a novel by Stendhal. Even the irrationality of being punished for doing what he

would have been disgraced for not doing becomes an occasion
for ironic persiflage. Thus the basic theme of the sketch is set as
incompatibility, and the whole dialogue of soul="moi" and
body="l'autre" develops the freedoms of this uneasy conjunction. But in developing its airy felicities, the soul comes also to
feel the fragility of the social texture; its wings are touched with
the chill breath of various voids. One of the most striking episodes of the fantasy (so different from the rest that one almost
suspects the guiding hand of brother Joseph) describes a ball-
room scene in which a crowd of exquisitely dressed and beautifully polite people are diverting one another. Suddenly there
enters "a polar bear, a philosopher, a tiger," or some other in-
human beast, who cries out: "Miserable human beings, you are
oppressed, victimized, unhappy, bored! Arise!" And he goes on
to suggest various ways of enlivening the party — the musicians
to smash their instruments over one another's heads, everyone
to out daggers and cut throats in the name of universal liberty.
How many of the charming company would respond joyously to
such an appeal? The thought appalls him; society is a howling
wilderness and the human heart a vacuum of sterile boredom
which accepts blindly any hideous suggestion. Then there is
Mme. de Hautcastel and her mirror or sequence of mirrors into
which she disappears, to the discomfiture of her lover (xxxv);
and there is the void of solitude within the room itself, into
which all the projections and recollections of the hero are forever threatening to disappear. Over these abysses de Maistre
dances very lightly, moralizing playfully like Marvell's "easy philosopher." His arch and conscious style, his diminished gestures
and small resolutions are tactics in a Fabian action against
whole series of *néants* too dangerous for direct confrontation.
In its dispute against the body, where the soul comes off so
badly (xxxix, xxxx), we are not far from feeling that consciousness itself is a stranger within the material world; the body has
its own exquisite associations, memories, and logics which the

soul can only interrupt and disturb. "Je" very nearly changes name as well as position to become "l'autre," as in Rimbaud's classic discovery of self-alienation. The arrival of faithful Jo-anetti the valet, and the grateful business of breakfast choco-late, are seized upon almost joyously as handles to get back into the routine of everyday life. "I have travelled widely in Con-cord," said Thoreau, with a certain sturdy American confidence that when you got through Concord you were bound to find yourself in some pretty authentic country. But Captain Xavier found perils even in the narrow circuit of his room, where the unsteady dimensions and erratic impulses of his imagination threatened always to betray him into some venture, within or without, too vast to be traversed, too deep for escape. That "vaste espace toujours ouvert devant moi" may be either an asy-lum or a dissolution; the author's ardent, unwilling admiration for Milton's Satan (xxvii) is most stirred by the tantalizing question of what it must mean to launch oneself into chaos and void. But de Maistre's trifle, while recognizing all the epic ges-tures, diminishes them, and keeps our eyes out of the abysses all around us by its own tiny exercise. It is an early version of the anti-voyage.

The anti-voyage prudently prevents one from encountering Nothing (or anything else dangerous), at least directly; actual imaginary voyages sometimes bring the hero up against the void as against a blank which outlines the purity of his striving or the special character of his achievement. Stories which culminate in the frustration and ultimate defeat of the strenuous seeker nat-urally have a touch of the tragic about them; a hero who is too good for the common forms evokes feelings of guilt and terror when he suffers from his search for uncommon ones. The higher his aspirations and the deeper his fall, the more apt it is to seem an ethical and therefore a tragic pattern. But specifics sharply modify these abstract reflections. The Ancient Mariner, for instance, conforms to neither of the "pure" types. His voyage has no announced objective; he sails simply because he is a mariner, he is relieved to have escaped with his life, but he must pay for his escape with periodic confession. The mood of the poem is tempered toward a festive sobriety in the acceptance of this world's goods, as if the Mariner, having once committed himself to a perception of the irrational void (whose theater is the vacant waste of the ocean, whose index is the blank, white, omnipresent moon), could never shake permanently free of it. For this poem, Nothing is the test to be passed; the albatross, a mere indicator itself, projects against the blank of the ocean, in the reflected light of the moon, issues not only of life and death but of salvation and damnation. Confrontation with Nothing (the isolation of the ship, the solitude of the soul) thus acts to magnify issues which in social life would be lightly passed over. What will the wedding party be eating at the banquet but stuffed roast goose? The murder of the bird is a moral crux only because it takes place in open ocean, under the aspect of eternity; for this reason too, its equivalents are not rational human equivalents. The trivial crime is visited with a monstrous retribution which, by a skewed and distorted logic, falls most heavily on the innocent bystanders. The Mariner's atonement is vicarious. Because it is unpredictable and alogical, the judgment is exotic. It fulfills the story's expectations, for we do not travel to the South Pole merely to learn that honesty is the best policy; at the same time, it suggests transcendence and ultimate truth, for that judgment which we shall face in the final loneliness will be by a law which it is presumptuous of us, in the here and now, to try to understand. Within the poem, it suffices to note, dream plus supreme existence triumphs over mundane plus domestic values, not merely in fascinating the Wedding Guest away from his ceremony, but in imposing itself — intermittently, forever — on the Mariner and his listeners. Thus life is seen as an episode the ultimate meaning of which is revealed in an episode-within-the-episode; the void of the voyage is a porthole opening on eternity.

On the other hand, Baudelaire's "Le Voyage" (written early in 1859 and added to *Les Fleurs du Mal* in the second edition of 1861) is a poem *against* voyages and indeed against the very possibility of voyages. The energy of Nothing appears as the precondition, texture, end, and meaning of the voyage — which, for the very reason that it is a voyage from, through, and to Nothing, can never properly become a voyage at all. The poem is ironic and negative from the instant of its dedication to Maxime du Camp, whose bouncy *Chants Modernes* (1855) had begun with the blithe phrase, "Je suis né voyageur." . . . Baudelaire's composite voyage is defined almost at once by the motivations of those undertaking it; their aim is only to get away from something (a "patrie infâme," "l'horreur de leurs berceaux," or a "Circé tyrannique") — or at best they are driven by mere restlessness:

> ceux-là seuls qui partent
> Pour partir.

But in fact these are merely their real reasons for traveling; their ostensible reasons are the familiar liberal delusions of improvement, progress, and self-betterment, summed up in an ironic reference to Cabet's *Voyage en Icarie* (a rationalist, materialist, communist Utopia) as the goal of our souls' seeking. The voyage itself is inept and clownish; pursuing visions of delight, the mariners founder inevitably on sand-bars, and since their goal is continually shifting, they end by trying to sail in all directions at once. Adrift and bewildered, whipped like giddy tops by evershifting desires, they have forfeited all pretense to the classic art of navigation. Now, distancing the voyagers from first to second person and presuming them returned from their travels, the ironic poet asks for an account of their discoveries; and Section IV of the poem is given up to a fragmentary recital of their souvenirs, all tarnished by boredom or triviality. So far in the poem, the travelers have been "cerveaux enfantins" and the poet a mocker; but in Section VI he brings in another sort of report, from a different and more inward voyage. What is described is the eternal monotony of universal and unredeemable sin — a reign of hypocrisy, disease, self-degradation, and fraud which underlies all changes of atmosphere. This state of universal unchanging stagnant horror is the mirror image, as it were, of universal progress, and in fact an image of existence not much more intricate or interesting than that of hopeful Maxime du Camp. Automatic stagnation is a form of automatic progress. If there is to be a voyage which gets anywhere (and for the poem, development of some sort is a necessity), it must surpass both these visions. Neither by motion nor by fixity can one escape time, the vigilant enemy. Thus the poet, rather than have no goal, makes Nothing itself his goal; the final apostrophe to death invokes the only power under whose auspices a significant voyage can be made. The idea of exterminating oneself in order to gain a new sensation does not seem, in its literal application, very carefully considered. But its expression in the poem serves to register an impasse growing out of revulsion, not only with the greasy commonplaces of flesh and blood, but with those of decision as a whole. The poet's final demand to be shown, whether in heaven or hell, "du nouveau," sounds deliberately trivial; it is in effect a denial of representation and of poetic method itself. It gestures with conscious slackness toward an ultimate on the other side of the unknown, to which all the categories are irrelevant. There is nothing to be said about that sphere except that it is different. From so remote a perspective both fixity and change appear as the incidents of an ennui inseparable from life itself, as equivalent opposites. The final op-

tion which the poem symbolically makes is for transcendent annihilation rather than banal, on-and-on nullity. The poem's
closing gestures are consciously empty, for its elected destination is somewhere — anywhere — out of this world; it provides
a fitting and conscious end to the collection in which it appears.

"The Hunting of the Snark" (1876), which has become of
recent years a much more serious piece of humor than it ever
was for the Victorians, imposes on the design of the voyage a
new and sinister pattern; it presents Nothing, not as an obstacle
to be eluded or a test to be passed, but as a predatory potential
of the goal itself. Though the Bellman and his crew have five
infallible signs for recognizing Snarks, there is no way to tell a
Snark from a Boojum until it is too late — in fact, there is no
way at all. This is characteristic of the whole undertaking, in
which no means is ever proportioned sensibly to an end. The
crew's manifold skills are entirely irrelevant to the task at hand,
the ship sails now backwards, now forwards, the Bellman gives
contradictory orders and for navigation uses a map which,
though pleasantly intelligible, is a perfect and absolute blank:

> 'What's the good of Mercator's North Poles and Equators,
>   Tropics, Zones, and Meridian Lines?'
> So the Bellman would cry: and the crew would reply,
>   'They are merely conventional signs!'

Yet despite this indifference to prudential logic and the elements of natural fact — or more properly because of the comic
convention that lucky innocents lead a charmed life — the
quest has so far succeeded miraculously. It is of course all quests
in one, a tempting of destiny by a crew of sacred imbeciles
whose irrational agreement upon a final goal which is all things
to all men is no stranger than their diverse senses of the way to
reach it. But if this crew, united merely by the "B's" of their

names (a signal instance, this, of what Pope and Professor Lovejoy called the Great Chain of Being), and so identified as essentially a crew of plosives, has prospered so far, it is only that they may be led more rapidly to the culminating disaster, itself a "B." (It is in effect the but=end or purpose of which Baudelaire wrote in "Le Voyage," which, "n'étant nulle part, peut être n'importe où.") Emerging from nowhere in response to no summons (like those other fabled voyagers toward a fateful objective, Childe Roland and Captain Ahab), engaged in an insane enterprise looking toward what may be either a vague good or a permanent annihilation, they encounter the last number of their own sequence, the Boojum. Supreme reward (Snark) and ultimate catastrophe (Boojum) are only verbally distinguishable, as eternity is conveniently approached through its likeness to annihilation. And it is the Baker, that sacred idiot who cannot remember his own name, who was warned by his aging uncle against Boojums but could not remember to repeat the warning in English, it is the Baker who is predestined to encounter the Boojum. Void adventuring boldly into the world encounters void, ineluctably — or at least what the Baker encounters, though for others it might be Snark, proves for him Boojum. The eminent Snarxist Martin Gardner defines Boojum in these terms:

> The Boojum is more than death. It is the end of all searching. It is final, absolute extinction. In a literal sense, Carroll's Boojum means nothing at all. It is the void, the great blank emptiness out of which we miraculously emerged; by which we will ultimately be devoured; through which the absurd galaxies spiral and drift endlessly on their nonsense voyages from nowhere to nowhere (*The Annotated Snark*, New York, 1962, p. 23).

That the Baker represents the human race emerging miraculously from the cosmic void will perhaps be felt as a romantic

extrapolation from the text; but the presence of void within, behind, and about the poem is of its essence, and there is not
really much difference between a medium-sized void and a great
big one. The Bellman's venture has neither a starting point nor
a coherent method nor an objective; like a pair of violins unac-
companied, its two counterpointed themes, of inconsequence
and inevitability, poise with the necessary perilous fragility only
when raised over an emptiness. As Milton's Satan makes his
way through chaos, so the Bellman and his crew are continually
confronted with irrelevance and menaced with a fall; as they
mimic the adventures of human life (itself a voyage from void
to void), their lunacies are invaded by an abrupt and violent
principle of accident which at the end of the poem has taken
full command. The Banker can be rescued from the Bander-
snatch at the very moderate expense of his sanity, but the
Baker's vanishing is ultimate, like that of Oedipus. It implies
not merely that the quest is foolish and the man fated, but
more exquisitely (like Kafka's fable of the man before the
law), that only he could discover the Snark for whom it was
bound to prove a Boojum. The conditions of the problem were
such as to lead inevitably to the destruction of its solver, while
those who were immune to the consequences could not solve it
in the first place. The poem's metaphorical action represents
two interlocking binds; for obvious reasons, its pattern of self-
defeating success has a special fascination for us these days.[1]

1. The great social paradox of our time — the transformation of supreme
national power into a supreme national inhibition and limitation — is mirrored on all sorts of levels in the popular culture of the day. Ours is an age of
non-performance or anti-performance; we measure a man's wealth by the ex-
tent of his credit, i.e. his debts, and his worldly success by his position in hier-
archies which increasingly inhibit freedom of individual action. In humbler
spheres we rejoice in singers who by deliberate intent do not sing or sing
badly, fighters whose interest lies wholly in their patent ineptitude as fighters
(ditto baseball teams), painters who refuse to paint, writers who recite or
mope instead of writing, plays in which nothing happens, stories without

Being fantastic, the action of "The Snark" takes place by tacit definition within the realm of an undefined psyche, where one neither expects a consequence nor resists an association. The freedom of assertion first acquired under the protection of "nonsense"-writing is now a common liberty of fiction; in effect it permits an elastic, adaptable fable which under new circumstances freely takes on new features. The adventure of the Bellman makes use of physical questing largely for narrative backbone; but as it winds through many appended and incidental voids, void opens before it as a vortex, drawing irresistibly forward and finally swallowing the story's agents. Its ability to release the suggestive power of void is only one of this pleasant poem's pioneering distinctions.

Another instance of Nothing at work in an action of quest and voyage (this time a reversed voyage) is provided by Henry James's novella "The Beast in the Jungle" (1903). The action of this retrospective analysis springs from John Marcher, a man haunted by the sense of a special destiny. This destiny is plainly not splendid, possibly it is terrible, but in any event he knows it will be special. He enlists the sympathetic interest of May Bartram, too-apt namesake of an intrepid tropical explorer; and they wait together, in spiritual companionship, for the happening. After some years she dies, having indicated to him that, whatever the event may be, she has perceived it, and it is too terrible to communicate to him. Returning to her grave as to the last remaining center of interest in his life, he discovers, in the glance of a passing mourner at another grave, the flare of an authentic grief. Contrasting with his own cold, veiled egotism the naked sorrow of one who had loved a woman for her own

events — and a telling little machine so constructed that when wound up it will reach around to its own switch and turn itself off. The inversion of the sexes — boys who pride themselves on not being masculine and girls who pride themselves on being so — is no doubt part of the same process. But this is a scene from another opera.

sake, John Marcher senses at last that "he had been the man of his time, *the* man, to whom nothing on earth was to have happened." The extraordinary fate has befallen him without his ever knowing it; what he took for nothing (mere absence of experience) turned out, long after the event, to have been Nothing (an active, aching failure of experience); and mere numb disappointment turns, as he flings himself face-down on the tomb, into mortal anguish.

It will not have escaped the avid collector and categorizer of Nothings that for James the experience of the Boojum does not have to be sought, only awaited — for a long, long time, to be sure. The voyage is not through space, only time, within which Marcher marches, a bit heavily, in both directions, and its ending is so indistinguishable from the approaches to it that it arrives surreptitiously — "happening," in the exterior sense, without anyone's being able to recognize or render it, except so far as the habitual abstractions and qualifications of James's afterthought style, and Miss Bartram's shuddering reticences, may be counted a rendering. In fact, it is, properly defined, a wholly inward event, a judgment rendered from irrevocable distance on a failure to appreciate the import of the absence of an experience. This is abstract enough in all conscience; the theater of metaphysical adventure having been transferred not merely to the consciousness of Marcher but to the retrospective arraignment of his own failure of consciousness. Yet for all this inwardness, the void which John Marcher uncovers in himself has a strong and simple (one might almost say Puritan) moral coloration. He has been selfish and egotistical in his dealings with May Bartram, sacrificing her to an expectation which was, in effect, merely a disguised attitude of self-importance. He is a bad, heartless, selfish fellow — much worse in his idiosyncrasy than other men, and therefore subject to judgment as a conspicuous failure by standards which "average" men pretty well fulfill. That Marcher should be illumined, after a lifetime of labyrinthine self-deception, by a casual glance from an anonymous and perfectly characterless citizen suggests the precariousness of his void. If truth be told, there may well be something contrived and factitious about this celebrated story — of which the chief villain and malevolent agent is once again time. For the chief poignancy of the situation derives — does it not? — from John Marcher's extraordinary obtuseness in delaying his own perception of the truth about himself long beyond the point where he could do anything with it. One is not altogether comfortable with the sense that our hero's long-drawn-out mental strain (covering little less than half a lifetime) brings him merely to a point of awareness which a normally attentive reader will have attained by page seven — i.e. John Marcher is a pompous ass. We know through biography of an extraordinary instance of moral obtuseness, amounting almost to idiocy, on the part of Henry James with regard to a quietly enamored female compatriot. That wretched episode may well be the germ of this story, but so far from improving it, the information casts some doubt on its major interest for us. An encounter with Nothing has here become a grounds of private self-reproach, a point of personal blindness which does not exist dramatically except to the retrospective discovery of the introspective beholder. Meanwhile, what is all too apparent to the reader can have no function at all in the narrative. (It is not wholly true that in love the unselfish man takes what he wants; but something like the reverse is true, that the selfish man is he who refuses to want.) In any event, if it is a self-indictment, the story gains only additional overtones of self-deception from appearing as fiction.

Wiredrawn and manipulated it may well seem, this special American view of Nothing; certainly it is Puritan in its conversion of Nothing into a moral indictment, and its sense that the

truth of this indictment must be run down by the individual
conscience before a remote, lonely, and private court. (The
American often appears as a moral volunteer, with rudimentary
value-diagrams but an intricate, tenacious, insatiable conscience
— hence, perhaps, his fascination with the private eye, whose
ingenuity in running criminals down contrasts with the rough-
and-ready simplicity of his judgments.) The European Catholic
tradition, on the other hand, presses men more closely with a
public Nothing; as the nineteenth century draws to a close, obsessive and paranoid moods become increasingly evident. A dramatic poem of Emile Verhaeren, the first of the *Villages Illu-
soires* (1895), illustrates the point. "Le Passeur d'Eau" is a
study in motion and immobility. Clenching an emblematic
green reed between his teeth, the ferryman sets forth, responding to a vague call from a female figure who fades into the
mists; he struggles to reach her as she retreats, his muscles taut,
his back bowed. One oar breaks, he struggles on; the rudder
snaps and is carried away — with furious obstinacy he still
struggles forward, the voice which calls him becoming ever
more urgent. Empty windows watch him, lonely towers look
impassively down on

> Cet homme fou, en son entêtement
> A prolonger son fol voyage.[2]

His last oar breaks, he sits exhausted and helpless on the bench,
his head bowed — looking up only to see that his boat is just
where it always was, that he has never left the shore. For whatever enigmatic value it may possess, he still has the green reed.

Verhaeren, sensing history as massive, finds Nothing oppressive, exterior, and very present. It need not be sought. The
voice calls, the ferryman tries to respond, but is locked to the
shore by the current. He has a momentary illusion that some-

2. This mad man, persisting in carrying out his mad voyage.

thing has happened or can happen, but it fades. The pressure which immobilizes his voyage before it even starts may be history in the large sense or his own personal past — at any rate it is irresistible. Another of these nightmare vignettes, reminiscent in their dark distortions and moods of the graphics of Edvard Münch, offers a gloss. "Le Fossoyeur" describes an old man standing in the midst of an immense plain, digging graves and burying in them a steady stream of corpses which descend on him. They arrive from his personal past — his dead hopes, his dead courage, dead memories and miseries, crimes, mania, terror, and dead remorse. The bells never cease tolling, the gravedigger cannot shovel underground fast enough the rotten bodies which overwhelm him:

> Et tous les jours, par les chemins dolents,
> Ils arrivent les cerceuils blancs;
> Infiniment, ils arrivent vers lui de loin,
> Du fond des bourgs, du fond des coins
> Perdus, dans la campagne immense;
> Ils arrivent, suivis de gens en noir,
> A toute heure, jusques au soir,
> Et dès l'aube, leurs longs cortèges recommencent.[3]

This is a special kind of voyage which Verhaeren depicts, for as the conscious mind stands still and drudges, it is acted on by a stream of reversed experience out of its past; like the ferryman, the gravedigger is bound to a task which his own history renders impossible and absurd. Yet both figures are on a voyage of the mind, though a static and passive one; like Proust's water-lilies,

3. And every day over the mournful roads they arrive, the white coffins; endlessly they reach him from the distance, from the depths of the market towns, from the depths of the corners lost in the immense countryside; they arrive, followed by people in black, at every hour till late at night; and as dawn breaks their long corteges start to flow again.

they are in unmoving motion against the tide of their own existence. And thus Nothing for Verhaeren is not an abstract end to be sought but a weighty condition to be endured, not a moral but a dramatic state. Similarly, in the course of A Rebours (1884), Des Esseintes tries to take a voyage to London, finds himself anchored to the conditions of his own mind, but devises triumphant substitute-experiences. At an English café in Paris he swallows some fog, a beefsteak, and some ale, listens to some English talk, and returns home with an immense comic sense of having tricked his body into believing it has completed an arduous voyage across Channel. The grotesque mechanical substitutes for natural processes and "real" life which he exuberantly invents almost counter the weight of that deep revulsion which is forcing him toward Baudelaire's journey — anywhere out of this world. But though his mind can deceive the body in details, it cannot escape the conditions of inhabiting a body like millions of others; in solitude, distance, and inversion, it remains riveted to the universal fetid facts of animal existence in the nineteenth century. In one of the great moments of A Rebours, Des Esseintes looks in his mind's eye across the pullulating mass of fertile Paris corruption, sees it spawning, breeding, and festering like an immense, disgusting yeast-culture — turns from it in utter horror, yet returns to it, and at the end of the book is being forced to "accept" it. Verhaeren expresses much the same sense of bestial doom (perhaps, in addition to inhabiting the same culture, both authors had been reading Zola) in a moving and terrible poem about a journey undertaken by an animal — in fact a cow. Marked with a white cross on her brow, she is led placidly through the cold dewy morning, down familiar lanes, across flat fields, through the village and up a little hill — it is a slow and very peaceful progress through the fresh countryside, till abruptly she is pushed into a red and steaming room full of hot bloody corpses. She stops, looks past

the room, and out the open side of the abattoir to the rising
sun. At that instant she is stunned with a hammer-blow:

> elle tombe,
> Mais son dernier regard s'est empli de soleil.[4]

This is a poem about a cow, but not just about a cow. The
doomed voyage it describes — but it is a process rather than a
voyage — does not so much culminate in Nothing as confirm a
null already chalked up. The cow — and within the poetic universe, she stands for life itself — was only called into existence
(either physical or literary) with an eye to the moment of her
death. This death is brute utilitarian cancellation. The rays of
level sun which dazzle the dying cow offer no more transcendence than mitigation of her fate; if anything, it is an irony that
the sun glances with indifferent glory on the scene in the shamble,
and fills the cow's dying eye with a radiance which only confuses her. As one cycle completes itself, a different (and utterly
indifferent) one gets under way; apart from their *coup-de-théâ-
tre* effect, the level rays of the sunrise seem to say something
quite chilling about the busy horror in the abattoir.

Reporting back on the wider worlds which he had seen
through a momentary void in this narrow one, the Ancient
Mariner could invoke eerie but authentic sanctions for an ethical code on this small stage; his adventure into Nothing yielded
good, practical, moralistic harvest. Baudelaire's adventure, if it
was to represent anything but a shift in the old ennui, had to
surpass ethical categories altogether, outreaching humanity, morality, and the representable, yet amounting to not much more
than a negative nostalgia. Its concern is with extremes, which
have a proverbial way of meeting, here represented by a trivial
demand posed of a limitless ultimate. The fable of the Snark,
on the other hand, is largely a joke about first premises; parallel-

4. She drops, but her last glance is full of the sun.

ing the story of Oedipus, his buried fallacy hoists the Baker
with splendid plosive effect as a result of his own strenuous endeavors and final success in the great action of the fable. The
story of John Marcher pushes regression even further. Not only
is it a backward voyage, in time rather than space, but Nothing
figures in the adventure as the denial of humanity implicit in
undertaking the quest at all. Verhaeren denies first the possibility of the voyage, then the freedom of the voyager to wish his
own voyage, and finally the humanity of the voyager, who was
never anything but an object in the first place. Regressing thus
from the climax to the roots of the voyage-action, Nothing swallows up the imperative by which it was previously defined, like a
snake eating itself tail-first.

V

Baudelaire and Leconte de Lisle:

Nothing Multiplied

A problem in reading Baudelaire is the apparent absence of positive ideas and verbal inventions sufficient to justify his evident importance as a poet. One source of this missing "importance" may be found in the area of psychic gestures, the adventures of a fluid self in a porous universe where Nothing functions as Heaven, Hell, Indifference, Nirvana — and several other dramatic properties, as well.

Like deQuincey and Poe, Baudelaire often engages in a fascinated, perilous game on the verge of various voids; the general failure to abstract from his work anything in the shape of a coherent "philosophy" invites one to look in the direction of this psychic juggler's act for explanations (no doubt still partial) of his hypnotic power. There are more voids in his cosmos than in those of his predecessors; he is more deeply involved in them; and their geography is more difficult to envisage as they are often contiguous or inverted. But these difficulties may offer some reason for hoping that the causes one uncovers in this area may be more or less proportioned to a conclusion which is itself of some complexity.

Where, then, are some of Baudelaire's favorite and characteristic Nothings to be found — and under what terminology? "L'Ennui," "le Gouffre," "le Néant," and perhaps "l'Infini" offer themselves at once, and may be considered in order. A first question about "l'Ennui" might well be why, in the opening poem "Au Lecteur," among seven hideous beasts representing "la ménagerie infâme de nos vices," this sinister figure, cruel, sentimental, and narcotized, should be included as an eighth and climactic vice? Stupidity, no doubt, is a sin in perfectly orthodox circles (Aquinas, *Summa*, Part II, vol. 1, quaest. xlvi, art. 2), but boredom seems more like an affliction. Why is it the worst of the vices? A good bourgeois reason would be that we should love our neighbor, take an interest in his welfare, and so not be bored because healthfully occupied in "making the world a better place in which to live." Not a great many commentators have taken "Au Lecteur" in this way, but it is surprising that anyone has; and the point is rounded out by showing that Ennui "rêve d'échafauds en fumant son houka," ["dreams of scaffolds while smoking his hookah"] in order to emphasize that the final end of moral deterioration, boredom and selfishness, is sadism. "Harassed by the need to fill an infinite vacancy [*vide*], spleen culminates in cruelty." [1] This interpretation points the accusing finger directly at Baudelaire himself. It is a possible reading, but it is not consistent with patterns of Baudelairean thought and expression elsewhere. The notion of Baudelaire lecturing himself on his moral failings in a poem directed "Au Lecteur" is not particularly impressive. But if we consider its placing in the structure of the poem, ennui seems to assume a rather special position. The various other vices of which Baudelaire accuses "nous" [2] are, though vaguely indicated, all rather strenuous, hence probably conscious. The vulture and the jackal are carrion-eaters, scorpions and serpents are venomous and insidious, panthers and lynxes ferocious; only monkeys are, rather harmlessly, lascivious and parodic. An ordinary bookish reader is not touched by such fiendish, melodra-

1. Robert Chérix, *Commentaire sur les Fleurs du Mal*, Paris, 1962, p. 13.
2. Of the poem's ten stanzas, the first eight all use some form of the first person plural; the ninth stanza is impersonal, and the tenth turns with a heavy accent on the second person singular.

matic figures (like the unmeasured ragings of a revivalist preacher) until his contemplative perusal of *Les Fleurs du Mal* is allied with, and shown to mask, some of these fiercer and more cannibalistic impulses. Seen as an image for making this connection, ennui becomes a vice of the prurient reader, who comes, yawning and cruel, to read Baudelaire in search of entertainment or emotional exercise. And the last line of the poem gains double impact from this view, for it says not only, "You are as bad as me," but also "I am as bad as you; for I have looked into the pit of my own self only to see and boast of what could be found there for the book which is before you; we are conspirators, inevitable hypocrites in the very act of honesty."

But ennui calls for still more positioning because, though it looks like an extreme, as the eighth, last, and worst of the vices, under another aspect it is a mean. In abstract pattern, the sacred has two poles, the pure="Ideal" and the impure=Pariah; both are equally opposed to the profane, within which ennui exists and by which it is defined. Ennui is simply the consequence of seeing things not as sacred but as autonomous or indifferent. Specifically, it is the reflection of the outside world, indifferent to the furious sacred drama of Baudelaire's inner life; stretched upon the rack of more extreme contrasts than Flaubert imposed on it, Baudelaire's ennui is yet the same fat, complacent, empty image of humanity, its vulgarity heightened to vindictive cruelty. It is in this context and with these overtones that Baudelaire most often uses the word. In "Tu mettrais l'univers," it is the "femme impure" to whom he says, "L'ennui rend ton âme cruelle," and in "Le Possédé" he invites her to be still, be gloomy, "et plonge tout entière au gouffre de l'ennui." [3] Both passages use the word "ennui" to describe the self-absorption of the merely natural woman in the

3. "L'Amour du Mensonge" uses "ennui" in the same dramatic sense; for partial exceptions, see "La Destruction" and the second "Spleen."

face of the lover's sacred fury or adoration; ennui is a quality of
the indifferent Other, and so it may probably be in "Au Lecteur." In the "ménagerie de nos vices" (which is also the book
to follow), Baudelaire will represent himself as the animals, and
seems to allow the reader a privileged and exempt position (and
a human form as well) because he is a mere spectator. But
"ennui" must then be his, so that it may be shown to contain in
its languor all the other vices — and so pave the way for the last
line of direct accusation.

Yawning, indifferent, and empty, the world reflects back at
Baudelaire's frenzied attraction-repulsion only its own torpid,
half-conscious self-satisfaction. He sees it, or would like to see it,
dramatically, as lit from two directions by the fires of hell and
certain azure rays of the Ideal. Even here, however, pops up still
another void which keeps things off balance. Only one of the
extremes between which the void world of ennui balances is directly represented. "Au Lecteur" makes no specific mention of,
nor even a direct allusion to, God or Ideal. "Satan Trismégiste"
is very much present, as is the explicit "Diable." Why no grace
within this poem, why none of the familiar Christian aids
against temptation and sin — guardian angels, saints, sacra-
ments, sacred symbols, Mary, Jesus? On the literary plane, i.e.
the plane of contrivance, it is clear that Baudelaire simply excluded these properties; on the biographical plane, one could
invoke Mme. Baudelaire's second marriage, horrid usurping
General Aupick, the lost paradise of youth, and so forth; on the
broad plane of spiritual history, one could talk of the progres-
sive dissociation of wisdom and virtue from the divine, their
tendency during the nineteenth century to find autonomous,
secular justification — the divorce, in a word, of the arts from
that theology to which Saint Bonaventure had married them.
Against these backgrounds, the poet-dandy of Baudelaire, as
hollow and functionless gentleman, acts an ambiguous role —

his hollowness testifying to a human condition, his loneliness corresponding to the isolation of a laboratory, his rigid authenticity evincing a fidelity beyond reward or comfort. He is a proof of the human mind. His ability to exist on style alone is a defiance of nature — including his own nature, which he modifies freely in response to his mimetic impulses, his responsiveness to what can be "made of" subjects. Because Baudelaire existed within this personal void of artistic indeterminacy, he could (and, in the larger sense, had to) avoid the official counterbalances, the ecclesiastical squaring-off of his intellectual structure. Its shifting imbalances are deliberate and permanent elements of its fascination, i.e. it is perverse.

God is on the reticent side in "Au Lecteur." There cannot be a devil without a God, otherwise the devil would *be* God, but to make God's existence depend on this strain of reflection is to attenuate him remarkably. Other *Fleurs* are more explicit about adducing angels or the Deity himself — for instance, "L'Examen de Minuit," "Le Rebelle," "Un Voyage à Cythère." Doubtless He exists, therefore; but whether in any capacity relevant to us is an always reopening question. From poem to poem, from document to document, Baudelaire changes position; and with each shift the meaning of the profane sphere of everyday, the world or non-world of ennui, changes. If it is instinct with correspondences to spiritual truth, we must be alert to grasp them. But if the Ideal is as remote as the concept "pariah" implies, if the effort to grasp correspondences has suffered defeat, then the most we can hope for is a strict, authentic "conscience dans le mal." If there is an afterlife with rewards and punishments (as "La Mort des Amants," for example, finds it convenient to suppose), then "vice" and "virtue" have a meaning to which the whole concept of "ennui" is magnificently impertinent. If there is not an afterlife (as "Le Mort Joyeux" most certainly imagines) — but the consequences of this alternative are best looked at through a second area of void, "le Néant."

"Le Jeu," deriving from a print by Carle Vernet, displays senile avidity in a pack of aged harlots and decayed gamesters; having described them, the poet, by an unusual turn, describes himself observing them:

> Moi-même, dans un coin de l'antre taciturne,
> Je me vis accoudé, froid, muet, enviant. . . .[4]

And his envy of these pathetic old specimens — the men trafficking in their frayed honor, the women in their tattered beauty — becomes the full theme of the poem:

> Et mon coeur s'effraya d'envier maint pauvre homme
> Courant avec ferveur à l'abîme béant
> Et qui, soûl de son sang, préférerait en somme
> La douleur à la mort et l'enfer au néant! [5]

One reason for the poet's encounter with himself is clearly to gain a sense of distance from the scene; but it raises questions of geography and relationship. An "antre taciturne" is a somewhat highflown expression for a quiet foyer. As for the activity of the gamesters, which has been static not to say mechanical all through the poem, it seems somewhat exaggerated by a phrase like "courant avec ferveur," while the cold, sterile passion of the gamester does not accord very well with the ardent phrase "soûl de son sang." One had not the impression that there was blood enough in the casino for a proper *soulerie*. But these phrases would be less jarring if the game were metaphorical; to introduce a concept from "Le Gouffre," it might be a game of Numbers and Beings. Two relevant quotes from "Fusées" may sug-

---

4. I saw myself in a corner of the silent cavern, leaning on an elbow, cold, mute, envious. . . .
5. And my heart was terrified to be envying many a poor man, rushing eagerly into the yawning abyss, and who, drunk with his blood, would prefer in the end misery before death, and damnation to void.

gest the flexible potential of these metaphors: "Everything is number. Number is in everything. Number is in the individual. Drunkenness is a number." And in connection with the act of sex: "A deplorable game, in which one of the players must necessarily lose control of himself!" If sex can be a game and drunkenness a number, there is no reason why the activity in "Le Jeu" need be limited to baccarat and *vingt-et-un*; the conjunction of males and females, the discordant overemphasis of "ferveur" and "soûl," accord much better with a game of sex and life in their profane, everyday aspect. The idea of numbers suggests the limited quality of this existence, yet in its monotonous repetition of combinations it is infinite; gambling, says Baudelaire in describing the original print, is a "passion at once violent and contained" ("Quelques Caricaturistes Français," *Oeuvres complètes*, ed. Pléiade, p. 995). Gambling may then stand for an "abîme béant" of the here and now, of a vapid and profane existence. The choice made by the players, of "douleur" and "enfer" over "mort" and "néant" is metaphysical, not vocational or avocational; so seen, the title takes on special ironies. The game is a desperate gamble, a cast of the dice. The "antre taciturne" then becomes a little less inflated, through reference to an unusually specific adjective, "clairvoyant," in the previous line, applied by the poet to himself. His cave should be prophetic, sibylline; but it no longer resounds, as it used to, with prophecies and denunciations, it is not only lonely in its perspective but unfrequented.[6] Poised above two contrasted abysms, it constitutes a third sphere of void and neglect. Presumably anything is more authentic than the sphere of "jeu,"

6. The imagery of both "Le Jeu" and "Obsession" may be clarified by reference to that of "Les Ténèbres," the first of four poems grouped under the title "Un Fantôme." There the poet describes himself as inhabiting "caveaux d'insondable tristesse" within which he is condemned "à peindre, hélas! sur les ténèbres." The image invites reverberations from various analogues, such as Plato's cave, Porphyry's account of the cave of the nymphs, and the cave of Aeneas' sibyl.

but the poet's wondering envy of those who can passionately, even drunkenly, shun "néant" suggests a void-fascination of his own.

The indeterminacy of "Le Jeu," poised between fascination and contempt, prepares for the issues of "Obsession," the first of three poems in the edition of 1868 which are directly addressed to various voids. The sonnet's theme is correspondence, a continuing, inescapable, mutual correspondence in the act of consciousness between the internal and external worlds. Great sighing woods terrify the poet because the wail of their *De Profundis* wakes an echo in his heart; the ocean is hateful because in its enormous laughter can be heard the bitter laugh of the beaten man, full of sobs and insults. Even the night would please him only if it could be had without the stars which, in their light, speak a language already known. What the poet seeks (in thudding monosyllables) will arouse no echoes at all in his soul:

> Car je cherche le vide, et le noir, et le nu.

The void is a condition to be sought because it frees us from the sounding-box of a finite universe and from all the reverberations of our sad selves. It has no official status within the Christian scheme, corresponding most nearly to the Buddhist Nirvana. There are of course accepted paths for attaining Nirvana, but Baudelaire (like most Europeans) has no notion of embarking on them, so it is not surprising that his search for the void ends in failure:

> Mais les ténèbres sont elles-mêmes des toiles
> Où vivent, jaillissant de mon oeil par milliers
> Des êtres disparus aux regards familiers.[7]

7. But the shadows are themselves canvases on which live, leaping from my eye by the thousands, creatures long lost with familiar features. (Contrast these "regards familiers" with those of "Correspondances.")

This animated world fills the void of the self with correspondent noises; in revenge, the puffed-up self fills the void with inescapable images. The tyranny of those "regards familiers" seals the poet's failure to escape; "le vide et le noir et le nu" are simply not available to him, because he brings to them the perception of haunted eyes. It is an interesting twist to the idea of spiritual failure that one cannot even have Nothing, and it is deepened by the sense that any Christian who seeks Nirvana must already have given up on the harder path of ascent. In a famous passage of "Mon Coeur Mis à Nu" Baudelaire declares that in every man at all times there are two simultaneous postulations, one toward God, the other toward Satan. Invoking God, or spirituality, evinces a desire to rise in the scale of creatures; invoking Satan or animality bespeaks the joy of descending. But whether the deep impulse toward void which is frustrated in "Obsession" represents rise, fall, or evasion (there are some grounds for all three views) remains cloudy. Deliberately so, no doubt; for to be truly void, the void the poet seeks must be morally neutral or at least equivocal. The "regards familiers" need not be supposed glances of explicit reproach; if they merely recognize his existence, they remind the poet that the soul's burdens are not easily laid down. Strange and intricate self-defeat! in which escape to an easy void is blocked by the claim of a more frightful and immediate one. But it is a potent parable for modern man, who (like Father Bob Cowley, in *Ulysses*) often finds his only defense against one debt (=guilt=fall=void) is the claim of another.

"Le Goût du Néant" maintains till the last stanza a gracefully elegiac and slightly archaic tone, nicely reminiscent of Ronsard. But sleep, resignation, and picturesque melancholy (perhaps parodic) give way in that last stanza, first to slow engulfment by the snows of Time, then to the apocalyptic motion of the avalanche:

Et le Temps m'engloutit, minute par minute
Comme la neige immense un corps pris de roideur;
Je contemple d'en haut le globe en sa rondeur
Et je n'y cherche plus l'abri d'une cahute.

Avalanche, veux-tu m'emporter dans ta chute? [8]

Here the ecstasy of surrender, which in the Christian structure belongs properly to God, but in case of need can be transferred to Satan, is evoked by an image of total moral neutrality. The slow buildup of snow, which encases and rigidifies the body and then carries it furiously down a sudden slide assumes personal death as the final destination of human time. For Baudelaire, "néant" is particularly the end and enemy of time; it swallows especially that long, heavy end of time which is the past and its memories. Not only does it annihilate time and hence perhaps the awful weight of moral judgment (as, for instance, in "De Profundis Clamavi," where once again Baudelaire yearns for the easy oblivion and moral neutrality of a brute beast); even as mere void it promises an end to consciousness which can only be of suffering. To put the matter prudentially, if we are already in Hell, death has a very good chance of being a change for the better. "La Squelette Laboureur," by inverting this idea, demonstrates its importance; the vision of skeletons at work with shovels (and presumably "making the world a better place in which to live") suggests to the poet that "le Néant envers nous est traître" — the sleep of death may be uneasy.

Thus "néant" when it is real comes to be simultaneously a terrifying and a deeply desirable state. It is self-destruction, it is self-fulfillment; it envelopes a number of less capacious terms

8. And time swallows me, minute by minute, as snow engulfs a slowly stiffening body; I look down from on high at the world in its roundness and no longer expect the shelter of a shed. Avalanche, will you carry me off in your fall?

like "l'oubli," "l'inconnu," and "l'insensibilité," as well as secondary attributes like "ténèbres," "silence," and "vertige." Sometimes the poetry itself, with its possibilities of imaginative metamorphosis, becomes an effort at annihilation, as in the second "Spleen," where the poet insinuates himself into the emptiest and deadest things, first in his immediate surroundings, then in his imagination, by way of illustrating his spiritual vacuity. And in this fascinated circling around an inner precipice, we verge upon Baudelaire's favorite image of annihilation, the multiform, multi-directional "gouffre."

"Everything is abysm" says "Le Gouffre" compendiously, after invoking the example of Pascal, who carried his own portable "gouffre" around with him; and indeed the thought of being swallowed up by action as well as inaction, by thought, memory, desire, by all forms of self-commitment, runs through Baudelaire's biography as through Poe's. He was forever being poured forth, to his own unspeakable dismay. The ego, which German romantics had shown as adapted to athletic divisions and reduplicative stunts, shrinks here in terror from its own fluidity. In whatever it undertakes, it is bound to get lost. Man's liberated soul staggers through its jungles, like Little Black Sambo, careening from the jaws of one tiger into those of another, from the sense of absolute loneliness under the stars to a terrified sense that in the toils of humanity one's ego may flow away and disappear for good.

In "Le Gouffre" itself, a special quality of the pit is its gift for extending itself in many directions. "L'Irrémédiable" is perhaps a fuller exploitation of "gouffre" as that shaft of guilt through which the soul sinks helplessly, surrounded by monsters and grotesques, lit only by its own unwavering conviction of guilt. But in "Le Gouffre" the void is above as well as below; the shore toward which one struggles is a quicksand, as the sea into which one sinks is bottomless:

> En haut, en bas, partout, la profondeur, la grève,
> Le silence, l'espace affreux et captivant. . . .[9]

There is no appeal against the endless, elaborate nightmare which God scrawls at the bottom of the poet's nights, for in that image the heights and depths of existence are united against him. Urbane readers may not be shocked to find Satan taking over some of the functions of the Christ; Jean Prévost, at least, was comforted to find that when Baudelaire blasphemed he did so as a Christian (*Baudelaire*, p. 73). But when God himself is shown using his wisdom and power to drag one of his creatures into the pit, it is not altogether naïve to feel disturbed.

Sleep, then, is forbidden the poet, for through the wall of sleep God conspires against him; and when he looks out through the cracks and openings of his world,

> Je ne vois qu'infini par toutes les fenêtres.

Everywhere else in *Les Fleurs du Mal*, "l'infini" is an emblem of divinity, of the ideal, of joyous escape from "êtres et nombres." The "Hymne à la Beauté," though professing indifference as to whether beauty descends from heaven or rises from the pit, emerges from the "gouffre" or drops from the stars (and one notes how assuredly this poem distinguishes up from down), nonetheless professes confidence that its gestures

> m'ouvrent la porte
> D'un Infini que j'aime et n'ai jamais connu.[10]

It is the punishment of Delphine and Hippolyta (rather pompously pronounced, to a modern taste, in the second *Femmes damnées*) that they must renounce forever the infinity which

---

9. Above, below, everywhere, the deep, the shore, the silence, the space horrible and predatory. . . .
10. Open to me the gate of an Infinite that I love and have never known.

they carry within themselves. It is, if not specifically "l'infini," at least "le goût de l'éternel" which the platonic "Hymne" to Mme. Sabatier attributes to the lady's blessed influence.

But in a poem like "Le Gouffre" one feels "l'infini" itself turning from a consolation to a demand, from a source of comfort to a threat of terror and loss; and with it can be associated other poems like "Le Couvercle," where heaven becomes (by an inversion more serious than blasphemy, an inversion which has contaminated even the limping versification) the lid of a pot or a coffin — something which clamps a ceiling on man's aspirations and renders them actually vulgar:

> Plafond illuminé par un opéra bouffe
> Où chaque histrion foule un sol ensanglanté. . . .[11]

Even more sinister in its cold inhumanity, "Les Aveugles" describes the blind who wander forever through a "noir illimité" while the city bellows, sings, and laughs around them. By a kind of irrational tropism their faces are turned continually upwards toward the heavens:

> Vois! je me traîne aussi! mais, plus qu'eux hébété,
> Je dis: Que cherchent-ils au Ciel, tous ces aveugles? [12]

Especially in the "plus qu'eux hébété" there is direct self-reproach; if they, who cannot hope to see anything, look to heaven, why not I? But the contrast also carries an implication that only those people stare into the heavens who are unable to see them, or anything. There is, indeed, no hint that anyone, however acute his vision, will really see anything in heaven; and the overpowering image remains that of the blind man, shuffling through endless darkness, straining by a true instinct

11. A ceiling decorated with a comic opera in which every actor treads a bloody ground. . . .
12. Look! I am wandering too! but, duller than them, I ask: What are they looking for in the sky, all these blind men?

to see what he is prevented by irremediable accident from ever glimpsing. The cruelty of the hand which made the blind spectral markers of an instinct they cannot hope to gratify is scarcely concealed — actually, it is deliberately mirrored in the cruelty of the poet, a cruelty which has shocked some readers of this poem. Finally, in "Le Rêve d'un Curieux," which like "Le Couvercle" dates from the third edition of the *Fleurs du Mal,* the poet imagines himself suffering the final indignity of which a disordered, irrational universe is capable. Death is described here under the image of a theater curtain before which sits an audience, including the impatient poet:

> J'étais comme l'enfant avide du spectacle,
> Haïssant le rideau comme on haït un obstacle, . . .
> Enfin la vérité froide se revela:
>
> J'étais mort sans surprise, et la terrible aurore
> M'enveloppait. — Eh, quoi! n'est-ce donc que cela?
> La toile était levée, et j'attendais encore.[13]

"Néant," "gouffre," "idéal" and all their associated ideas reduce themselves in an instant to a Swiftian practical joke, with the Deity snarling contemptuously, "Go, go, you're bit." Whatever it is that lies the other side of the supreme adventure, it is less, much less than Nothing. Nothing, true Nothing, we can conceive of the poet greeting with a certain voluptuous abandon. Eternity, infinity, the swoon of oblivion, would at least be no anticlimax; but that death should be only, so to speak, a ticket to a third-run movie is a frightful humiliation. And this, or something like this, may well be what the enigmatic last line of "Le Gouffre" implies; for "ne jamais sortir des Nombres et

13. I was like a child, greedy for the show, hating the curtain as one hates an obstacle, . . . at last the chilly truth appeared: I was dead unremarkably, and the terrible dawn enveloped me. — Well, is it only that? The curtain had risen and still I was waiting.

des Etres" is to despair even of "néant" as unreachable and to proclaim the profane inescapable. Critics have been reluctant to see this triumph of the profane over the collapsed, identified voids of "néant" and "infini" as a terminus of Baudelaire's thought, because it looks like an anticlimax. Artistically, indeed, some of the poems in which it is expressed (particularly "Le Couvercle" and "Les Aveugles") are stylistically slack. But when the polarities start to collapse on which a man's world is founded, it may well be that the poetry of that world (particularly if, like Baudelaire's, it is a poetry of polarities) will collapse too. Not all at once, or without the possibility of spasmodic revivals — of which "Le Voyage," though much less schematic and summary than "L'Imprévu," seems a more fitting example — but in the end totally.

In summarizing Baudelaire's adaptations of Nothing to his poetic cosmos, we take note naturally of God's absence or only enigmatic presence, his refusal to commit himself to Baudelaire; but that is an old familiar anxiety, and the innovations are really elsewhere. They lie in a certain drainage and seepage of the self into a world which is porous and hydroptic; in a confusion, i.e. a flowing-together of voids which have actually become value-centers; in a representation of exoskeletal humanity as echoing within to great echoes without; and in a profound loathing of the limited human condition, an almost frightening openness to the resonance of any sphere not this. Structurally speaking, Rimbaud is perhaps right when, speaking as a "voyant," he reproaches Baudelaire with being "trop artiste," too preoccupied with a form which in the end has about it something "mesquine." But it may be argued that this form is deliberately hollow, so that voids can grow up within the poem and be felt against its structure. As a tension against threatening spaces, Baudelaire's not-always-sequential thought develops; it most often takes the form of a passive reaction in which any apparent solidity, or even a more remote quicksand, is invoked against the nearest "gouffre." Like deQuincey and Poe, Baudelaire is always summoning up the mobile reserves. The wider gaps between poems, the shifting values assigned symbolic and verbal elements — though sometimes more puzzling — are probably of less literary interest; spiritual biography, it may be, will very largely account for them. But the use of void within individual poems as technique rather than subject-matter fills them with a negative energy which is easy to feel but hard to define. It may explain, as much as these things can be explained, our sense of the extraordinary discrepancy between his felt importance and the meagerness of what we can find in his positive ideas and verbal techniques to justify it. He has the ragged elegance, and also the gift of eloquent, empty gesticulation, which one remembers from those little figures who populate the dark corners of Piranesi's etchings.

Ideas often serve a lyric poet better as façade and pretext than as substructure; what is allowed to peep through the interstices of his thought works more dramatically than the thought itself. Our sense that Nothing is an energy which Baudelaire can barely control, that it imposes itself on him and his thought to their imminent peril and ultimate ruin, lends depth and drama (perhaps factitious depth and drama) to his verse. Leconte de Lisle, no less preoccupied with Nothing, offers a notable contrast in his handling of it; he presents it as an element of a landscape which he himself securely controls and manipulates. Very frequently the foreground is a barbaric or exotic scene. "Les Hurleurs" describes a pack of meager, mangy curs quarreling over a clutter of dead bones, with an arid desert behind them, a wild ocean in front of them, and the dead moon rising overhead. "Les Eléphants" presents a long string of elephants trekking across the red, hot sands of a desert. The dogs are surrounded by Nothing, and the echoes which their yelps rouse in the depths of the poet's soul, "du fond de mon passé confus," evoke a moral or at least dramatic meaning for the scene. The elephants, wherever they have been, clearly don't like it there, and are going back as fast as they can. The cause of their weighty, wordless horror is only to be inferred, but it is strongly implied; as with the dogs, it seems to be some immense vacancy in nature which is now impelling them back toward their "pays natal," wherever that is. And like the dogs, the elephants are only present in order to witness, to point at, something which the poet's portentous reticence is intent on giving no name.

Truncated gesture and enigmatic, eloquent fact work well too in a poem like "La Fontaine aux Lianes," which opens and closes as a tranquil description of a tropical landscape. It is a charmed and romantic scene, a glade of enormous trees, warm and murmurous and maternal, through whose branches one can barely see the eternal snows of mountains. In the foreground a pool wells up among water lilies, reflecting quiet skies and mysterious birds. We are almost lulled into expecting sonorous meditations and nostalgic complaints, when it appears there is a corpse in the fountain. A young man lies there dead, as a result of no specified violence, making no plea for pathos, just dead with a bitter and perhaps ironic smile on his face.[14]

Il était de ces morts que bientôt on oublie,[15]

says the poet, not without a little bitterness of his own. But he is right; and after brief speculation on the young man's origins and troubles, the poet forgets him and returns to a vision of nature's blazing, indifferent splendor, leaving the corpse in the fountain, unexplained and without consequences.

Because it is at once lucid and enigmatic, the poem sustains a

14. The suggestion is latent that he has committed suicide, and it is reinforced by an earlier version of the poem which included specific reference to a romantic suicide, that of Stenio in George Sand's *Lélia*.
15. He was one of those corpses who are quickly forgotten.

satisfying number of suggestions; [16] but the image of the fountain as translucent tomb is central to most of them. It suggests,
among other things the thinness of that sense-continuum which
is "nature." Metaphors like the "suaire de l'onde" and the
"fosse bleuâtre" imply a sense that the void one thought was
beyond nature is actually within it — that infinity can be found
by reaching into a shallow pond — and perhaps that the difference between the young man living in nature and the young
man dead in nature is less than one had supposed.

A last instance of Leconte de Lisle's void-mindedness is
found in Flaubert's favorite poem, "Midi." The poet here takes
high noon as his setting. The fields lie thick and peaceful, sighing under the breeze and drinking in the sunshine. Ruminating
an endless dream, the cows lie still, and all nature seems heavy
and replete with physical content, wrapped in a thick blanket of
its own *Dinglichkeit*. But the poet, turning abruptly against his
scene, warns the reader to bring neither joy nor bitterness to
this landscape:

> Homme, si le coeur plein de joie ou d'amertume
> Tu passais vers midi dans les champs radieux,
> Fuis! la nature est vide, et le soleil consume:
> Rien n'est vivant ici, rien n'est triste ou joyeux.
>
> Mais si désabusé des larmes et du rire,
> Alteré de l'oubli de ce monde agité,
> Tu veux, ne sachant plus pardonner ou maudire,
> Goûter une suprême et morne volupté;
>
> Viens, le soleil te parle en lumières sublimes;
> Dans sa flamme implacable absorbe-toi sans fin;

16. A rather similar poem by Rimbaud, "Le Dormeur du Val," by saving
the wounds which have killed the young soldier for the climactic last line,
makes a more limited and pathetic appeal. Leconte de Lisle's poem is about
a pool with a corpse in it — Rimbaud's is only about the tragedy of war, the
pathos of death, blighted young lives, etc.

> Et retourne à pas lents vers les cités infimes,
> Le coeur trempé sept fois dans le néant divin.[17]

Nature's indifference to human interests is a major theme of the poem, and might well have occupied it entirely.[18] But the poet's most interesting theme is an interplay of voids. A preliminary emptiness is required in the viewer, who then qualifies for a bath in the divine void where he will be made *really* empty. Dipped seven times in the element of fire (like Achilles, whose mother dipped him alternately in ambrosia and flame, to burn away his mortal nature), such a man is at last empty enough to endure human life — made impersonal and as it were divine. Not surprisingly, the author of "Les Montreurs" returns from his venture into the heart of darkness which lies within the shower of light, confirmed in his aristocratic disdain for the swarming impurities of flesh and blood.

The mood of "Midi" was not transient for Leconte de Lisle; one finds echoes of it and approximations to it throughout his poetic canon, and the *Derniers Poèmes* of 1895 are still deepening a tonality first found in *Poèmes Antiques* (1852). His disdainful fatalism toward things of this world is more Buddhist than Buddha, for he does not believe in purification or release, pantheism or metempsychosis. The vision of Nothing is for him a black pit, not any form of ecstatic reunion with any conceiva-

17. Should you be passing through the radiant noontime fields, if your heart is full of joy or bitterness, flee — for nature is void and the sun devouring. Nothing lives here, nothing is sad or gay. But if, skeptical of tears and laughter, changed by oblivion of this frantic world, no longer capable of a curse or a blessing, you yearn to taste a last gloomy delight — then come; for the sun speaks to you in sublime rays. Absorb yourself endlessly in its implacable fires, and return at last slowly toward the miserable cities, your heart tempered seven times by the heavenly void.

18. It has been argued with good probability that "Midi" derives some of its point from a dialogue with Leconte de Lisle's compatriot Lacaussade. But, so far from impeaching the originality of "Midi," its relation to Lacaussade merely emphasizes Leconte de Lisle's reach beyond the nineteenth-century banalities. "Midi" does not take part in a debate, but transfigures it.

ble godhead; for he does not recognize any first substance or divine essence, even unintelligible, with which we will finally be reunited. The tissue of life is nothing but error and illusion, and its only authenticity is the assurance of its ultimate nullity:

> . . . le néant final des êtres et des choses
> Est l'unique raison de leur réalité.[19]

Thus Nothing becomes not only the end of existence but a principle to be recognized within existence, a source of assurance against the follies and despairs of existence. In addressing a dead poet (Gautier), he declares:

> Moi, je t'envie, au fond du tombeau calme et noir,
> D'être affranchi de vivre et de ne plus savoir
> La honte de penser et l'horreur d'être un homme.[20]

From what lofty vantage-point it is possible to consider thought a disgrace and humanity a horror is one of those questions which poets, perhaps fortunately, do not have to answer. Then as now there was plenty of *bassesse* to turn up one's nose at; but categorical and undemonstrable disdain risks in the end seeming forced or monotonous. Perhaps this is the price one pays for a certain sort of sincerity. In any event, Leconte de Lisle managed to sustain in his verse an attitude toward Nothing which in practical life could have had only a sudden outcome, and even transcended on occasion the theme's inherent tendencies toward baldness of statement varied with rhetorical overlay. Whether success in handling this corrosive subject lies in striking a controlled and weighty tone is less clear. It may well be that the monolithic solidity of what Mendès called Leconte de Lisle's "Nirvana furibond" is both the most impressive and the most limiting aspect of his obvious talent.

19. The ultimate Nothing of beings and things is the sole reason of their reality.
20. I envy you, deep in your calm dark tomb, your freedom from life, from the shame of thought and the horror of humanity.

VI

Masks, Screens, Guises:

Melville and Others

Prepared vision has been conditioned by an intermediate agent, whether mask, screen, or guise: some definitions. It makes various use of Nothing, as a base from which to measure creative delusion, as a springboard to imaginative freedoms, as a mirror to shut out society or illumine oneself, as a destiny to be sought or shunned.

The flowing together and ultimate identification of Everything and Nothing sounds, at first, like one of those exaggerated word-games which a critic who aspires to be thought sensible must be careful to mention only in a tone of distant levity. But it has roots as old, at least, as Rousseau, and is not really a paradox but an enthymeme:

> In fact, man, being greedy and limited, so constructed that he desires everything and obtains little, has received from heaven a consoling force which brings close to him whatever he desires, subjects it to the sway of his imagination, renders it present and sensible to him, actually makes it in some sort his, and to sweeten even further this imaginary ownership, modifies it at the whim of his passion. But all this splendor disappears in the presence of the object itself; nothing embellishes the actual object in the eyes of its possessor; one never images forth what is already beneath one's eyes; imagination makes no play with what one actually possesses; illusion ceases where enjoyment begins. In this world, the land of chimeras is the only one worth inhabiting; and such is the nullity of human affairs that, outside the one self-existing

Being, the only beautiful thing is that which has no existence at all (*La Nouvelle Heloïse*, VI, 8).

So writes Julie d'Etange, become Mme. de Wolmar, to her ever-agonized Saint-Preux. The world of things, practical objects, here-and-now arrangements, can yield only a meager experience; the mind must create its own delights, and the freer it is from the fetters of sense, the more it will create. Thus the experience of (physical) Nothing is the only path to the delights of an (imaginative) Everything. The nineteenth century is full of witnesses following this road toward solipsism (which might itself be defined hyperbolically as a condition in which Nothing becomes Everything). From Julien Sorel to Des Esseintes, from Keats to Mallarmé, from Novalis to Ibsen, they all testify that anticipation, imagination, and memory (any relation as long as it is *distant*) are richer experiences than experience itself. Forced to possess fully his heart's desire, the romantic cries involuntarily, "N'est-ce que ça?" But if by fortunate circumstance he is immured in a cruel dungeon, or denied access to his beloved by unbreakable taboo, he wraps the precious thought in the richest folds of his imagination, and creates. The nineteenth century is full of ecstatic isolates worshiping neutralities wrapped in projections.[1] These projections are made through a third agent, which if it stands close to the projector we call a mask, if in the middle distance seems a screen, and if on the object can be called a guise. A sort of deception or self-deception lies at the heart of the process, but we are in a position to

---

1. A dramatic instance is provided by D'Annunzio's *Trionfo della morte* (I, iii–iv), when Giorgio Aurispa suggests to his mistress Ippolita that they celebrate the second anniversary of their affair at Orvieto; and he describes to her what the town will be like — cold, quiet, lofty, with that immense echoing masterpiece of the Duomo at one end. But, having had the best of Orvieto in imagination, and fearing to dilute this exquisite impression, they promptly abandon the project and go for their anniversary to Albano Laziale. Cf. analogous non-experiences of Des Esseintes and Count Axël d'Auersperg.

speak categorically of truth and falsity only if we suppose the projector must be looking at the thing in itself, and that his prepossessions are ultimate. But neither condition need hold. As every hypothesis is a filter of random reality, so every filter may be in the nature of a hypothesis, subject to the correction of an antithesis and the adjustments of a synthesis. How better to see patterns, the "reality" of which is not to be denied, even though under full daylight, to the uninstructed eye, they may not be apparent? Only by following Don Quixote in his indefensible folly does Sancho Panza make the great and real discovery that it is his own essential nature to be loyal.

But the dialectic of literature may exploit by questioning as well as by exercising devices of projection and filterage — mask, screen, and guise. In Anderson's story about the Emperor's new clothes, it is a little child who sees that the monarch is stark naked; he speaks with the authority of nature itself, and besides, as the story is intended for children and we grownups are mere intruders, we are reluctant to question the flattery. We accept the joke that the pompous monarch was indeed naked and did look silly. The collapse into mere common sense is perhaps too easy to be wholly comfortable; [2] of the same mode but contrary tendency, books like Great Expectations and Madame Bovary destroy obsessive projections in order to permit the appearance of a higher, a more austere, and perhaps more authentic insight. Either the perceiver finds he is not who he thinks he is, or the object is not what he took it for, or the way to it is not what it

2. Those rascals the artisans, if they had studied romantic critical theory, might easily rebut that their weaving was not done for the eyes of children, that the true test of weaving can never be the unprepared eye of an innocent, that the finest weaving is done, not with gross material rags, but within the mind of the onlooker — and so prove that the emperor had never been naked at all, the child was simply childish in expecting material clothes. (A trip to the Folies Bergères would show him that a person may be very substantially clothed in a couple of spotlights.)

seemed to be. Sometimes this is a novelistic truth, sometimes it would more properly be called anti-novelistic, since it grows only from the defeat of the novel's perceptions and puts irrevocable end to the novel by destroying its values. When he has absorbed the full, clear radiance of divine grace, Don Quixote is no longer a subject of fiction. Thus it is in the perilous interplay of perception that fictional destinies are worked out. The uncertainties of their working are often accentuated by the proximity, in one direction or another, of a vigorously operative Nothing.

As his approach to experience was characteristically indirect, the novels of Stendhal (e.g. *La Chartreuse de Parme*, 1839) make use of a rich repertoire of screens, masks, guises, and indirections. The Prince of Parma reigns through a social mask modeled on the deportment of Louis XIV; Fabrizio uses Saint Jerome and the terminology of heavenly love as a screen through which to express his profane passion for Clélia Conti. The Duchessa Sanseverina, ardently devoted to her handsome young nephew, has laid hold of a handy guise under which to prosecute a more tender affection. Fabrizio, as is well known, first makes love to Clélia through an actual physical screen; and the whole action is determined by the circumstance that Stendhal's hero must assume the mask of an ecclesiastic. This crucial mask, however, poses a question. The Prince, in his quizzing of Fabrizio (Section 7) tries to reach through the young man's pious mask, and fails. This is not surprising, indeed the episode is conventional spy-story routine, and we are allowed to think that our hero has simply outwitted his suspicious inquisitor. But shortly thereafter Fabrizio pauses in a church to thank God for his escape after killing Giletti (Section 12); and on this occasion the author himself tries to reach through the mask of Fabrizio's religiosity, reaches and probes into the things of which his character is or may be aware, and fails to find the discrepancy which he expects. Fabrizio is not a hypocrite, he has simply received a Jesuit education, which "forms the habit of not paying attention to things that are clearer than daylight." He is therefore unconscious of having conspired to commit simony. He is conscious that murder is a fault, and sincerely repents of having killed Giletti, even though in self-defense; but he does not condemn himself as a priest who has killed a man in a public knife-fight over a loose woman. Fornication and simony are not for him occasions of hypocrisy, because nobody has even raised for him the question of whether priests should be sexually continent or connive for offices. The answers to these questions are clearer than daylight, and he is wholly unconscious of them.

When one describes Fabrizio's mind in this way, it sounds as if one were saying that he was not a hypocrite because there was no thought for the mask to conceal. But this is not true; the lines of demarcation between his shrewdness, even cynicism, and his naïveté are simply arbitrary. And the problem is complicated by the circumstance that perfectly "natural" behavior on his part often serves, in specific social circumstances, as black hypocrisy. When he goes to call on Archbishop Landriani, it is in perfect simplicity and by the connivance of a lucky accident that he has himself announced by a deaf footman as a young priest named Fabrizio. But already the poor Archbishop is at a hopeless disadvantage in that humility-contest to which (in Stendhal's eyes) all priests are committed. "A del Dongo kept waiting in my ante-room!" It is his perfect sincerity in one context that best serves Fabrizio as screen or mask in another. His uncontrollable tears over Clélia give him a splendid reputation for saintliness; and the little worn black coat which he wears is an even more intricate exercise of innocent policy.

In the first place, we do not know why he wears this ostentatiously humble garment, in fact we learn only quite suddenly from Conte Mosca (Section 26) that he has been wearing it for some time. As Coadjutor-with-eventual-succession, he would

normally wear something more splendid, in a court where even
flunkeys dress elaborately and are elaborately described (Section
28, at the beginning). But this retrospective introduction of a
disguise — as if it had been worn but scarcely noticed hitherto
— removes it from the conscious and purposeful game of advantage which Fabrizio and his mentor Conte Mosca have been
playing. To be sure, the little worn black coat functions fa-
mously in that game. There is exquisite social duplicity in having scapegrace Fabrizio esteemed more saintly than the Archbishop, in having his snobbery triumph over the other's simplicity and in the name of simplicity itself. A triumph of these
ironic inversions occurs when the exasperated Archbishop
actually has the bad taste to accuse his Coadjutor of *hypocrisy*
— the accusation being patently correct (more correct than he,
poor man, can possibly know) and totally absurd at the same
time.

But the little worn black coat, though it is a weapon in the
social war, is not just that. It is the badge of a mute, enigmatic
grief, a deeper disgust with the world than anyone but Clélia
can fathom. It is, as it were, a miniature prison within which
Fabrizio discovers and creates himself. As Julien Sorel's buried
poetry flowers in prison, Fabrizio's blossoms under the little
black coat. It is a baroque poetry, we gather from the short description of his sermons, emotional and florid and rather like a
spiritualized opera. But there is no longer any question now of
imposing on people; Fabrizio no longer has anything to gain by
playing a part, at least he can gain nothing which he values by
playing this particular part. In fact he has gone beyond the light
of the Conte and Contessa Mosca, as well as that of Parma society, and all the values of their special game, the name of
which is see-and-be-seen. Declining all the gambits of light,
Fabrizio follows Saint-Preux in seeing that his self can feed in
full liberty only in darkness, only on its deeper and former

selves; he turns away from the world of experience. Where does his passion for prisons start and his love for Clélia leave off? They have been interwoven, from the very beginning; his first thoughts of her were linked with the idea of prisons. Not only so. The darkness into which Fabrizio is turning at the end of the book links back, imagistically, through the prophecies of Priore Blanès about a prison which is his destiny, to tie up with that long-forgotten tree which once represented his self. The instinct of darkness has grown like a tree inside Fabrizio; it is not a learned habit, it is something that was there from the start. He flirted with the Spielberg as with fatality, sought out the Prince's prison as by natural instinct, and found perfect happiness there; when he is finally liberated, it is toward other and more private prisons that he necessarily moves. His choice is made, not out of perversity, but for reasons which he cannot or at least does not make clear. They are "reasons" which the reader is required to invent after the fact, as the little black coat pops into consciousness after it has been worn for a long time, and reasons must be found for its appearance. The book which is, as a rule, immensely explicit in accounting for motivations — which distinguishes in quite surgical detail levels of awareness and measures of intention — seems intent on keeping as dark as possible about Fabrizio's crucial turn to darkness. There is of course a deep inherent instability in Fabrizio, as in most of Stendhal's heroes, but to make the terminal act of the book gratuitous on Fabrizio's part, or expedient on the author's, is to truncate the novel radically and unnecessarily. The choice which is made through the modality of the little worn black coat is not willful or perverse, it is rooted in the book's development so deeply as to be inward and voiceless; it is not so much a rejection of opportunity as an acceptance of destiny. And for this effect there need be no emphasis, not even a statement that the character's motives are obscure or that his nature has changed — suffices a purely artistic void. The more momentous the action, and the slighter the evident motivation, the more a reader must presume that what looks like a mask really answers to something in the unvoiced, unexplored remotenesses of the character. (The author's professed incapacity to understand his own character is a more transparent gambit in the same game.) So that in effect this mask — the little worn black coat — which Fabrizio puts on to conceal his character from friends and enemies, and within which his true nature grows, serves by its very negativity to create in the reader's imagination a sense of distance, strangeness, and echoing profundities within the character. Neutering motivation just when motives become crucially interesting, the coat's *impenetrability* achieves the special impact of a deliberately unsounded note in a sequence, where in one taut diphthong the ear both hears and fails to hear the sound it had been led to anticipate. A more emphatic and less emphasized Nothing we shall be hard put to discover.

What begins as a concealing screen becomes an instrument for suggesting the deepest truth of which Fabrizio is capable; the contrary process, of making the truth serve as a screen, is a well-known variety of equivocation, and also has its uses in fiction. Melville's Confidence Man (1857) in one of his many guises sells presumably fake stock to a gullible fool by reminding the victim that he may be talking to a swindler. This suggestion clinches the deal. "If you were other than I have confidence that you are," says the sucker with peremptory magniloquence, "hardly would you challenge distrust that way." And he evolves on the spot a splendid set of syllogisms to show that he need not examine the books of a company before investing in it:

"But you had better. It might suggest doubts."
"Doubts, may be, it might suggest, but not knowledge; for how, by examining the book, should I think I knew any more

than I now think I do; since, if it be the true book, I think it
so already; and since, if it be otherwise, I have never seen
the true one, and don't know what it ought to look like"
(Chapter 10).

It is an argument which grew grey in theology before ever it was
applied to commercial ledgers, so its speciousness is amply dangerous, doubly provocative.

The fragile bubble of "confidence" is forever being jabbed,
but never quite exploded, in this teasing, static, insinuating
story, by darts of suspicion and mistrust; the confidence man,
who is in turn almost everybody on the boat, becomes in the
end nothing less than a metaphysical principle, a bottomless
doubt. As we first enter into the story, it seems possible that one
swindle or another will explode, one boob or another will realize
that he has been tricked. But as the swindles multiply, the
chance of any one of them being successfully exploded fades
away and out of expectation. The confidence man himself has
little to gain from many of his operations (both victims and ob-
servers remark this fact), and in the later episodes he seems absorbed in the metaphysics of swindling to the neglect of the
swindle itself. Thus there are several potent Nothings at work
in the story. The screen of confidence through which innocents
choose to see things is reduced by persistent insinuation —
without anything so gross as proof or confrontation — to shreds
of delusion, grounded on Nothing, through which everyone
can see except the victim. But beneath the sleazy screen of confidence, and the only alternative to accepting it, is the limitless
pit of misanthropy. Disabused of confidence in others, a man
cannot be merely clearsighted, he must hate, and live to his own
fixed, timeless hatred. This seems to be the clear significance of
an apparent digression on Indian-hating in Chapters 25–28.
The Indian-hater has fallen out of the world of confidence=
faith, and entered on an existence of unchanging ferocity. He

has disappeared into his own mind, and died to this world, as surely as any anchorite.

How evident that in strict speech there can be no biography of an Indian-hater *par excellence*, any more than one of a sword-fish, or other deep-sea denizen; or, which is still less imaginable, one of a dead man. The career of the Indian-hater *par excellence* has the impenetrability of the fate of a lost steamer. Doubtless, events, terrible ones, have happened, must have happened; but the powers that be in nature have taken order that they shall never become news" (Chapter 26).

As there can be no biography of the Indian-hater, there can be no fiction about him either. So long as his vision was open to something besides Indians, so long as he discriminated one Indian from another, there might be reason to tell his tale; but monomania has no story, and all its episodes are the same. The price of failing to believe in "confidence" itself is collapse into this gaping hole which one feels staring Melville in the face throughout his story. (Joseph K. in *The Trial* has an intimation at one point that the crime of which he stands accused is nothing less than guilt; Melville's characters are asked to confide directly in "confidence." The middle term, the substantive of crime or faith, has dropped out of the logic of their predications.) By their blithe imperviousness to rational evidence, his caricatures provide a kind of screen for the artist himself, or at least a way of delaying a conclusion which his mind clearly found horrible in itself and deadly to his art. And it is this sense of something out of control working directly under the surface, crazing the appearances of the story and distorting them, but being for the moment held back, that gives this queer prolonged sketch its Gogolesque vitality.[3]

3. A close and disturbing parallel from the plastic arts is the elder Pieter Breughel's "The Misanthrope" (Capodimonte Museum, Naples), which

The Confidence Man is not the usual avenue of approach to Moby Dick (1851), though linkages are amply apparent. Ahab is a monomaniac probing the screen of the ostensible (an Indian-hater among the whale-hunters), and there is a raging cynic with a wooden leg (emblem of instability as well as impotence) who appears briefly in The Confidence Man. The crew of the Pequod like the passengers of the Fidele constitute a representative deputation of Everymen; both books work on the dynamic of a threatened, long-delayed confrontation. But a primary and immediate difference is stylistic; apart from a somewhat mannered lyrical patch at the start of Chapter 16, much of The Confidence Man is desultory, and some of it parodically flatulent in the writing. With rare intervals, the style impedes, as much as it can, appearance of a theme to which all style is inadequate. In Moby Dick, on the other hand, styles are the theme; or, to flesh out this paradox, much of the narrative energy goes into fabricating a dialect, an idiom, a verbal mask or façade which will adequately suggest (if not render) an experience, one name of which is Nothing.[4] A whole sheaf of these masks or dialects is made available to versatile Ishmael, who speaks alternately like a crackerbarrel philosopher and King Lear, like a lecturer on comparative anatomy, a hayseed humorist, Koheleth the preacher, and a nineteenth-century melodramatist. The effect has sometimes been described as pastiche, and so it sometimes is; but it also serves the purpose of fixing an elusive quality or combination of qualities which no single style could en-

---

portrays the lank, indrawn, black-robed misanthrope lost from the gray world in his own faceless thoughts, while a mad-eyed little man ensphered in the globe itself cuts his purse.

4. The discussion which follows owes some of its assumptions to Mr. James Guetti, formerly a graduate student at Cornell, whose thesis on Melville, Conrad, and Faulkner I profited by supervising. But as I write without his text to hand, I must hope not to trammel up his consequences too desperately.

compass. The heart of mystery is of course the white whale; and as we approach him, we are struck to see that most of the people who have any knowledge of him have been somehow fractured by the experience. Elijah, Ahab, Pip, the vision-haunted crew of the *Jeroboam,* the no less distanced and decimated crew of the *Town-Ho,* all suffer some sort of impressive mental derangement as a result of affronting the whale or his ocean. That fact alone summons up misgivings about Ishmael, whom early in the story we learned to trust as a humorous, companionable fellow. But apart from the ultimate consequences of seeing the whale (which are so ruinous to sanity as to raise the question whether he has ever really been perceived), we soon find the approach to this large mammal is beset with obstacles only to be surmounted by metaphors, paradoxes, rhetorics, dialects — in a word, verbal legerdemain. He has so many guises and disguises that the very existence of a knowable substantive nature comes to seem dubious.

Meeting with the ghostly *Goney* off the Cape of Good Hope, Ahab asks for news of the white whale; but the speaking-trumpet slips from the other captain's hand, winds howl, waves rise, and no answer ever comes to the query (Chapter 52). Trying to describe and catalogue the whale, Ishmael slips into a system of classification so playful, so intimate, so inconsequential and full of holes as to be a parody of an arrangement — starting with a basic, perhaps willful, taxonomic blunder of egregious proportions, when he includes whales among fishes. It is the obvious and deliberate inadequacy of the categories in the "Cetology" chapter which aims to convince the reader that the whale is elusive of all categories — as it is a whole battery of phrases like "grand hooded phantom" (Chapter 1), "outrageous strength with an inscrutable malice sinewing it" (Chapter 36), "unexampled intelligent malignity," "morbid hints and half-formed foetal suggestions of supernatural agencies," "the monomaniac incarnation of all those malicious agencies which some deep men feel eating in them" (Chapter 41), "the heartless voids and immensities of the universe" (Chapter 42), and "dim shuddering glimpses into Polar eternities" (Chapter 104), which suggest that the whale's real quality lies somewhere outside the categories of common sense. Ishmael has had a vision of the whale before ever he hears of him — an innate, therefore, and private whale. And as the story proceeds he invests the animal with continuously vaguer and more tremendous attributes, insisting meanwhile on the inadequacy of all words to do him justice:

> It was the whiteness of the whale that above all things appalled me. But how can I hope to explain myself here, and yet in some dim, random way explain myself I must, else all these chapters might be naught (Chapter 42).

A list of things which are white and also terrible, no matter how far prolonged, will never establish that whiteness is terrible; the catalogue with which Melville tries to "explain himself" is hopelessly, and no doubt deliberately, irrelevant to the fact which it pretends to demonstrate. This is one way in which Melville is continually suggesting another order of experience, a totality which is not the sum of specific qualities, a dimension which is not the total of finite magnitudes.

The slow development of many miscellaneous, irrelevant whale-approaches in the opening and middle sections of the book parallels the long, devious passage of the whaling vessel itself. Ishmael frequently combines, to pleasantly comic effect, the characters of mariner and scholar, creeping up on the whale in one capacity and trying to encompass him in the other, invoking all the resources of philology and adventurous action, simultaneously. But every verbal strategy for approaching the whale, every intellectual scheme for controlling him, is inadequate:

> Dissect him how I may, then, I but go skin deep; I know him not, and never will. But if I know not even the tail of this whale, how understand his head? Much more, how comprehend his face, when face he has none? Thou shalt see my back parts, my tail, he seems to say, but my face shall not be seen. But I cannot completely make out his back parts; and hint what he will about his face, I say again he has no face (Chapter 86).

Faceless, written over with undecipherable hieroglyphics (Chapter 68), proposed by the Bible itself as the very type of a mysterious and unfathomable power, ubiquitous, immortal, incomprehensible, the agent of an intangible malignity, the white whale is not to be seen through his disguises, nor is even his species to be understood. His mere dimensions are inconceivable. Ishmael undertakes to report on a whale-skeleton he once observed and measured, but though he does give a few carefully indefinite dimensions, it is only to insist on their utter inadequacy; and indeed, the very circumstances which make measurement possible render it useless:

> How vain and foolish, then, thought I, for timid untravelled man to try to comprehend aright this wondrous whale, by merely poring over his dead attenuated skeleton, stretched in this peaceful wood. No. Only in the heart of quickest perils; only when within the eddyings of his angry flukes; only on the profound unbounded sea, can the fully invested whale be truly and livingly found out (Chapter 103).

Not only the white whale and whales in general are unknowable — we cannot tell the simplest thing even about the nature of the whale's spout, since, says Ishmael, "I have ever found your plain things the knottiest of all" (Chapter 85). But then Ahab too is a mystery, concerning whose "deeper part" we are given to understand that "every revelation partook more of significant darkness than of explanatory light" (Chapter 106); and so is Queequeg, written over as he is with tattooings containing "a complete theory of the heavens and the earth, and a mystical treatise on the art of attaining truth" (Chapter 110). And Ishmael, who is continually protesting that he does not know or cannot possibly express this or that, or that some quality is beyond his measure, unfathomable to his thought, uses these protests systematically as a way of suggesting precisely what he says cannot be expressed:

> How it was that they so aboundingly responded to the old man's ire — by what evil magic their souls were possessed, that at times his hate seemed almost theirs; the white whale as much their insufferable foe as his; how all this came to be, . . . how to their unconscious understandings, also, in some dim, unsuspected way, he might have seemed the gliding great demon of the seas of life, all this to explain, would be to dive deeper than Ishmael can go (Chapter 41).

This is to make of duplicity a literary principle. By multiplying his rhetorical devices and at the same time denying their efficacy or relevance, by suggesting vividly a number of things he says he does not know, by adopting various dialects (as of Milton, Shakespeare, and the Bible) and then protesting that none of them are adequate to his theme, Melville creates a vast, reverberant shell of a book. The great genius of the sperm whale, we learn, "is declared in his doing nothing particular to prove it" (Chapter 79); here no doubt is an Emperor's-new-clothes joke, but the whale's inversion is characteristic of Melville's own rhetorical method, where irrelevance or inadequacy of strenuous expression is offered as evidence for magnitude of conception.

About this sort of book there is always controversy, for some readers cash the blank check without thinking about it, while others (and not necessarily the best readers) examine it suspiciously and turn it back finally as unpayable. Like the bones of the whale, Melville's book is not to be measured coldly, anatomically; if it is a triumph at all, *Moby Dick* has to be the triumph of an illusion and suggestion in which the reader co-operates a little more than passively. Its distinctive effects are hypnotic and incantatory — it flourishes before us words like "profound," "mysterious," and "unbounded," which denote little but gesture largely. And on the plane of verbal pantomime *Moby Dick* may be a momentous experience, although (or perhaps because) it never succeeds in defining lucidly its own elementary antagonisms. Whether Ahab is a maniac (as Ishmael repeatedly says he is) and the whale a mere dumb animal; whether Ahab is a visionary (as Ishmael says he is) and the whale an emblem or agent of some supernatural power; whether Ahab's satanism is or is not a form of worship, and then of what or of whom — all these problems are raised, elaborated, half-answered, but then qualified, rendered half-serious, and finally left unclear. For the antagonism between the eagerly grasping mind and elusive reality is fundamental to all other antagonisms in the book; so that it is the book's ultimate failure after exhaustive efforts to express its theme which is presumed to constitute best evidence of its success in handling it.

Many of the epithets and images which surround Ahab and the whale are redolent of voids and infinities; when the rhetoric turns to epistemology, it is often to suggest that behind the façades and masquerades of this world one finds deadly void, icy infinity, and irrelevant impersonal process:

> "O, thou clear spirit of clear fire," cries Ahab; ". . . I own thy speechless, placeless power; but to the last gasp of my earthquake life will dispute its unconditional unintegral mas-

tery in me. In the midst of the personified impersonal, a personality stands here. . . ." (Chapter 119).

The "personified impersonal" is probably Nature; setting his own "personality" directly against her, Ahab implies that everywhere outside his own self she is dead or lives with only borrowed life. And in the famous chapter on the whale's whiteness occurs a dramatic bundle of suggestions, that this color "by its indefiniteness shadows forth the heartless voids and immensities of the universe, and thus stabs us from behind with the thought of annihilation"; that it is "a colorless all-color of atheism from which we shrink"; and that whiteness reveals under the colors of nature the charnel house, the leper's pallor, of the universe. At the cost of some urging (for a universe stripped of color would be, not white, but black), white thus becomes a multiple metaphoric window opening on Nothing. But it reduces the book's import to make the whale emblematic of a specific threat, even void, or Ahab's quest the impulse to verify a specific speculation. They are the sum of their suggestions, or perhaps a little more; the book knows no either-or, only a both-and. And the clogged allegory of the final pages is as it were a confession that the totality of its suggestions cannot be summed or epitomized or even rendered. The struggling bird nailed to the sinking masthead, the coffin bursting from the vortex, the orphan-searching *Rachel*, all this machinery merely mimes and gesticulates toward a conception which has retreated beyond even suggestion. These actions are the mere dumb-show of allegory. And it is in this larger use of Nothing — in the context of conscious verbal insufficiency — that Melville seems most clearly to continue the tradition of Poe's prestidigitation and to anticipate an artist of verbal collision and mental impasse like Faulkner. What is particularly easy to see in Melville is the operation of a Nothing which needs no expression, which creates itself by being automatically "beyond" whatever splendid immensities the author's vocabulary is capable of. It can be described under the image of a balance, on one side of which the author ostentatiously heaps Everything — and which yet holds level. What can be on the other side? and how much does it weigh? The burden of reconciling these suggested answers is laid on the reader; multiple unexplained imbalance becomes a literary principle.

VII

Mallarmé

Not a topic, not a technique, nor yet a repertoire of strong
effects, Nothing is an accepted and pervasive presence in
the poetic universe of Mallarmé; interstices of void provide
perspective depth, significant distance between, and significant
distortion of, poetic constellations.

The filtering of Buddhist ideas, ideals, and attitudes into the consciousness of the West during the nineteenth century is a story the broad outlines of which are still in darkness or under dispute. Particularly among the poets who clustered about the *Parnasse contemporain,* one finds a vogue for the props and postures of Oriental resignation which verges perceptibly on attitudinizing and pastiche. What, for instance, could be stranger than to find M. Catulle Mendès, that one-man anthology of styles and effects, preaching in "Le Conseil du Sofi'" a doctrine of total passivity and resignation? Everyone is fastened to the wheel of life and the world of appearances, declares this elegant fabricator of occasional gestures, and is doomed to be reborn into it in an infinite sequence of boredom:

O lassitude enfin de voir encore les cieux!
Le roi, de qui l'orgeuil en la pourpre défaille
N'envîra plus l'amant désabusé qui baîlle
Dans le perfide lit des femmes aux beaux yeux! [1]

1. O weariness of seeing the heavens continually! The king whose pride grows weak under the purple will no longer envy the cynical lover, yawning in the treacherous bed of attractive women.

Having wearied of desire, one must be a motionless rock, over which wind and tide will break; with eyes shut, ears deaf, senses dead, one must renounce existence. Indeed, the poet says, with more than Persian enthusiasm, if a vulture perched on your head should claw out one eye, you should not open the other to see what is happening. Your reward will be Nirvana:

> Et bientôt, à la source unique retourné,
> Où le néant avec soi-même commune,
> Tu participeras à la paix infinie,
> Delivré de renaître et n'étant jamais né.[2]

Mendès can only be described as a Buddhist by vogue; Henri Cazalis, who published most of his literary work under the pseudonym of Jean Lahor,[3] was an Orientalist of more sincerity and greater interest, whose work has affinities enough with Mallarmé's to serve as a partial introduction to it. Cazalis was a man of many abilities and many careers. With a degree in law, another in medicine, an interest in what would nowadays be called "public health," and sufficient Oriental scholarship to write a well-reputed history of Hindu literature, he maintained a steady and productive career in literature. His *Livre du Néant* (1872) is a series of prose poems about everything and Nothing. Disdaining the systematic approach to so spacious a pair of topics, Lahor swarms over them, using aphorisms, parables, homilies, epigrams, and inventive translations with conscious

2. And shortly, returning to the one origin where void communicates with itself, you will enter into limitless peace, free from rebirth and never having been born.
3. Neither of these names was devoid of literary meaning for the poet. His *nom de plume* was taken from the capital city of the Punjab, seat, as he felt, of Indian mystic learning. As for his "real" name, it evinced spiritual kinship with Muhammad ibn Muhammad Abu Hamid al-Ghazali, an eleventh-century Arabian mystic, parts of whose poetic work Cazalis claimed to have translated in the second section of the *Livre du Néant*. Al-Ghazali, it is hardly necessary to say, never wrote a line of verse in his life.

inconsistency. His attitude toward "néant" is as various as his technique. At first, void tends to be a source of conventional horror and dismay. In one of his most compelling fragments he describes a slave ship, on which, lest the cargo die of despair, a few of them are occasionally brought up on deck, made drunk, and encouraged to caper and sing. Moving through the night to the sound of this barbaric, artificial revelry, while an occasional dark figure slips into the shadows and thence into the ocean, the slave ship is a gruesome emblem of a doomed world. But gradually the mood changes. *Néant*, it appears, can be overcome by asceticism, meditation, and love; it may not even have to be overcome at all, for

> par la magie du rêve ou la splendeur de tes passions, le néant de ton âme puisse être, comme le Néant universel, glorieux, sublime, magnifique et *divin!* [4]

Thus, somehow, the void consciousness comes to triumph over consciousness of void, and the mind is entitled to rejoice in the fragility of its own empty coherence. The world is mere illusion, to be sure; it consists of nothing but impressions and sensations, at best. No doubt this sensation of the fragility of the veil should lead to horrified rejection of its falsity and corruption. One stream of Cazalis's thought runs in this well-worn groove.[5] But another conclusion is to accept the thin tissue not only of things but of consciousness as valid and even exhilarating ex-

4. through the magic of dream or the splendor of your passions, the void of your soul may become, like the universal void, glorious, sublime, magnificent, and divine!

5. "La Pitié du Bouddha," sketched in prose in *Le Livre du Néant*, is a full-fledged poem in *L'Illusion*; it contrasts the Buddha's perfect indifference to a courtesan in the full flower of her beauty with his tenderness for her when she is old and ugly and foul, and understands ". . . que tout est vain, / Que toute forme n'est qu'un songe / Et que le monde entier comme le corps humain / N'est rien qu'un douloureux mensonge" [that everything is vain, that every form is a mere dream, and that the whole world, like the human body,

perience. One's ego may be a mountain which hides the sun, but, *tel quel*, it is not devoid of interest; illusion may be a horizon, a norm of value. A sort of provisional and ironic humanism thus grows out of the enormity of one's despair over the human condition, one cultivates a deliberate superficiality:

> On the surface of the brain are the layers of nerve cells whose vibrations create my sensations, thoughts, and dreams. And this surface of existence is the whole of existence. The complete ego reaches its high-point there, in becoming conscious of itself; the body, with all its tissues and organs, exists only to sustain and nourish this delicate surface, which alone in the whole creature thinks, dreams, and commands, which alone suffers and enjoys.
>
> And on the earth itself, note the position of animate life — it is on the surface that the nerve-cells of consciousness are spread, like the glittering foam of the ocean-waves, a precious foam, a dust and delicate substance for which this entire world seems to be made, since it furnishes, along with self-consciousness, consciousness of the world's grandeur and its misery, its joys and its sorrows (*Le Livre du Néant*, pp. 151–2).

That the world's body exists only to culminate (*aboutir*) in certain delicate and unstable shadings of consciousness gives to that consciousness a precious ironic dignity, and to its most nuanced expression, in poetry, the status of precious error. One finds Cazalis moving in his later treatments of illusion (see, for example, *La Gloire du Néant*, 1896) toward an ecstatic, tremulous pantheism which embraces even the delusive veil of appearance. His verbal skills did not suffice to weave those intricate void-enlacing webs toward which his philosophy pointed; but those of his friend Mallarmé most assuredly did.

---

is only a mournful lie]. Or again "L'Enchantement de Siva" portrays the seduction of Siva by Maya; in the instant of their embrace he sees her as "un putride amas de chair, d'os et de sang," drops her in horror, and plunges once more into the "gouffre du vide."

One can scarcely approach the figure of Mallarmé without trepidation and misgivings. Fifty years of hermeneutics have not produced many areas of clear agreement among the critics beyond that original one that the poetry is of a terrifying complexity and the prose provides no facile key to it. Yet Mallarmé is an author for whom void provides a — perhaps the — central experience; from its emplacement at the heart of his work, it rays out in a spectrum of directions through modern poetry, modern prose, modern critical theory. The perilous presence of Mallarmé is not to be escaped; let us therefore close with him and his dealings with a void which was neither cosmic nor comic, neither religious nor social, but intimate and ontological. These adjectives imply that the characteristic scheme of a fully developed Mallarmé void includes few large gestures or grand trajectories. There is, perhaps, a quiet room, a single object isolated on a bare table, and Mallarmé looking at it — a peculiarly active transaction which no perfunctory phrases will adequately define; and the object, like the viewer, is either empty within or surrounded by emptiness without, or both—like a jar in a painting by Morandi. All Mallarmé's perception of the carefully chosen, precisely defined objects in his world is haunted by an emptiness, as a result of which perception is a dangerous venture, intricately compounded of memory, distance, misgivings, while expression is inevitable shipwreck at best.

What did Mallarmé's sense of void grow from? Neither biography nor criticism can say with any sort of assurance. There are conjectures. The earliest poems of all show no trace of a void, but not much is to be inferred from this absence of an absence, for they are mere schoolboy verses. But — perhaps as a result of two untimely deaths in his intimate family, perhaps because of some sexual guilt, perhaps from a loss of religious faith, the depth of which is particularly hard to sound — for whatever reason, void settled upon his world and invested it completely, before the poet reached his majority. The two sonnets "Angoisse" (originally "A une putain") and "Tristesse d'été" invoke, along with certain deliberate Satanisms of evident Baudelairean inspiration, the imminence of "néant" and its close connection with sexuality. Apart from specific social circumstance, Mallarmé's early notions of "néant" derive from contrast with an "idéal" which is inconceivably remote and inaccessible. This failure of mind before the remote perspectives of "idéal" — which provokes in the "idéal" itself a certain cold, aloof irony, and in the poet something like terror — finds poetic expression in such poems as "L'Azur" [6] and "Les Fenêtres":

De l'éternel azur la sereine ironie
Accable, belle indolemment comme les fleurs,
Le poëte impuissant qui maudit son génie
A travers un désert stérile de Douleurs: [7]

So begins the one poem, and the other concludes:

Mais hélas! Ici-bas est maître: sa hantise
Vient m'écoeurer parfois jusqu'en cet abri sûr,
Et le vomissement impur de la Bêtise
Me force à me boucher le nez devant l'azur.

Est-il moyen, ô Moi qui connais l'amertume,
D'enfoncer le cristal par le monstre insulté
Et de m'enfuir, avec mes deux ailes sans plume
— Au risque de tomber pendant l'éternité? [8]

6. Mallarmé's own explication of "L'Azur" is found in the *Correspondance*, ed. Mondor and Richard (Paris, 1959), pp. 103–5. There is an interesting irony in Mallarmé's founding his poetic method so largely on Poe's "Philosophy of Composition," which was, of course, a hoax. There is no particular reason in logic why a poetic work of great integrity and rigor should not be suggested by and founded on a fraud — but not just any fraud. It is an interesting fulfillment of Baudelaire's judgment that one of Poe's real greatnesses was as *farceur*.
7. Eternal blue's quiet irony, lazy-lovely as flowers themselves, stuns the poet, helplessly maligning his gift through a sterile desert of despairs.
8. But alas! Down-here is ruler; its ghostly presence disgusts me sometimes

The windows which should admit "l'azur" and should open to provide access to it, in fact shatter its image, and force the poet in with "Bêtise"; "azur" itself is nothing in effect but a threat of forever falling into a pit without bottom. "Néant," then, is more than an individual abyss; it is a common ditch into which we are dragged by the "ésprit d'Impuissance" [sense of Impotence] which haunts modern man. Already too, the link between fall and ideal has become so deep and reciprocal in its working that fallen and faded things are precious to Mallarmé because they provide evidence (otherwise sparse or nonexistent) that the "azur idéal" still exists or at least recently did so. But in "Las de l'amer repos" a flower which has fallen from heaven and faded while its perfume evaporated, after some hesitations and equivocations in the first sketches of the poem, finally dies; and this death is only symbolic of a larger invasion of "néant" amid the Parnassian solidities of this early verse. We are moving into the full Mallarmé cosmos of icy virgins, mirrors which catch and freeze images, cold jewels, lofty glaciers, remote stars, silences, refusals, absences, and abstentions. Of this world the fiercely worked-over "Ouverture ancienne" to *Hérodiade* is the first expression.

Explicating a text so knotty, intricate, and ambiguous is quite out of the question in the present limited context; to establish the importance of void it will suffice to note merely the major themes of the Nurse's opening Incantation. Her speech begins with the word "abolie" and repeats it in the second line, varying the gender, "aboli" — Hérodiade the swan is abolished, and so is the pool of her tears, the mirror in which she has seen herself, the ambience in which she has existed. Dawn breaks on a deso-

---

even in this safe refuge, and the foul vomit of Stupidity forces me to stop my nose in the face of the blue.

Is there a way, oh myself who know bitterness well, to break through the crystal insulted by the beast, and take flight on pennonless wings — at the risk of falling through all eternity?

late and empty landscape, a room from which the aroma of fad-
ing roses is slowly disappearing. Within the vacancy of this
mournful landscape, the memory of a former voice, painfully
and wearily, without the aid of a verb, tries to raise itself in
song; but it breaks, falters, is forgotten:

> Et, force du silence et des noires ténèbres
> Tout rentre également en l'ancien passé,
> Fatidique, vaincu, monotone, lassé,
> Comme l'eau des bassins anciens se résigne.[9]

The song which the Nurse recalls was "parfois incohérent,"
and in imitation the "Ouverture" itself becomes deliberately involved, grammatically and rhetorically. What the Nurse must
describe is absence, the afterglow of a presence, a milieu from
which life has altogether, but just recently, disappeared. The
folds of Hérodiade's bed linger like the perfume of her hair;
and the thought recurs of her remote father, struggling through
piles of unburiable corpses, blowing his dark silver trumpets
furiously at the cisalpine pines. He is perhaps an evergreen
himself, this reverberant ancestor, but a very distant one, and
his rustle scarcely disturbs the dim light in which the Nurse
comes to doubt whether she is living through a dawn or a dusk.
As for Hérodiade, in her final imagined gesture she is "exilée
en son coeur précieux," hiding her head under her wing in
order to see more clearly

> les diamants élus
> D'une étoile mourante, et qui ne brille plus.[10]

That the general theme of the poem so meagerly sketched
here is a world of void needs no laboring; Mallarmé himself

9. And, through the silence and black shades, all things return together to
their past, prophetic, beaten, monotonous, weary — as the water of ancient
pools sinks back.
10. the chosen diamonds of a star which is dying and no longer shines.

said as much in a letter of late April 1866 (*Correspondance*, pp. 207–8), that "en creusant le vers" for the "Ouverture ancienne" he had fallen into two "néants," one outside and one within him. These "néants" are abundantly felt in the poem itself; but in the mere fact of their presence they are neither new nor startling. Mallarmé's handling of the theme has fascinated (and, it must be admitted, repelled) readers chiefly by virtue of his verbal textures and strange imaginative angularities. The language is dense, taut, and difficult; it suspends the modifier at an acrobatic distance from its substantive or hangs it at an impartial distance between two possible substantives, it stretches the thought over great irregularities of subordinate clause, it sinks subject and verb almost out of sight under festoons of qualification, it inverts and distorts word-order, its metaphors metamorphose wildly as if to demonstrate that not only the relation of analogy, but any relation of analogy, can hold, it hangs out perilously unsupported appositions, and leaps across yawning parentheses down vast winding staircases of abstractions related to abstractions related to abstractions. Finally, the development of thought takes place through a series of image-links which, if they are often highly abstract and theoretical, are often quite private and sometimes unexpectedly blunt and physical as well. A speculative thought struck off by the mind becomes a human head struck off by a sword, hesitating in its trajectory between *azur* and *ici-bas*; a fold in drapery becomes a thought turned back on itself, an evidence of intimacy, a gesture both of modesty and fecundity, and in its alternate opening and refolding a physical representation of the dialectic. These multiple possibilities of innuendo not only provide for the reader of Mallarmé's poetry a tantalizing exercise of interpretation, they also give to verse of the most abstract and intellectual quality a hard surface and that special metaphysical energy which comes from superficial harmonies overridden or boldly disregarded. In addition, the unexpectedly literal and physical images represent the tissue of material things — blunt and often irrational — imposing a lattice on a texture of woven abstractions, behind which lies the deeper darkness of void itself.

But it was not simply the appearance of void as an outside phenomenon, or as a theme for expression, which preoccupied Mallarmé during the years from 1866 to 1870; during this period he ventured his own actual identity against the presence of Nothing. The definition of "néant" which he took from Hegel made this sense of testing almost inevitable; for, says the philosopher, "nichts" is reality without concept (*Logic*, par. 87) — it is thus a deficiency of mind before unbroken reality. On the other hand, this very subjectivity of Nothing makes possible, if one takes the dialectic seriously enough, the involvement of Nothing as an active element in the very creation of the universe; it is one of the two antithetical theses from which thought itself takes flight. A curious concretizing this of the idea of Nothing, a granting to the concept of active powers,[11] which, however, did not prevent it from seeming to threaten closely Mallarmé's personal survival. He moved, almost convulsively, into the deepest darkness of an intellectual night — there to struggle, with the dubious aid of Hegel, after a problematical self-realization. It was during this period that he wrote to a friend, "I may say further, but for your ears alone, that I still need . . . to watch myself in this mirror in order to think, and that if it were not before the table on which I write

11. An earlier instance of this process is found in Dr. William King's *De Origine Mali* (1702) where, obviously with the phrase "creation *ex nihilo*" in mind, the learned Archbishop argues that every creation is descended from God as its father and from Nothing as its mother — the mother being thus the source of all earthly imperfection. This gambit moves the origin of evil back one stage from matter, its customary locus; what other advantages it provides is not very clear.

this letter, I should return once more to Nothing [*je re-deviendrais le Néant*]" (*Corresp.*, p. 242; cf. "Igitur," Section III).

His first step in reconstituting himself after the frightful sensation of a universe and a self gone dead was to immerse himself in total subjectivity; imitating Hegel and his predecessor Fichte, Mallarmé set himself to think his own thought (*Corresp.*, p. 240). But in order to see or define himself at all, to keep from draining away like water into the infinite spaces of black void, there had to be a first gesture, if only mental, of limitation. Such a gesture would enable him to divide himself into subject and object, and, in several different senses, to reflect upon himself. Hence the importance of the mirror, either literal or figurative,[12] in this period of Mallarmé's thought, as well as of the fold, which images the mind turning back on itself and generating a dialectic out of its own self-awareness. The drama of Hérodiade, so far as its final form can be guessed from the various sketches and unfinished versions which Mallarmé left behind, was to enact this moment of rebirth, this achievement of self-possession out of despairing self-knowledge. Hérodiade, seen unawares by the eyes of John Baptist, has suffered symbolic rape before the poem begins; in an instinctive reaction of *pudeur*, she turns away from all human life, rejects the three efforts at *rapprochement* of the Nurse, folds her head swanlike under her wing, and lives to her own consciousness. But in a moment of fury and revulsion, she has ordered the decapitation of the saint; and this act, complexly double in intent and consequences, results in her veil's being ripped:

12. Among the figurative mirrors was his wife. One sees him, as early as 1862, planning that Marie, after a couple of years of marriage, "sera mon reflet" (*Corresp.*, p. 53) and later, when they had in fact been married a while, announcing with satisfaction that "Marie . . . c'est moi, et je me revois dans ses yeux allemands" (*Corresp.*, p. 151).

Le glaive qui trancha ta tête a déchiré mon voile [The steel which cut off your head has ripped my veil]. (*Les Noces de Hérodiade*, ed. G. Davies, Paris, 1959, p. 136)

This second, and rather less metaphysical, rape is actually a division of her person in two. She becomes subject and object at the moment and by the act which sends the head of John Baptist into its brief orbit of rise and fall, and produces that gory sunset heralding a new night of Nothingness. But in this drama of an instant, Mallarmé apparently intended that she should seize the still half-animate head, cradle it on her knees, and seek in its glazing eyes both the reflection and the recognition of herself.[13]

How to manage this transition from the mirror which passively reflects, and which is in effect the mere contrived agent of the seer, to the recognition of active, independent *others* and the recognition of one's self by others (and how to make all this evident in the fully completed but evanescent consciousness of Saint John), was evidently one of the problems which posed Mallarmé's dramaturgy. Philosophically, the matter was far from insoluble; in Hegel particularly he found hints that full self-possession could be achieved only through a negation which was itself negated, by an arbitrary act growing out of a fully-realized despair. A cast of dice, for example, might be a self-creative response to the despairing recognition that chance prevails unalterably in the universe; fully realized, the disease is its own cure. "Destruction was my Beatrice," he told Eugène Lefébure (*Corresp.*, p. 246); in the submission of himself to the drama of self-destruction and self-reconstruction he found both a poetic theme and a personal perspective on all experience. But

---

13. Decapitation, for a thought-tormented man like Mallarmé, and a thought-tormented age like the nineteenth century, has one perfectly apparent meaning; but a careful analysis of the theme would very probably yield subtler and more sinister shades of significance.

how for Hérodiade this prescription could be made to produce that *other* which she so desperately lacks, and how the whole process could be made dramatically or even poetically tangible, these are problems on which Mallarmé's poetic venture shipwrecked. Some sort of leap or creative gesture, it seems, the heroine was to have made; and it would be out of her rediscovery of her authentic self, and celebration of her new existence, that her final dance was to have been created. A strange, almost motionless duality must have been the theme of this last dance, representing the dialectic of self-generated, self-observed existence. The light of her life having been lit at the prophet's gory sunset, she would create in her dance a new artifice, celebrate a new harmony, and even forget the victim of her crime now that his existence was, as it were, subsumed in hers. But though one can see how the *Hérodiade* might almost have expressed in its intricately knit lines the full ontological crisis of Mallarmé — and was clearly intended to do so — the fact is that the poet came to understand the full import of his creative venture only after it had come to irreparable disaster.

But the dimensions of Mallarmé's crisis are underestimated if it is confined to a single poem, even a single poetic crackup. The low point of his spiritual arc is represented by the tangled anguish of *Igitur*, posthumously published, and only to be described as a dramatic gesture of spiritual suicide. All reconstructions of this incomplete set of unfinished sketches are tentative, but a rough scenario can be detached and fixed at least partially. The time is midnight; the scene a solitary room from which a staircase leads downwards; the props a mirror, a candle, a clock, and a vial of "néant" or alternatively a pair of dice; the hero a naked skeleton of logical relationship. Compressed from one direction by immediate consciousness of the past, and stifled from another direction by the future's failure to fulfill itself, Igitur exists in "pure time, or boredom, rendered unstable by

the malady of the ideal"; and under these pressures, augmented
by his own bitter sense of "Impuissance," he disintegrates in his
own consciousness, disappears from his reassuring mirror, and
escapes from public time into a time measured only by the
"horloge de son âme." His bitter fragments must now be re-col-
lected so that he may live in an abstract and permanent idea of
himself; and something like this he seems actually to accom-
plish, for the harsh wind of "néant" ceases to blow, the
draperies no longer writhe, and the new Igitur begins to live or
die for himself in the act of blowing out his candle. He has discovered his idea of himself, but only by going outside of time
— has committed an exterior suicide and lit an inner light, but
only by accepting "néant" as his medium and making within it
the limited gesture, half of defiance, half of acceptance, which
Mallarmé loved to symbolize by a cast of dice within/against
the laws of chance. The meaning of the gesture is reinforced by
an alternative, and apparently equivalent, gesture which in the
sketches Igitur was to have made, drinking the vial of "néant."
Both acts are acts of folly (=drunkenness=absurdity=literary
creation), since accident is bound to prevail over any gesture to
affront it. But the gesture is made anyhow, as an act of internal
witnessing; and it seems that in the act of death, Igitur, like
John Baptist, was to attain supreme self-knowledge. But when
he sits down amid the ashes of his ancestors, and closes the door
of their tomb on himself, the knowledge he has attained is
rather less evident than the despair it brings with it.

Though Nothing is everywhere and all-important in Mallarmé's great spiritual crisis of 1866–70, though its mark is on
everything he wrote during that period, and continues to be felt
for the rest of his life, yet one may usefully ask how necessary
an element of the whole experience it was. And here a certain
skepticism is called for. For Mallarmé submitted his mind to
Nothing as to a test, and one is permitted to think that in other

circumstances it might have been the idea of God, infinity, eternity, one's own begetting, or some other transcendence, which he would have invoked. Any infinite concept which a finite mind cannot conceive, or finite language express, might have served the same broad purpose. Having wrestled with it for a while, he could then have returned from the glacial altitudes of intellectuality to find — still handy for his use and acceptable after his anguish — a kind of provisional, skeptical humanism not very different from the one on which, in fact, he settled. And of course any argument which opposed this rough-and-ready view of the matter would be paradoxical to start with, since it would consist of attributing a special positive value to the non-experience of Nothing. Yet the paradox may be worth affronting, if only to get us away from a rough-and-ready Mallarmé, a notion before which paradoxes pale. For Nothing did have a special value in impressing itself on Mallarmé instead of being sought; it compressed the mind instead of stretching it, because it stood outside any system of rewards. Its challenge was peculiar too in requiring the discovery of an ultimate inwardness (a subjective diamond, an interior sun) — something deeper than a change of heart, nothing less in fact than a reconstitution of the whole individual economy. It offered less to work with, but committed one to less in the way of prefabricated values than any other concept. No doubt "néant" was in the air, and an occasional phrase like "le néant moderne" shows that Mallarmé himself was not unaware of a vogue. But the evident authenticity of his struggle and the hardness of its terms (his battle was not for freedom, not for advantage, not for "happiness," but simply for a chance to exist) made of him a specially sensitive index to the modern dilemma. No other test-concept would have served quite this purpose quite so well as Nothing.

Wherever it came from, the fact of Mallarmé's extraordinary

spiritual grace is not subject to question; and its reverberation against the memory of this pure metaphysical anguish produced a legend the more fascinating because it was avowedly not for everyone. He had been tempered in the bath of "néant"; and though this image, with roots at least as deep as Leconte de Lisle's "Midi," has become almost a cliché of our time, it corresponds to a favorite metaphor of the poet's, and, so far as we can tell, to something like the realities of a personal history. On the crudest level, there is the biography. If not because of his long wrestle with the demon of vacancy, at any rate immediately after it, Mallarmé emerged as a crowned and mage-like personality. Driven in something like disgrace from a provincial school at Tournon, he had been an inhibited and mentally muscle-bound exile in Besançon and Avignon; abruptly, once the center had been crossed, he moved to the capital, found suitable posts there, became (in time) the revered center of those weekly conversations in the rue de Rome, acquired a dazzling mistress, and took up (most unforeseeable of metamorphoses!) the editorial direction of a ladies' fashion magazine — for which he himself provided, under suitable pseudonyms, all the editorial copy. All of which would be nothing, or less than nothing if it were not for the sparse, continuing miracle of the poetry — a fragile, intricate, yet wonderfully chaste filigree of thought.

The point has been made that Mallarmé the redactor of *La Derniére Mode* and Mallarmé the elaborate, elusive position-player of the late poems, are not polar opposites. Apart from the continuing recurrence of identical themes in the poetry and the journalism (what the lady readers made of them it is agreeable to imagine), there is a deep ironic reservation in all Mallarmé's later writing. He does not really believe that the world he is writing about exists at all. At least if it exists, it exists only provisionally, as a convenient fiction which is dependent for its reality on the poetry which expresses/creates it. Behind this transparent screen, if we had the slightest impulse to push or peep through it, *néant* would once again yawn. But Mallarmé and his chosen masks do not usually want to break it decisively. Thus the whole interest of the faun, to take an obvious instance, is that he does not quite know whether he has captured the nymphs physically or in his revery. But in pushing this retrospective query, with the aid of all the witnesses he can summon (enigmatic foliage, for the most part), he reconstructs the event as it might have happened, moving it forward from his first discovery of the nymphs to the climax of erotic possession — all the time leaving a lingering doubt as to whether his song is creative or mimetic. He is dreaming the capture deliciously, and no more needs assurance of its "reality" than he needs actual wine to drink:

> j'élève au ciel d'été la grappe vide
> Et, soufflant dans ses peaux lumineuses, avide
> D'ivresse, jusqu'au soir je regarde au travers.[14]

The breath with which he blows up the skin of the empty grape is nothing less than his own avid desire of drunkenness, the "serein souffle artificiel / De l'inspiration"; but, once blown up, the grape is luminous, and a full day is not too long to spend looking through it. A particularly elegant balance is struck by the phrase, "O nymphes, regonflons des souvenirs divers" — where the nymphs, who are themselves partly imaginary, are asked to help the faun puff up Memories, a request which implies not only that mere memory is insufficient in itself, but that there may be a question of other memories than those of short term and physical foundation. Since the poem is always glancing reflexively at its own existence, these hesitations and indirections give it a wonderful air of floating unsupported in an elastic atmosphere of indeterminacy.

14. I raise to summer skies the empty grape, and, blowing into its luminous skin, thirsty for drunkenness, I look through it till night falls.

The faun's characteristic action of peeping through the luminous screen or fringe of things, always precious to Mallarmé, grows in importance in the later work. Foam, lace, leafage, the fragility of glassware — whatever delicate tissues permit passage of something evanescent and "éblouissant" — are textures of preference for him. Words themselves, jolted by radical metaphors and violent syntax out of their accustomed contexts, become multivalent and transparent, first as puns and anagrams, then through a series of connections so tenuous and intuitive as only to be symbolized by the relationships which make up a constellation:

> To set up an exact relation between images, and then let a third aspect detach itself from them melting and lucent presented to insight. . . .
>
> ("Crise de Vers," *Oeuvres complètes*, p. 365)

The technique can be justified by appeal to the dialectic (as can just about anything else), but it also constitutes a first and seminal principle of the art of symbolic suggestion. In all symbolist writing the distance between the metaphors and the difficulty of connection (accentuated, usually, by the specious exactness of preliminary and often irrelevant connections) constitute the ground out of which suggestion flowers. Another special quality of Mallarmé's work, of which Yeats particularly was a close imitator, is the use of a limited group of images, constituting almost a closed cosmos, images which are repeated from poem to poem in varying contexts and with controlled emphasis — so that the significant distances come to include those between individual poems, and even an apparent trifle may be a microcosm of the poet's whole universe. (From the aspect of critical method, this is why the best commentary on any given poem of Yeats, for instance, is generally a couple of other poems by Yeats.) For this reason, as well as for the special

charm of the poem itself, and its relative simplicity, the little
sonnet "Salut" may serve to sample the quality of ripe Mallarmé, rather than the more impressive and worked-over
"Tombeaux" or "Coup de Dés." The occasion was a banquet
for the staff of the magazine *Plume*, over which Mallarmé presided in February 1893, and to which he recited this sonnet:

> Rien, cette écume, vierge vers
> A ne désigner que la coupe;
> Telle loin se noie une troupe
> De sirènes mainte à l'envers.
>
> Nous naviguons, ô mes divers
> Amis, moi déjà sur la poupe
> Vous l'avant fastueux qui coupe
> Le flot de foudres et d'hivers;
>
> Une ivresse belle m'engage
> Sans craindre même son tangage
> De porter debout ce salut
>
> Solitude, récif, étoile
> A n'importe ce qui valut
> Le blanc souci de notre toile.[15]

The first word of the sonnet, *Rien*, may be deprecatory (what I
am going to say is a mere nothing), but it also serves to set a
scene which is familiar as that of other poems, "A la nue
accablante" and "Un Coup de Dés"; the ship has just sunk,
leaving no trace ("rien") but a bit of foam — which is the

15. Mere nothing, this foam, maiden verse to mention only the cup/cut; so
in the distance a school of sirens drowns itself numerous upside down. We
navigate, oh my different friends, I long since at the helm, you the proud
prow which slices the wave of thunders and winters; a fine intoxication leads
me, fearless even of its pitch, to rise to my feet, raising this toast/salute —
solitude, reef, star — to whatever it is that repays the blank/white concern
of our canvas/sail.

froth of champagne in Mallarmé's glass, as well as an immediate suggestion of the poem he is reciting. It is a trifle, delicate but intoxicating and translucent; as for the ship, which has already met disaster and of which the foam is a last trace, it must be presumed a venture of thought (this image will be reconfirmed in the last part of the sonnet), perhaps shipwrecked on the reef of materiality (the occasion of this occasional poem) or of expression. In any event, the abrupt "rien" emphasizes a qualitative change wrought by the first word. Having had the free ocean of open possibility to swim on, represented by a clear white page, the poem's first act of being — represented characteristically by the minimum commitment of the word "nothing" — is its shipwreck. The verse is therefore virgin like Venus Anadyomene but also like the Virgin Mary, in whom an incarnation took place as anguished as the poem's. Yet the next line by pouring the foam into a cup, breast-shaped, modifies this virginity. "A ne désigner que la coupe" makes multiple reference to the cup holding the champagne, therefore to the literary form in which the thought is newly cast; it designates the "coupe" of the verse, its abrupt concision (Mallarmé was forever cutting off the beginnings and endings of his poems, the prefaces and explanations; and his trimeter lines in this poem yield a great effect of truncation). Finally "coupe," with its emphasis on cutting and its connection with a "vierge," cannot help reminding us of Hérodiade, who by cutting off John Baptist's head gave him one last radiant moment of complete self-knowledge. The troop of sirens drowning themselves in the distance must be committing suicide, since sirens are creatures of song, natural swimmers, and in any case this troop "se noie." The flash of their white buttocks in the distant sun repeats, upside down — à l'envers — the shape of the champagne glass. There are other "envers" in the situation; the cup is drowning in its champagne, the song which here survives and derives from shipwreck is there drowned in it; there may even be a pun by which the sirens are drowned only poetically, i.e. *en vers*. But the recurrent emphasis is on self-destruction as the basic action of thought becoming poetry; one recalls Mallarmé's statement that destruction was his Beatrice.

The second quatrain defines, rather literally, the relation of Mallarmé and his friends; he, "déjà sur la poupe," has been relegated to the rear-guard; they are the proud adventurers, leading the way, and the voyage is therefore nothing less than the adventure of thought and literature. As for the "foudres et hivers" of which the sea is composed, it is another, less amicable, version of the ocean, not to be reconciled with that earlier one which yielded the foam of champagne. The cold of winters and the peril of thunderbolts both constitute interdictions (perhaps natural and supernatural), which the artist must be prepared to defy; but to affront them is an act of boldness, almost of folly. At the same time, to invoke an ocean of thunders and winters is to attenuate all three concepts to the thin edge of transparency — to catch hold of them and link them by their overtones. In this elegance of intellectual domination over brute fact is dramatized the buoyancy of the "avant fastueux."

Lifted by poetic enthusiasm and champagne, the poet is carried into an "ivresse belle" which imperils his equilibrium (the floor of the banquet-hall, like the deck of a ship, is starting to pitch about) but encourages him to proffer his toast — which, in addition to being a salutation, is in its own way a recipe for salvation, a source of safety. The twelfth line of the sonnet I take to be an explanatory parenthetical appositional phrase, supporting and rendering specific the not-yet-expressed idea of the thirteenth and fourteenth lines. The three alternatives thus hung out in a grammatical void represent three motives for undertaking "le blanc souci de notre toile," i.e. for setting sail at all. "Toile" combines in a crucial ambiguity (like English "can-

vas") the idea both of a sail and a white artistic vacancy to be
filled. The toast then is grammatically completed with the deliberately vague invocation of "whatever" motivates the artistic
enterprise — by virtue of its compressed grammatical violence
"n'importe ce" is almost contemptuous in its dismissal of motivation. As the voyage on which all are embarked is reminiscent
in some ways of Baudelaire's (cf. p. 94), two of the alternative
intentions are within Baudelaire's grasp. Solitude is the motive
of those who sail to escape, the star is a traditional emblem of
aspiration. But the impulse specific to Mallarmé is the middle
one, the reef of shipwreck which his intellectual enterprise must
seek and find; it is a paradoxical disaster which represents
safety — and to this bold ruin the gallant gesture of the toast is
directed.

Mallarmé's perspective, as it emerges from this breaking of a
butterfly on the critical wheel, does not have much to do with
romantic admiration for lost causes; in his cosmos void is primary and "natural." It really is by foundering on the rock of
specific words that his thought generates that "tiers aspect fusi-
ble et clair" which invites our divination. The poet does not fall
into void as a result of a long search, he falls lamentably and
triumphantly out of it, out of something like the intense inane.
The truth is that Mallarmé was never very well domesticated to
existence on this planet — as with Shelley and Yeats, this is one
of his values for us. An odd but revealing biographical fact confirms the depth of malaise in the poet. For twenty years in the
rue de Rome he lived down the street from a railroad overpass,
which twice a day he had to traverse on his way to and from
work. In those twenty years, he confessed to a friend, he never
once crossed the bridge without repressing a strong impulse to
throw himself off it to his death. His desire for the void was neither artificial nor abstract nor literary; it grew out of a basic,
inalterable disgust for material existence. Mallarmé simply felt

that his basic self was conditioned to another sphere; he was, in this life, like a watchmaker with incurable elephantiasis. In all the "Tombeaux" which it became inevitably his duty to compose, something like this feeling finds expression: the true existence of the artist is manifested only when he sheds the vesture of his personality and the mundane forms in which he has momentarily disguised himself, to become a pure and essential *oeuvre*. Such an *oeuvre* Mallarmé had himself been, since about the age of twenty-three; he was a book, or more properly the book, to the possibility of which his whole life was a witnessing. But the dialectic of his living in this world toward that *oeuvre*, of his steady progress toward a faceted outlook within which feeling and thought, the temporal and the eternal, were perfectly fused, was also an achievement; and no doubt it was his listeners' awareness of this, quite as much as their perception of the sonnet's delicacies, which made "Salut" such a tumultuous success at the banquet of the *Plume*. By an ancient tradition the art of dying well is nothing less than the art of living well. It was in fulfillment of a paradox as elementary as this that Mallarmé's preparation of himself for eternity became a morality for those who perhaps knew eternity less intimately and immediately than he did.

Thanks primarily to the testimony of that exotic fellow Des Esseintes, but also for the very human reason that Mallarmé's point of departure was hard to conceive and never explicitly explained, there has been a tendency to suppose him a man who strained continually to write verse ever more hermetic and esoteric — a man who was, so to speak, on an outward spiral and continually moving farther out. Yeats may have been such a man at one time, and Baudelaire may have wanted to be; but Mallarmé's subtle dialectic bound him more intimately, I think, to the things of this earth. Getting back gave him more trouble than getting out. In that highly discreet "Autobiographical Letter" which he prepared at the instance of Verlaine, he gives a characteristically tentative, ironic, elusive account of his own poetry in relation to the age:

> At bottom, I consider the present age as one of transition for the poet, who has no reason to traffic with it: it is too much given to languishing and premonitory bubbling for any task except working with mystery in view of sooner or later — or never — and from time to time sending to the living one's visiting card, stanzas or a sonnet, in order not to be stoned by them if they suspect one of knowing that they have not existed (*Oeuvres complètes*, p. 664).

What seems most exquisite about this balance of attitudes is the poet's wry acceptance of the forms and conventions of life, its calling cards, as the price of exemption from that savage lapidation to which, as his own name must have reminded him, pioneers of a new faith are liable. It seems he lived at best on tenterhook relations with "ici-bas," propitiating its surfaces but always aware of something bigger and tougher behind them. Perhaps that is why his poems do not assault Nothing (or any other topic) as a theme to be labored, but move with an easy elegance behind the often rocky syntax toward an assured vision of things. Domestication in Nothing provides for Mallarmé not a substance of discourse but the occasional glint of backlighting which outlines a hard edge, suggests a dimension, and renders the world of his poetry unexpectedly and permanently luminous.

VIII

Liebestod

Immolation by passion offers gratifying imaginative access, in the late nineteenth century, to varieties of moral, material, and spiritual void.

In the course of his scornful, summary repudiation of Wagner ("The Case of Wagner," 1888), Nietzsche accuses the composer of the *Ring* of stumbling into optimism through the blandishments of Schopenhauer, and then rationalizing this accident into his actual destination:

> A way out of the difficulty finally dawned on his mind. The reef on which he was wrecked — how would it be if he interpreted it as the *goal*, the ultimate purpose, the real meaning of his voyage? To be wrecked *here* — that was a goal also. *Bene navigavi cum naufragium feci.* . . . And he translated the *Nibelung's Ring* into Schopenhauerism. Everything goes wrong, everything goes to ruin, the new world is as bad as the old. — Nothingness, the Indian Circe, makes a sign. . . .[1]

Doubtless anyone who has adjusted to the conception of Schopenhauer as an open door to optimism will have few troubles with the Indian Circe. An Indian would be more likely to interpret Circe as the Greek Maya, the weaver of circumstances which seduce the soul (Odysseus) *away* from its true goal, Nirvana or Nothing. But Nietzsche's altered emphasis expresses a first truth about the Wagnerian void, which, in fulfill-

1. "The Case of Wagner," Section 4, tr. T. Common.

ment of a tradition as ancient in Europe as in India, is feminine, seductive, sexual — in a word, orgiastic. Voluptuous abandonment of self, whether to love or death or both at once, has a history as old as folklore, instances of it are familiar from Novalis and Keats (to look no further back), and it achieves classic expression, not on Brünnhilde's funeral-pyre, but in the ecstatic rites of *Tristan und Isolde* (1865).

M. de Rougemont would persuade us that the Tristan-myth had inherent powers from the beginning when secular love acquired sacred overtones by way of the Albigensian heresy. So it may have been; medievalists have not swarmed overwhelmingly to support the theory. But whatever extraordinary powers the Tristan-myth had, it did not manifest them fully until Wagner stripped the fable ruthlessly of its accumulated incidents to concentrate the tangled episodes of the medieval tale in a few splendid scenes. These wholesale reductions, which impose on the materials of the story a full qualitative literary change, are all in the direction of compression and thick texture. Act I of the opera, for instance, represents roughly the last hour of the voyage from Ireland. All of Tristan's previous history, and Isolde's — amounting to some twenty years of incident, in the prose narration — is sketchily summarized in retrospect; the fatal potion is drunk as the ship arrives in Cornwall. Act II omits such bedroom agilities as the substitution of Brangäne for Iseult on the marriage night, and Tristan's leap across the flour-strewn floor; it omits, equally, major episodes of discovery, escape, three years in the forest, the sword-exchange, return to court, various episodes of clandestine meeting, and the incident of Iseult's trial by ordeal — as well as the whole story of Iseult-les-blanches-mains and Tristan's white marriage. We have instead a single ecstatic rendezvous, interrupted by the arrival of Mark and concluded by Tristan's fatal wounding at the hands of Melot. In Act III, Tristan has been tacitly translated to Brittany, Iseult-les-blanches-mains still being absent.

The story of her jealousy and the mixup over white and black sails is omitted entirely. Tristan dies as a result of deliberately tearing the bandages from his own wounds at the approach of Isolde — he says he conquered Morholt with wounds and will conquer Isolde with more wounds. (No previous version of the myth offers precedent for this conceit, for the mood which inspires it, or the action which accompanies it.) Finally, after suitable sword-play and word-play by underlings, and the timely arrival of Mark, Isolde perishes with an eloquent aria on the corpse of her lover.

Thus brutally reduced, we see in Wagner's opera three essential occurrences: drinking the potion, keeping the fatal rendezvous, and dying the death. They all lead ineluctably in the same direction. One thing the Tristan story had in all its early versions was dramatic conflict; whatever its defects of unity and control, it was in the highest degree a story of people torn. Their tortuous twistings were what made Tristan and Isolde so "human" and so "interesting" — in the sense of contradictory, weak, unpredictable. (These are the "absurdities" of the story — uncontrollably passionate lovers, having an openly adulterous affair, who, alone in the woods, sleep voluntarily for three years with a sword between them, yet remain flexible enough, in the matter of honor, to trick God himself with an equivocation in the ordeal.) But conflict is precisely what Wagner omits. Not only does he omit it, he deliberately avoids it. Tristan drops his sword when attacked by Melot; Isolde never has any crisis of conscience over whom she belongs to. Mark tries to raise the question of honor at the end of Act II, with his querulous "How could you do this to me?" —

> Mir dies?
> Dies, Tristan, mir?

— but after the king's long expostulation, the only reply he gets is in the nature of an evasion, a putting-off:

O König, das
kann ich dir nicht sagen;
und was du frägst
das kannst du nie erfahren.[2]

Wagner's characters are not in conflict with one another or with themselves, they are in perfect, immediate, instinctual rapport. The world, to be sure, does not understand the lovers, nor they it; but this division is so deep that dramatic conflict is out of the question — there is merely (as above) mutual incomprehension, which words can scarcely even attempt to define. Tristan and Isolde feel no evident shame or remorse, no impulse to justify or explain or even defend their love against its direct assailants; they simply sink into it, as into a dark, luxurious, naked infinity, and that is what the great duets of the second act are about.

The first remarkable thing about these arias is that they occur in the second act, which implies that Nothing is not a blank wall, a terminus, but a landscape to be explored in depth, and the next is that they are musically and metaphorically so opulent and extended. It is frequent and easy in opera to have hero and heroine endure their trials till the end of the fourth act and then, in an ecstatic brief duet, opt for oblivion (via rope, knife, or poisoned goblet), as a way of getting offstage to thunderous applause. But the great Hymns to Night which fill the second act of *Tristan* are voyages of visionary discovery — with supreme confidence they launch into Nothing as into unbounded space. "Das Wunderreich der Nacht" (lines 1195 and 1598) is not only a world but a cosmos, a galaxy. The customary thing is to say that Wagner has his lovers investigating Nirvana, Buddhism, non-existence; but what they find is more than that, it is a gigantic equivocation, a cosmic paradox. For, in

2. Oh King, that I can never say, and for the question you ask you can never find an answer.

the absence of the garish and deceitful light of day, their world
is lit by an inner glitter, where

> leuchten lachend
> Sterne der Wonne (1266–7) [3]

which shine within the heart. They are not escaping the world
of will, they are transcending and transfiguring and interiorizing
it; and to convey the effect of this transcendence the language
of paradox is invoked in ever-tighter, ever-more-rhythmic bal-
ancings of contrast and comparison. The games of counterpoint
and antithesis culminate first in a declaration of independence,
the lovers are a world to themselves:

> selbst dann
> bin ich die Welt:
> Wonne-hehrstes Weben,
> Liebe-heiligstes Leben,
> Niewiedererwachens
> wahnlos
> hold bewusster Wunsch (1284–90). [4]

The emphasis upon "Wunsch," conveyed by its climactic positioning, is not to be mistaken; absolute non-existence, for which
the lovers passionately thirst, implies an eternity of desire and
conscious ("bewusster") longing. Positive unconsciousness, if it
is not a contradiction in terms, is the full content of all those
passionate paradoxes which culminate, as a second climax, in an
exchange of identities:

> Tristan du
> ich Isolde,
> nicht mehr Tristan (1430–32)

3. glitter the laughing stars of bliss
4. even I, then, am the world: the web most sacred to bliss, the life most
holy to love, never-again-awaking, illusionless, pure and conscious desire.

— so Tristan; and Isolde confirms the metamorphosis. Self-fulfillment through self-annihilation, victory for will through denial of will, life eternal as a result of deliberate death, ecstasy through ascesis, light through darkness — the effect of all these swiftly multiplying paradoxes is to suggest a world outside thought, a world of exploding, potent consciousness which mere language is unable to contain. Wagner was able to pack the idea of annihilation with so much positive experience (including, of course, the wordless immensities of the music) that a reader of the libretto may wonder why he never uses any of that splendid nuptial terminology and transcendental imagery which lay ready to hand in the Book of Revelations. But his avoidance here was doubtless deliberate. Part of his tactic was to steer clear of everything suggesting a Christian afterlife, judgment, reward and punishment, apotheosis. For the mystery to which his lovers are initiated is one which they themselves create, free of all ready-made systems and established values. It is a mystery defined carefully in negatives, contradictions, and vague figures — metaphors of night, infinity, eternity, fusion, dissolution, and exclusion. M. de Rougemont finds two wrong interpretations of Wagner's opera holding the field, one which sees in it a romance of vulgar adultery, the other which sees in it a triumph of Schopenhauer's yearning for the void. As alternatives they are doubtless wrong, but, put together, they are perfectly right; and there are easier ways of getting them to adhere than through the Albigensian heresy. One major function of the terminology of Nothing is to sterilize desire beyond the grave of its Christian connotations, good or bad, orthodox or heretical. (The loves of the angels, or, for that matter, of the devils, are to be no part of the story.) Another function of Nothing is to heighten the values of the romance by making them inaccessible, mysterious, and highly charged; those who disdain the world and all that is in it must have seen something beyond it which is precious indeed. And still another function is to provide a terminal to which, across a suitable space of mind, the spark of electric desire can be made to leap in a rhythm of paradox. There must be something "out there" for the spark to leap to; its leaping is presumptive evidence that there is something "out there"; the distance it leaps is a measure of the pressure of current behind it. And yet there is no doubt that the intellectualizers are "perfecting" the circuit, in the sense of "rationalizing" it, when they fill in (with such items as the Albigensian heresy) that last little gap, that calculated interruption, which is the reason for the whole thing.

Tristan und Isolde fed a fire which was already burning vigorously in the nineteenth century, and toward the end of the century it turned into something like a general conflagration. Nothing would be easier than to pile up lists of romantic disasters in which late-nineteenth-century authors imagined the glow of transcendent love momentarily illumining a world of lowering doom. In most of his later plays Ibsen showed heroic conscious love involving almost automatic suicide. In Villiers de l'Isle-Adam's Axël, Axël von Auërsperg and his cousin Sarah reject the direct way of the church and the occult teacher, discover one another, look momentarily on the world which lies before them, and promptly commit suicide out of a sure sense that life can hold nothing beyond this moment but bitter decline and anticlimax. While the world collapses about them in pain and shame, Launcelot loves Guinevere, in Tennyson as in William Morris as in A. C. Swinburne. A remarkable ballad of Swinburne's called "Les Noyades" summarizes the pattern in an image; the speaker, a sixteenth-century Huguenot warrior, declares himself ecstatically happy to be chained to an attractive girl and tossed with her into the Loire to drown. Such a demise, he seems to think, has everything. Giorgio Aurispa, in D'Annunzio's Trionfo della Morte, is inspired in his love for

Ippolita by the example of Tristan and Isolde; his love for her, haunted from the beginning by the premonition of death, cannot possibly terminate in any gesture but suicide — to which, however, he manages to add the agreeable stimulus of murder. It was during the nineteenth century that Paolo and Francesca, those not very interesting doomed lovers, attracted an immense sentimentalizing interest which expressed itself in pictures, poems, and enthusiastic hermeneutics. And what is the story of *Pelléas et Mélisande* (1892) but another Paolo-and-Francesca story enlarged to the point where its contours start to go fuzzy? Weeping, wincing, and lost, Mélisande is from the beginning a creature from another sphere. Married to rough Golaud, frozen and miserable in his land of shadows, she seeks out Pelléas as he seeks her, indifferent to the taboo of kinship, careless of practical consequences, because their love is the pathway to death. The herd of sheep baaing in the distance on their way to the slaughterhouse, the subterranean pool of death beneath the castle, the massed premonitions and forebodings of Maeterlink's dramaturgy, all make clear the goal of the characters' striving. And when, knowing Golaud to be lurking in the shadows with drawn sword, they deliberately move into the moonlight for a last embrace, they are merely filling in a pattern which existed from the beginning of the drama or from outside of it. Their void is nothing like the opulent explorations of Tristan and Isolde, rather it is the long-sought end of a lingering disease; the love they claim to seek is scarcely more than a transparent verbal disguise for the death of which they are avid.

Unhappy lovers are always with us, and in piling up these sentimental suicides of the late nineteenth century, I intend no more than to suggest a certain tonality. Passion consuming to the point of destructiveness became in the 1880's and 1890's a literary mode. Paul Bourget, in his *Physiologie de l'amour moderne* (1891), specified cruelty as a distinctive component of modern, as against old-fashioned love; but this was a belated recognition of what had long been apparent. All extreme passion, when it wants to convince someone of its extremity, picks up elements of sadism or masochism or both. As far as the realities of the situation go, western Europe in the late nineteenth century was an age in quest of new sensations, or new evidence for old sensations, and erotic gigantism was one formula. Precisely because it was an old and tired formula, imaginative extravagance was often invoked to fill it. (And because everything had been vainly invoked to fill it, the next generation was ready to think there was "nothing in it.") Probably in the first half-century after *Werther*, when the heroic mode of passion was relatively new, people took it more "seriously." At all events, lots of portentous young men and chlorotic young ladies seem to have committed suicide at that time, in a practical way, for aesthetic or sentimental reasons (M. Louis Maigron, in *Le Romantisme et les mœurs* provides some of the details). The late nineteenth century, less fresh in its responses, found passionate annihilation a theme available for literary elaboration, and made of it in some instances a grandiose convention, in others an occasion for ingenuity and artifice.

But if personal love turns, with the rotten romantics, toward ever-hollower gestures (culminating in the echoing verbal flux of D'Annunzio), we are pointed toward a very different conjunction of sex and Nothing by the work of Zola. *Germinal* (1885) is typical in making of animal sexuality a yawning, insatiable force, in which all men's intentions, ideas, and identities are lost. The impotent overseer Hennebeau who rides despairingly through nocturnal countrysides surrounded by noises of happily fornicating miners (IV, vi) provides an interesting premonition of a D. H. Lawrence predicament, and perhaps too clamorous a symbol for delicate literary stomachs. But the mindless force of earthly fecundity is symbolized, not only in gross females and animalistic miners, but in the central character of the mine itself. This great black shaft does so many suggestive things — breathing, swallowing, spewing forth, digesting, gestating and entombing the characters — that, as often in naturalistic fiction, it becomes more impressive as object than the personae as alleged people. Its power to negate humanity leads to a positive sort of Nothing. In any sense it may seem a little odd to invoke Nothing in connection with a book which is so fat with textures and thick with verbal effects — which tries so hard to render for its readers the exact sensual experience of something. But there is real void-worship in Zola's abasement before the blind, brutal fact of fertility. All efforts to rationalize human relations come to ruin, the men who think enough to protest are killed off or twisted out of all usefulness (Souvarine, Etienne, Maheu), and we are left with an image of fecund, indifferent, exhausted earth spawning forever Jeanlins and Bonnemorts — any creature will do, as long as it can survive, as long as it isn't human, that is. Bonnemort the walking coal mine, so impregnated with rock-dust that he is already half-petrified, retains enough strength to strangle Cécile Gregoire in her young beauty (VII, iv), and Jeanlin, the crippled gnome, lurking in his cave, steals and murders for pleasure. To show life "triumphing" on these terms is to rouse in the reader (who feels himself defeated in those very qualities which make him a perceptive reader) a sense of irrelevance and nullity. Though there is hyperbole here, there is also a literary device; human void is only emphasized by the continuance of a mechanical process, as Binet's lathe bores into Emma Bovary's ear like an angry wasp. Only for Zola the irrelevant process is nothing less than life itself, the roar of generation, the sough and sigh of the mine, the cycles of filth, misery, growth, corruption.

   The same point is made in *Nana* (1880), where the corrupt, inexhaustible power of nature is embodied in one grand female who destroys all the men she gets hold of — all the more inevitably because for the most part indifferently. It is no random metaphor that the Comte Muffat, at the moment of clearest insight into his relations with Nana, feels a sudden burst of such terror that "he burst into tears, suddenly in despair, distracted, as if fallen into a great void [*vide*]" (7). "There's nothing left," he cries, "nothing left, nothing left" — and the momentary loss of a Paris whore really has something catastrophic about it, because Zola has so firmly in hand the hyperboles that Nana is both everything and nothing. The whole book, seen in this light, builds toward a contrast which becomes explicit in the last section. Seen from within, Nana's room is "invested with a voluptuous lust for annihilation" within which the Comte Muffat disappears, "trembling in the irresistible grip of sex, as he fainted before the unknown reaches of the vast heavens." But from the outside a disinterested observer like Mignon sees Nana's career as a heroic labor of immense macabre solidity, accomplished alone, with no apparent means at all. Mignon had seen, we are told, the Pont du Gard near Nîmes, "oeuvre cyclopéenne," and the great new port at Cherbourg:

> but that seemed puny to him, Nana exalted him more; and before her labors he rediscovered that sensation of respect which he had once known at a party given in the château of a sugar-refiner, a palace whose entire splendor had been paid for by a single commodity, sugar. For her it was another thing, a little ridiculous stupidity, a bit of her delicate nudity, it was with this shameful and mighty nothing whose force sustained the whole world, that she, working all alone without helpers or machines invented by engineers, she had just succeeded in rocking all Paris to its foundations and building this enchanted castle where cadavers slept.
> — Good Lord! what a tool! exclaimed Mignon. . . .

The expression is richly comic, yet the "rien honteux et si puissant" is a terrible and exact phrase, and the weight of Nana's work is the weight of the book itself, not far from epic. At the same time, Zola does not forget to show us the sensible, simple domestic animal — we see Nana in bourgeois slippers and dishabille, stopping round the corner to buy a bit of fish for dinner. In Zola's great novel, we are not far from Joyce's vision of Molly Bloom as the foul, ever-renewed, vulgar, inexhaustible earth, turning mindlessly on its axis in the midst of the icy void, exercising vast magnetic forces, and plucking men like flowers to wear helter-skelter on her indifferent bosom.[5]

Zola's prostration before the idol of woman as rotten, sensual, and fatal is nicely complemented by Ibsen's sense of her as athletic, idealistic, and fatal. Svanhild, the ferocious little heroine of *Love's Comedy* (1862) is an early exemplar of Ibsen's destructive female idealist. She encourages her suitor Falk to live his poetry instead of just writing it; his wringing the neck of her sparrow shows graphically what this means. But when he turns now to Svanhild in expectation of sympathy if not reward for his sacrifices to her ethical demands, he finds a new lesson to learn. His mistress is mad for categories; she wants no contamination of poetry with life nor of love with marriage, and has concluded a strict, business-like arrangement with an elderly admirer. Love triumphs only in renunciation, only when spiritualized into the world of memory; and the play ends, not with a coming-together (at least on any plane that can be represented) but with a separation, not with a tying of knots but with a sundering.

In the same spirit, Nora Helmer attacks her aesthetic, super-

5. The name "Nana" has some interesting overtones. Like "Gaga" and "Bébé" it suggests a baby-mother relationship, the idiotic repetition of bleating syllables suggests mental vacuity, and it comes very close to Spanish *nada*, nothing.

ficial husband Torvald, and with him all the conditions and conventions of stage-representation, in the name of a "true marriage"; her assault destroys the moral pretensions of a character, but also the very texture of a representation to which the audience had committed itself, and the curtain falls on a moral void of undischarged guilt.[6] Rebecca West by her promptings and insinuations and demands for a freedom of which she is herself incapable, destroys herself and Parson Rosmer; Hilda Wangel lures Halvard Solness to the top of his steeple in full assurance that he will fall; Hedda Gabler provokes Eilert Lovborg to shoot himself, and is distressed only that he does the job so ungracefully; mysterious Irene inveigles Professor Rubek up to the cold, destructive mountain-heights, where only bearhunters can survive, and where he is bound to seal a spiritual death with a material one. Over and over in these plays, the women represent ethical existence, a fullness of being from which the aesthetically-minded men shrink, but which imposes itself on them, generally with fatal effects. When they are not physical athletes like Hilda Wangel, they are moral recordseekers like Rebecca West. They climb mountains or are at home in the depths of the sea; trolls, or monsters of another species entirely (like the Lady from the Sea), they act to invariably fatal effect on the flatland men who tangle with them. Behind the frigid ferocity of their destructiveness lurks an idealism buried almost or actually out of sight. Judge Brack presumes to speak of "love" in the presence of Hedda Gabler; her response in the finished play is, "Ugh, don't use that sticky word." Only in the first drafts of the play, amid the fragments from Ibsen's workshop, do we find her original speech: "Do you really believe that anything so wonderful exists?"

It is a black religion of woman one sees in Zola and Ibsen;

---

6. For fuller elaboration of these brief indications, see my "Ibsen, the Fiftyfirst Anniversary," *Hudson Review*, Autumn 1957.

from an idol (sometimes a pink little Hellenistic idol, as in Michelet), woman has become a Moloch, a Juggernaut. Zola sees her as mindless and natural, a vortex; Ibsen, as an impulse to lofty instability, almost a vortex inverted. Neither leads in narrative terms to anything but the blank wall of death; there is no trace of the luminous transfiguration worked by Wagner. For Zola and Ibsen alike, woman is a touchstone revealing if not creating spiritual bankruptcy. In Zola, because she is natural, woman survives the destruction of mind; the man of (presumed) distinction is crushed by her as beneath an irresistible stream of traffic — negated, neutered, overridden. The Nothing he achieves is absorption in an enormous alien process; he is therefore exemplary in a negative and vindictive sense. In Ibsen, because woman is ethical, she is herself destroyed with the culture-bound, appearance-manipulating males to whom she is so deadly. For Ibsen, unlike Zola, woman's destructive quality is relatively independent of her sex. By their unfettered demands on life, Ibsen's women reduce the men they attack to paralytic states of glacial remorse; as in *John Gabriel Borkman* or *When We Dead Awaken*, physical death merely confirms a long process of death-in-life. For both, the worship of woman is the worship of a deadly disease; she is a sacred, fatal invalid, whether frigid or rotten, and her fascination lies in the assurance of doom which she provides. A great paradox of ancient origins but modern applications, that strength is weakness and weakness strength, finds early and portentous expression in this turn-of-the-century worship of woman.

For the student of Nothings, it must be confessed, there is little that is particularly distinctive about the void which a willing victim reaches through the doorway of woman. More intriguing is the line of development which leads to it — a line which runs from hatred of the conscious mind as overbearing and tyrannical to guilt and shame at its artificial and evasive inadequacies. This line of steadily augmented loathing felt by literary artists for themselves could be richly documented out of the late nineteenth century. In sketching it, one would want to consider the figure of the clerk, copyist, or hack as an artist who has died to himself (Bouvard and Pécuchet, Bartleby, the narrator of "Notes from Underground," Ulric Brendel, Torvald Helmer, Little Chandler, Jim the Penman, and so on). But contrasted with these hollow shells is a series of authentic and magnified females — voices of instinct, illiterate or simpleminded, not always particularly admirable, but largely and intuitively powerful to survive or destroy. Late nineteenth-century *nostalgie de la boue* is largely mingled with *admiration de la boue* and *horreur de la boue,* but the mud is chiefly fascinating as relief from the frigid, self-manacled mind. So arranged, by thematic antithesis, Ibsen and Zola represent complementary approaches to the same vacant final fact.

IX

The Picturesque of Nothing

Curiosities of baffled expectation, of perverse anxiety, of anti-action.

One of the more ample of *Les Diaboliques* (1850) by Barbey d'Aurevilley is "Le Bonheur dans le crime," a study of several different kinds of moral void. The tale, recited by a sardonic, unexcited atheist of a doctor, has to do with Mlle. Hauteclaire Stassin, daughter of a fencing master, named after the sword of Oliver, and brought up in a *salle d'armes*. She gives lessons to the Comte Serlon de Savigny. But he is married to Delphine de Cantor, and Hauteclaire's relations with the count (like all her relations with young men) are limited by the severe, impersonal code of the rapier. Then one day Hauteclaire disappears without explanation, without trace. The doctor discovers her some time later serving as the chambermaid Eulalie in the château de Savigny, where Delphine is languidly wasting away of an aristocratic non-ailment. Hauteclaire is clearly the mistress of Savigny; just as clearly, she is the master-spirit of their intrigue.

> Savigny, who should have had more, had in fact much less than she did of freedom, ease, and naturalness in a lie; but she! ah she! she lived and moved in a lie as the most flexible of fish lives and moves in the water. . . .

Fascinated by the hauteur of the personages and the squalor of the circumstances, the doctor engages in disinterested espionage, and is able to see, one night, Hauteclaire and Serlon in a private fencing-match, their form of love-making.

Eulalie-Hauteclaire poisons Delphine — by "mistake." Delphine knows she is dying at the hands of her husband and his mistress, and tells the doctor so; but commands him to connive at concealment of the crime, not for any kindly motives but from sheer class-consciousness. It would not do, she thinks, to have a convicted wife-poisoner among the nobility, contaminating a name she had born. Delphine "was . . . a real woman of V. . . , who knew nothing about anything [*rien de rien*] save this: that she was noble, and outside the nobility the world was not worth a glance." The doctor accedes to his patient's dying wish, Delphine's death passes as an accident, and after her husband's two prescribed years of mourning are over, Hauteclaire becomes the Comtesse de Savigny. The pair are idyllically happy, living on the estate where their crime was committed, snubbed by the local gentry, subject to horrifying rumors, but deliriously contented with one another, a model of domestic bliss. The only person who knows for sure the full story of their crime is the doctor, and they know that he knows; but they are plagued by no guilt, feel no remorse, and pass by the doctor in the Jardin des Plantes without even recognizing him. The story, which began with the lady outstaring a panther, ends with her outstaring conventional morality, the absence of conventional morality, the retributive Deity Himself.

The narrator-auditor, who recites the story as he heard it from the doctor, is horrified:

> I was stunned. . . . But, said I, if this story you tell me is true, doctor, the happiness of these people is evidence of a real disorder in the constitution of things.
>
> Order or disorder, just as you please, replied Doctor Torty, that atheist as absolute and assured as the people of whom he was speaking, but that's the fact.

There is no reward, there is no punishment, there is no reason to be surprised at the absence of reward or punishment.

The point of the story for the conventionally-minded narrator is this *bonheur dans le crime,* and the story plays maliciously with our expectations of a moral balance. The sinful couple are childless, and Doctor Torty throws out the teasing thought that this might be a form of judgment; but no, they don't particularly want children, finding their own love sufficient and undistracted without offspring. Indeed, domestic prattle as a style of happiness is made to seem rather paltry, next to their lithe and glowing elegance. Meanwhile, by contrast with the hard-shelled doctor, the narrator is made to look as naïve as Hialmar Ekdal musing flabbily on the injustice of things: "But after all, there's something monstrous, isn't there, in the thought that he [Old Werle] is to realize the true marriage" — as if only nice people had the right to earn happiness in this world; others ought to have the decency to slink off and be miserable. The protagonists of "Le Bonheur dans le crime" are neither diabolists nor diabolically minded; they are simply hard-headed aristocrats in a more active and vital sense than dead Delphine ever dreamed of.

Barbey's concern for the hard, abrupt, and decisive is illustrated in this story not only by the business of swordsmanship and the picturesque alternations of "Eulalie," who plies the needle for her mistress by day and the rapier with her master by night — elegant opportunity for epigrams on the uses of cold steel, which our author does not fail to pre-empt. It also appears in an extraordinary page descriptive of Mlle. Stassin's disappearance, a page of flourishes so extravagant and wit so cutting that it deserves reproduction:

> She had disappeared: why? . . . how? . . . where had she gone? Nobody knew. But what was clear was that she had gone. At first there was an outcry, followed by a silence, but the silence did not last long. Then the tongues cut loose. The tongues, long held back, like water behind a dam which leaps forth when the barrier is lifted, pours out, and whirls

the mill-wheel furiously around, began to foam and babble
over this disappearance, so unexpected, so sudden, so unbe-
lievable, which there was nothing to explain, for Mlle. Hauteclaire had disappeared without saying a word or leaving a
word for anybody. She had disappeared as one disappears
when one wants really to disappear — for it's not really disappearance to leave behind one something, as gross as nothing, which people can make use of to explain why one has
disappeared. . . . She had disappeared in the most radical
manner. She had made, not what people call *a hole in the
moon*, for she had not left a debt, any more than anything
else, behind her; but she had made what can very well be
called a hole in the wind. The wind blew and did not blow
her back. The mill of tongues, for all that it had to run empty,
ran on nonetheless, and began to bite cruelly into this reputation which had never given such an opening before. . . .

Her leaving nothing behind her, not even something "grosse
comme rien," from which others might discover something
about her disappearance, makes fine use of the vulgarism to
emphasize how thick and pointed a fact is this very absence of
an index; and the way in which Barbey's dandies, male and female, control the paradoxes of their own existence is nicely figured in the play of the images over the idea of emptiness.

Among his *Contes cruels* (1883), Villiers de l'Isle-Adam includes a crude but vigorous caricature which plays variations on
the same theme. "Le Désir d'être un homme" takes as its protagonist an elderly actor, who may or may not be representative.
Esprit Chaudval *né* Lepeinteur *dit* Monanteuil has reached the
age of retirement from the stage; and, looking back on all the
roles he has taken, he senses that they have been artificial and
conventional. He has mimed all the passions, but sincerely felt
none of them; has existed merely in the eyes of his audience.
Now that age forces him to renounce stage and audience, and
he is faced with solitary existence as a lighthouse-keeper, he

feels the need to re-enter somehow the ranks of humanity. To do so he needs to have had an experience, a real emotion; and he casts about, among the available candidates, for an emotion of which he is still capable. Remorse will do nicely, though, to be sure, it requires a preliminary crime. But this is no obstacle to his Gallic lucidity, and he proceeds, in a fine burst of enthusiasm, to think of the most atrocious and gratuitous one possible. It will be an arson so monstrous and so "désintéressé" that no one will be able even to suspect him. With regard to the police, he sums up his position in a grandiose line of pseudo-Corneille: he will be

Garanti du soupçon par la grandeur du crime! [1]

Nosing out a gasoline depot in a crowded Parisian *quartier*, he proceeds immediately to work. All goes according to plan, and M. Chaudval retires to his lighthouse aglow with the virtuous sensation of having done his duty and earned his humanity. Scarcely has he installed his meager belongings — including, naturally, a huge mirror — when word arrives of the success of his coup in Paris. The dead amount to nearly a hundred, dozens of miserable families are homeless, the whole district is blackened and smoldering: splendid! He settles back, with maniacal satisfaction, to await the torturing of conscience; and nothing happens.

> Contrary to his hopes and expectations, his conscience suffered no remorse. No specter came to haunt him. He experienced *Nothing, absolutely Nothing!*

Furious, he tries to manipulate and falsify his signal-light, in the hope of causing a shipwreck and rousing the specters of remorse. In vain, all in vain:

1. Secured from suspicion by the scope of the crime!

Useless outrages! Vain efforts! He felt *nothing at all*. He saw no threatening phantoms. He was no longer able to sleep, so deeply did despair and *shame* distress him.

And he cries out to God, begging to be haunted, begging to see, to see something, if only a phantasm, protesting that he has earned his torture. But the Lord grants him no such favor, and he expires, declaiming in histrionic style on his need to see specters, without ever understanding, says the author, that he was himself the thing for which he was searching.

Most of the *Contes cruels* have at their back an infinite animus against the entire nineteenth century (for example, Romeo and Juliet, holding an assignation in the garden, talk of nothing but money, Bienfilâtre's daughter is disgraced because she gives up whoring for love); and if he is allowed a bit of symbolic dimension as Faustian man reduced to his nineteenth-century proportions, the old actor avid for a real emotion may have a significance which is not wholly grotesque or burlesque.

The contrived element of both stories is the (unnaturally naïve) expectation that moral accounts will balance neatly over the short term; the sense that nobody will ever add them up, ever — that they might as well not exist — animates Byron's un-Byronic study titled "Darkness." This blank-verse declamation, dating from 1816, depicts the end of life on earth as a result of the sun's unexplained extinction. The human race proceeds to perish of cold in the immense, indifferent void of space, its last two survivors disappearing with a satisfactory shriek of horror at each other's ugliness. The moon dies in the sky, tides and seasons cease, and the world,

A lump of death — a chaos of hard clay,

spins on its infinite course through frigid darkness.

Written at Villa Diodati on Lake Geneva during July, 1816,

the poem was probably suggested by Buffon's theory that the world would ultimately smother under its own impacted ice-packs, for we know this image was much in Shelley's mind at the time,[2] and Byron was much in Shelley's company. It may further have been suggested by an end-of-the-world scare which ruffled Paris that very month, or conceivably it owes something to Grainville's *Le Dernier Homme.* But sources are really un-necessary for so commonplace a speculation; the earth's decay is an immemorial idea, and the sun's extinction is anyone's nightmare. (Actually, at the moment when Byron was compos-ing "Darkness," calculations by Laplace and Poisson had just placed the possibility of solar extinction some millions of years in the safe future.)

Less commonplace than the physical scene Byron depicts is the absolute vacuum of moral comment which he allows to in-vest his poem. God is nowhere in this cosmos, is not even men-tioned; individual reward and punishment are not only irrele-vant but wholly disproportionate. Nobody in the universe feels any interest in the extinction of the human race as a whole, let alone of individuals within it. For a man with a North-Country Calvinist background this imagined failure of retribution can-not have been wholly depressing; the indifferent universe lets man perish like a colony of grubs, but the God of John Knox would have hounded him through a wilderness of hells forever. The same gloomy exhilaration at the thought of absolute annihilation lights up James Thompson's *City of Dreadful Night* (1874). In the course of his wanderings through echoing desolation, the narrator of this poem comes, in Section XIV, upon a preacher who has good news to impart:

> And now at last authentic news I bring,
> Witnessed by every dead and living thing;
> Good tidings of great joy for you, for all:

2. Letter of 22 July to T. L. Peacock, *Letters of Shelley,* II, 513.

> There is no God; no Fiend with names divine
> Made us and tortures us; if we must pine,
>   It is to satiate no Being's gall (XIV, 7).

Disappointment over a retribution that fails to take place is exactly balanced by joy over a discovery that suffering continues and is meaningless; both are responses to a presumed death of God. Thompson develops his slightly stagy and eloquent attitudes toward a universe emptied of transcendental meaning in verses of stately and rather impressive tread:

> I find no hint throughout the Universe
> Of good or ill, of blessing or of curse;
>   I find alone Necessity supreme;
> With infinite Mystery, abysmal, dark,
> Unlighted even by the faintest spark
>   For us the flitting shadows of a dream (XIV, 13).

Humans used to think the heavenly bodies looked on them with scorn or sympathy, at least with some feeling; but the new perspectives are aloof and indifferent. The stars are all dead to us.

> If we could near them with the flight unflown
>   We should but find them worlds as sad as this,
> Or suns all self-consuming like our own,
>   Enringed by planet worlds as much amiss:
> They wax and wane through fusion and confusion;
> The spheres eternal are a grand illusion,
>   The empyréan is a void abyss (XVII, 3).

Yet for all its invocation of void, *The City of Dreadful Night* remains rooted in its four-square syntax, its weighty dogmatisms. Nothing could be stiffer and sterner than the moral dudgeon of its high Presbyterian atheism.

Should one venture a generalization, it might come out so: the failure of a moral guide left Catholics with a sense of emptiness in the texture of daily life, a hole in the conscience; the failure of a moral rule left Protestants with a sense of emptiness in the command posts of the cosmos, where the course is charted and the final balances, of profit and loss on the cruise, are cast up.

E. T. A. Hoffmann displayed, in "The Sandman," a mechanical woman whom the sentimental hero took for a real one and worshiped blindly till the hour of his disenchantment. Discovering her to be a mere puppet, he felt cheated and humiliated. But by the latter years of the century this notion had undergone provocative transformations. Des Esseintes is ready to fall in love with copper-corseted, raucous-voiced steam-engines, though puzzled by the form his ardor should take; and in Villiers de l'Isle-Adam's prophetic *L'Eve future* (1886) a hero appears who is no longer vulnerable to disillusion because he has actually learned to prefer artificial women over living ones. This peculiar version of post-Byronic world-weariness leagued with perverse science-fiction is largely stage-set in picturesque Menlo Park, New Jersey; its mage is an improbable, larger-than-life Thomas Alva Edison.[3] He is consulted on an intimate problem by an overwhelmingly wealthy and fascinating young Englishman, Lord Celian Ewald, who has suffered, and is still suffering, a rather special disillusion. The love of his life, Miss Alicia Clary, is unbearably beautiful, and if she were only *bête* as well, like a proper female, Lord Ewald would marry her and live a life of ecstatic bliss. Unhappily, she is *sotte* instead of

3. Villiers deliberately treated Edison as a mythical figure during his lifetime. In the background of *L'Eve future* there probably lurks a magician invented by Theophile Gautier for a short story called "Le Chevalier Double." By means of mysterious Oriental lore this exotic fellow can cause souls to change bodies. Finally catching on to what his own powers mean, he proceeds to kill the handsome hero and occupy his corpse — a twist which lends to the fable something of the character of a shaggy-dog story.

bête; she has a spirit so flat, vulgar, mediocre, and imbecilic, that Lord Ewald, when he thinks of her magnificent exterior, has the impression that it is inhabited by a complete stranger. (Having exhausted other expressions of shuddering disgust, he compares her to a bourgeois goddess, the goddess Reason.) Edison listens with Gallic sympathy to this recital, though he remarks, with mingled sympathy and amusement, that "for three quarters of modern humanity" this compound of bromide and commercialism would represent a Feminine Ideal (I, 17). But his special affection for the young lord, who it seems once befriended him in adversity, wins out. Hooked on his lady's exterior charms, but revolted by her lack of soul, the young man is on the point of blowing his brains out; Edison proposes that he wait three weeks in order to try one last desperate expedient.

This expedient, to which the young man is introduced at once, is a potential counter-attraction, an incomplete Andreid or artificial woman, incorporating all Edison's latest electrical gadgets. Her name is Hadaly, which we are told means "Ideal" in Iranian; she will be perfected in the image of Miss Alicia Clary (for Lord Ewald is of an ancient family whose members love but once and forever, therefore his new love must be identical with his old one), and turned over to her husband-owner. Though the dazzling Miss Clary is the living image of the Venus de Milo, Edison feels no hesitation before the task of matching her exterior appearance. He will imitate her physique, her features, her perfumes, her motions; he will reproduce her wardrobe and the least of her mannerisms, record the tones of her voice, provide an indistinguishable (and imperishable) replica of her entire person. What will task his invention is to give the Andreid an inner constitution, an emotional and spiritual life which will enthrall his demanding friend. This is a real test of what modern jargon would call his programming skills; but he faces up to it. The challenge is nothing less than that

Hadaly, set beside Miss Clary, shall appear the real and vital person, while the living girl shall seem an animated doll. A later development of this distinction sardonically contrasts the *real* with the *living* Miss Clary; but in effect ironic duplicities shroud the whole challenge. It is to be a test of Edison's magnificent technical powers, yet it also implies that the humanity to be rivaled is a meager mechanism. Under the circumstances, the outcome cannot remain in doubt; and in fact the challenge posed by Lord Ewald's despair — a mere skeleton on which the book's substance is loosely draped — is largely forgotten during long passages of excursus, revery, and speculation. Surface realism does not count for much here; Edison every so often quotes Hegel, and Lord Ewald understands what he is talking about. This is evidently the full flood of romantic fantasy.

When the philosophy of artificial woman is straightened out with a mixture of sophism, sarcasm, and sentiment, an explanation of her anatomy is in order; and here Villiers advances, with Miltonic relish, into the labyrinthine complexities of digestion, lubrication, control, and response. Once again defense is interwoven with attack. It is true, Edison concedes, that Hadaly's battery must be recharged periodically, and if this is not done, she in effect "dies"; on the other hand, bringing her back to life again gives one the exquisite sensations hitherto reserved for the divinity himself. It is true, too, that Hadaly's movements must be controlled by various buttons and levers, chiefly the several rings on her fingers and pearls of her necklace. But then even an ordinary mistress, says wise Edison, must be controlled by analogous mechanisms — by importunities and promises, some of which are harder on one's self-respect than the operation of a button. Hadaly is an artifice, but all women make use of artifice, and some already in large part consist of it; Edison catalogues the cosmetic and prosthetic devices with a zeal worthy of Swift. As for the notion that her pre-recorded twenty hours of conversation may prove dull after a while — some of it consists of literary masterpieces, which are immortal; some of it is deliberately vague, so as to fit into as many different conversational contexts as possible (and this arrangement provokes the lover's artistic ingenuity to invent ever-fresh contexts for responses like "long ago" and "too true"); and finally, says the proud inventor, what is wrong with monotony in love? Is it not the unchanged, unchanging moment of first ecstatic union that we all seek to recapture? In Hadaly that exquisite instant is frozen forever.

Though much is revealed, much too is withheld. Tactfully, Edison reserves certain arcane secrets of the mechanism, as its actual features are hidden by a veil, lest Lord Ewald have too many disquieting memories to overcome. There is a not-altogether-fortunate subplot, in which it is insinuated that somehow an actual living soul with special extrasensory powers has got entangled in the mechanism. But a mechanism Hadaly is and remains, though one capable of *tendresse* and even *pudeur*. And in a final, passionately anti-scientific apostrophe, Edison addresses himself in imagination to the modern age which, in creating Hadaly, he has deliberately burlesqued. The age has discarded its ancient beliefs, has made utility the test of everything, has dispensed with spiritual reality and accepted mechanical substitutes in so many other areas of existence — let it recognize the real tendency of its thought, and accept the hygienic and therapeutic value of a love-machine.

We need not follow out this shrill allegory to its busy dénouement in order to recognize Villiers's provocative intent. He is calling into question man's existence in those areas where he has been most apt to think himself unique, indispensable. A climactic scene presents Hadaly — in a speech pre-recorded by Miss Alicia Clary herself, who has been told she is rehearsing for a scene in a play — pleading with Lord Ewald to grant her the belief which will transform her into a woman, and him into a man. The last twist is pure Villiers. All existence, he proclaims, is a mechanism to which we give life by breathing into it a sustaining faith; the creature of flesh and blood is a mere rag and bone and hank of hair unless we create her by an act of faith, an act of adoration. And unless we provide some such spiritual clothing, not only for a specific woman or woman-excuse, but for the world as a whole, we cannot live, we are not men but suicides, anti-men. This emphasis on the fragility and willed quality of the saving illusion is a distinctive note in a very strange book. It does not very often march directly up to the topic of Nothing, and when it does so, its effects are mostly comic; but the cold wind of an icy and meaningless void blows through the picturesque machinery of the novel, and its representation of humanity as called into question, in its most intimate relations, by its own grotesque inventions represents an early expression of a now-familiar anxiety.[4]

Doctor Faustus (in Marlowe's melodrama) is living his last few minutes on earth before midnight strikes and the

4. Messieurs Chapuis and Gélis in their encyclopedic *Monde des automates* (2 vols., Paris, 1928) describe an immense variety of people- and creature-shaped mechanisms. The singing birds of Byzantium are here (rather poor creatures, alas), and so are a serried mass of androids capable of various tricks — talkers, reciters, singers, writers, drawers of pictures, players of musical instruments, and participants in various games. But in this whole gamut of achievements, one notes that the rarest is ordinary locomotion. Walking, as a complex cycle of partial falls, recoveries of balance, and responses to kinetic impressions, has been (or until 1928 had been) one of the hardest human activities to mimic mechanically. It is a rather meager triumph for humanity — particularly since walking itself is now rapidly becoming obsolete, even among people. So far at least we retain one minor superiority over the machines: we can switch them off. But on the larger scale, they can switch us off, and permanently. Among the forces making toward modern man's estimate of himself as null and void, the bald, brutal challenge of the machine is surely one of the most potent; perhaps the fact that it is so little represented in literature and so largely in sub-literature is best evidence of its seriousness.

devil comes to take his soul to hell. Stage time, which has hitherto been extraordinarily rubbery and mobile, suddenly comes much closer to "real" time, starts to be marked off, progresses steadily without leaps or gaps; it also assumes a central role in the drama, so that the most dramatic events on stage come to be the tolling of a bell in the wings and the sheer experience of waiting during which the audience can count on its pulses the passage of seconds and minutes. Meanwhile the protagonist talks. He talks, not as dramatic characters usually talk, to carry the action forward, but in despairing bursts which he hopes will somehow hold it back. Marlowe has his speech career wildly about under pressure of his hysteria; but in the silences when he does not talk at all, the audience can hear something more terrifying than talk — the passage of real time, to which stage time has been assimilated. This inversion of energies — the theatrical dialogue used to delay, if only symbolically, a development rooted in real time — has the special effect of rendering the texture of the drama itself diaphanous; and then the promised event has only to refrain from happening, and we have an interplay of Nothings sufficient to stock a Theater of the Absurd. An early play of Maeterlinck's, the one-act morality *Les Aveugles* (*The Blind:* 1891), offers an instance of the technique in undeveloped but clearly seminal form.

Maeterlinck's play opens with six blind men and six blind women, one with an infant, sitting quietly on stage. They do not know, though the audience does, that in their midst sits a dead priest, who has been their guide and guardian. They think he has gone away for a while, they discuss where he might be, and make a few feeble efforts to go in search of him. But they are afraid of getting lost or separated, and none of them had paid much attention to the priest's instructions, when he was alive, about finding the way. So there they sit, talking, in the depths of an immemorial forest, by the shore of an alien sea, not knowing where they are or how long they have been there, uncertain whether it is day or night, helpless to get back to the shelter and the three last nuns, if they are still alive — talking, talking aimlessly, as time passes. One of the bolder ones finally probes and prods around enough to discover that the priest is sitting dead in their midst; but even this discovery cannot much deepen their despair nor does it rouse them to do anything. Snow begins to fall. After a while, the youngest girl says she hears footsteps, which seem to stop in their midst. Who it is they do not know, and the audience in this matter is not only as blind as they but deafer. Stage-instructions mention no sound effects. Under the circumstances only one visitor can be anticipated, but no way of identifying him appears. There is no answer to the query of the blind, "Qui êtes-vous?" and the curtain falls on the empty cry, "Ayez pitié de nous," and the steady wailing of the terrified child.

The most interesting thing about Maeterlinck's little play is the way in which it makes the mere passage of time its central action, and opposes to this relentless progression the idleness of talk. An analogy in fiction is with the delaying-actions of Melville's *Confidence Man;* the device by which the narrator of Byron's *Don Juan* delays with his digressions the telling of his own story is an analogous tease. The anti-work-of-art plays straight against the expectations of the reader. (In a positive work, the reader collaborates with the author's controlled release of information; in negative work, the reader is led to expect more information than the author chooses to surrender.) In *Les Aveugles*, since all talk is doomed to futility, the progression is made by subsurface time measured against talk — much as, in the similar *Waiting for Godot*, expectation grows and becomes obsessive by standing still against the eddying currents of small-talk, horse-play, and heavy silence between Vladimir and Estragon. What is particularly useful about the expressive device is that it converts negative into positive forces at so many different levels. Particularly in a stage-situation, time is an almost tangible demand. An audience is assembled "for entertainment," focused by artificial darkness, the rule of silence, and immovable seats on a small segment of the 360 degrees; the usual stage play tries to placate their demands by offering "action." But *Les Aveugles* is almost the first play to act in its entirety as an escape mechanism — using the audience's expectations of action as a lead weight to which the play's speech offers resistance, while subsurface two times, stage and real in momentary collusion, march inexorably toward the promised end.

The reader who looked into F. H. Bradley's *Appearance and Reality* as it came from the presses in 1893 found himself in the abrupt presence of a tough, assured mind and a prose style bristling with barely suppressed belligerence. Bradley can be something of a lion in anyone's path, for his book comes at one in a no-nonsense mood and has a special way of being, without overt polemics, bluntly argumentative. Addressing the reader, more often than not, directly, Bradley tends to pick him up by the scruff of his logical neck, and force him to face the consequences of his metaphysical positions. *Appearance and Reality* begins, in fact, by requiring the reader to admit that he has metaphysical positions, whether he thinks them possible or not. Then it moves into a series of demonstrations, grouped under the rubric "Appearance," designed to show that most of the categories under which he attempts to grasp reality, including his notions of space and time, are self-contradictory and therefore mere illusion. In the second part of the book, under the heading "Reality," Bradley tries to redeem, in part at least, the devastating consequences of his earlier skepticism; and in the end, by a supreme effort, he does establish to his own satisfaction, the existence of a greater measure of reality behind or within the illusion — an elusive reality, about which we are surely in endless error, but about which we can predicate that it is one, coherent, and (at least broadly) perceivable. About this Absolute we cannot be in any doubt, for the simple reason that we do not have enough information for doubt. The act of doubting implies possession of two beliefs or sources of belief; and to know anything outside the cosmos seems incompatible with the definition of cosmos. All we have to go on is experience, all experience is of the cosmos, therefore we must be infallibly certain (precisely because of our ignorance) that a cosmos exists, though all our ideas about it may be mistaken. We cannot even, with Herbert Spencer, set aside one portion of it, for worship or wonder, as the Unknowable; about what we do not know at all we cannot even predicate that it is unknowable. Thus, at the end of nearly five hundred pages of hard-bitten argumentation, Bradley succeeds in establishing, not the knowledge of any particular thing, but what is for him a comprehensible and defensible assurance about things in general. The ontological argument traditionally expends immense energies to establish logically conclusions without which — if we did not know them instinctively — we would not get out of bed in the morning. Still, no one can look into Bradley's immense and athletic book without a sense of how radically the everyday object must have been called into question, if such extraordinary efforts were necessary to redeem it. Even supposing it a victory in the struggle to snatch a little hard reality from the smog of confusion and the gape of void, Bradley's book is surely a Pyrrhic victory. For a book of metaphysics, its impact was extraordinary — partly, no doubt, because the topic had been largely neglected by English philosophy, with its traditional pragmatic bias. By and large, Dr. Johnson's answer to Berkeley's doubts had been good enough for most Englishmen; and even so subtle and tenacious a thinker as Hume once confessed that he never had any questions about reality which were not satisfied by a good dinner. Bradley's preoccupation with the problem had its roots in post-Kantian German metaphysics; but he made rather a point of not uncovering them, and his own book was, in tone and vocabulary, pure blunt English. It was therefore an accessible book, one of the most accessible books on metaphysics ever written — and this added to its shock effect. To see a man struggling so hard, and succeeding so precariously, in establishing facts which generations of Englishmen had vaguely but easily taken for granted, must have been a sobering sight. It was the more sobering because Bradley was no crier of rhetorical doom — on the contrary, his entire book bore witness to a sustained effort at strict creative thought. His limited success in reaching the real, and the grounding of his final assurance upon nothing stronger than a form of ignorance, did much to move metaphysical void into the modern consciousness, via a side door, as it were.

By something less than an extraordinary coincidence, at the same time as Bradley was knotting up his logical networks at Oxford, Claude Monet was undertaking the first of his "series" paintings in France; and the indirect, unprogrammed effect of both projects was, from sharply differing angles of approach, to diminish the status of the object. Monet had, of course, been a radical in painting since his first shows: the very name of "Impressionism" seems to derive from the title of one of his canvases, painted in the mid-'seventies, and he had already borne the full storm of academic abuse for the "formlessness" of his paintings, his indifference to the ideal of the photographic likeness. For like Turner before him, and Whistler his contemporary, Monet was from the beginning a student of luminous decomposition. He loved to paint mists, clouds, twilights, and scenes in which a special hazy light served to soften and qualify the hard outlines of objects. His handling of color was on many occasions comparable to that of his precursor and supporter Manet; he insisted upon the colors of shadows, often used pure colors applied in flat patches, and radically lightened his palette. But he went far beyond Manet in allowing the play of light to disintegrate the objects on his canvases. And the most dramatic demonstration of this process occurred precisely in the great series-paintings (of poplars, hayricks, cathedrals) which he began to do in the late 'eighties and early 'nineties. "Les Meules" (1890–91) studied a group of hayricks under various lights, in various weathers, at various times of day; inevitably, the variations were so striking as to reduce the common denominator of all fifteen pictures — the underlying hayrick — almost to the role of tailor's dummy. The twenty canvases on which Monet recorded the play of light across the façade of Rouen Cathedral (1895) were even more dramatic in obliterating the object behind the process of illumination and vision. To capture that process in precise instants of time, Monet invented more and more elaborate strategies, frequently working on four or five pictures at once and reserving for each one a particular section of the day.

In itself, the act of painting the same scene twenty times over cried aloud that the scene was nothing compared with the evanescent light that qualified it. But in addition, Monet undertook to paint, as it were, on the viewer's retina by putting on his canvas what one can only call the objective correlative of a natural color. His paint imitated rather the impression made on the eye than the natural tonality making it; seen from close up, his paintings disintegrated into mere blobs of juxtaposed, though subtly related, color, while, seen from a distance, they composed a vibrating, shimmering unity of impression. Monet painted the motion of light-particles rather than the limit of the diaphane. "Never has a painter more resolutely denied matter," wrote Louis Gillet (*Trois variations sur Claude Monet*); and he went on to speak of the painter "giving himself artistic festivals in honor of indigent realities," and composing "one of the most beautiful hymns to universal Non-being." This, to be sure, is the voice of the nineteen-twenties, and it seems reasonably clear that Monet had no such elaborate philosophical program in mind, back in the eighteen-nineties. He was far from a metaphysician. Popular exaggeration has drawn the limits of his education too narrowly (he was neither analphabet nor incoherent of discourse), but his was a vigorous, inarticulate, intuitive nature, deeply rooted in the here and now. He was no more capable than Renoir of painting a picture for ideological reasons. Yet one uniform critical reaction was spontaneous, as far back as 1896, when André Michel (in his *Notes sur l'art moderne*) had been driven by the experience of Monet's painting to declare indignantly that, after all, trees and rocks did exist *really* — as if the painting had somehow called them into question.

There is some truth to the plea that Monet never set out to call things into question; there is more truth in the rejoinder that he effectually called them into question even without meaning to do so. But it is true also, and in the largest sense of all, that things have been getting less and less solid for the last hundred years. Clémenceau had the right idea when he invited critics of Monet to visit a laboratory and there inspect some of that lucent air and limpid water which they thought the painter was obscuring with the complexities of a private vision. He predicted that they would find Nature herself bubbling and boiling with Brownian motion. Even as he wrote, solid matter was ceasing to be solid, and becoming convertible into quanta and patterns of energy. In a word, what Monet called into question had long ceased, on other levels, to exist at all — as, under the converging impact of multiplied particular interests directed by no special skeptical intent at all, the solid core of objects in the world around man crumbled and everywhere gave way.

X

Some Instances of Boredom

As it shields or reflects the horror of an inner void, the bored man's immobility may be serviceable to the meditative lyric, but poses special problems for fiction. It may act as an anchor against which the story's energies tug or an obstacle against which they are, with comic irrelevance, stacked.

Characteristically, Nothing is encountered either far out, after an immense enterprise of spiritual or physical effort, or else in an act of intimate introspection at the bottom of one's heart. It is cosmic or contemplative, rarely either one exclusively, more often both in resonant tandem; but it occurs outside the middle range of social experience, it is the discovery of some sort of ultimate. Perhaps for this reason, it is often popularly regarded as a spiritual test, by which one hardens the soul to what is called the modern temper. By discovering Nothing, one has seen through, or to the bottom of, Something — hence, by easy extension, of Everything. Yet it is a purely defensive discovery; that is, the discoverer of Nothing is not to be suspected of trying to persuade, convert, or peddle, any more than his discovery can be criticized as tending to his advantage. Nothing, in fact, is *purer* than anything; by abstracting everything which is outside the potential for consciousness, one seems to gain an interior ultimate. Whether reduction is the way to define the ultimate self — whether in fact the ultimate self can be contemplated at all without contamination — is another question; it is at least arguable that the self exists only in action, that it consists of roles acquired in the process of doing things. One must then keep the self healthfully nourished with sensations and exercised in its multiple functions (avoiding the creeping paralysis of omphaloskepsis), lest this delicate agent dwindle into a vestige as odd as the vermiform appendix. But the discovery of Nothing at the root of the self erodes away all such healthy, calisthenic motivations; for the name of this Nothing is boredom, and cruel is his power. Like tuberculosis and venereal disease, it was one of the great tacit killers of the nineteenth century, a topic slow to rise to conscious expression and not easily adapted to literary representation, but all the more potent in its mute, deadly diffusion.

The word "bore" in the sense of ennui did not exist in English before the middle of the eighteenth century, and "boredom" as the resulting state is not to be found before the middle of the nineteenth. The thing itself, of course, existed from time immemorial — one sees animals like dogs and horses looking bored, and there is no reason to suppose yawning a recent human accomplishment.[1] Yet the classical languages have no term which corresponds strictly, though several are tangential. Greek ἀκηδεια is more akin to our "apathy," and Latin *taedium* originally meant "weariness" and later came to include the notion of "disgust." The native English word was of course "dulness"; it is the term used by Dryden and Pope in their literary satires, and in their hands it acquires a kind of massive, negative grandeur, a dark splendor which verges on the heroic. But, though they culminate inevitably in sleep, these literary inversions are too potent and too active to bear directly on boredom proper, which is allied with triviality and repetition and irrelevance, and which rises at its height to something like anguish.

1. Even wild animals sometimes appear bored — e.g. well-fed lions yawning through a hot afternoon, or rhinos in a sleepy lagoon; civilization does not cause boredom, it intensifies a condition whch in nature the pressures of gross appetite allow to appear only briefly and intermittently.

When first it appeared across-Channel, the verb "to bore" was popularly supposed to be of French origin, and therefore denoted the light, the decadent, and the monotonously trivial. (The actual etymology of "bore" is uncertain, but the concept if not the word had long been domesticated in France; "ennui" was a favorite complaint of the French lady of fashion, often accompanied with the specification that she was relapsing into "néant." [2]) To bore or be bored was a social, not a distinctively literary or intellectual activity; it implied, then as now, a wearisome profusion of unnecessary yet demanding details.

Being an attitude of detachment and indifference, boredom in England had about it a quality distinctly discreditable, even shameful, which it did not have on the Continent, and which it still partly retains in everyday usage. To confess oneself bored is, as it were, to confess oneself without inner resources and perhaps even ungrateful before the gift of God; it flies in the face of the crucial Puritan doctrine of the calling. We are supposed to know, by intimate inspiration, what to do in this world — if we don't, there must be something wrong with us. Nor is this judgment purely ethical; it is reinforced, in literary representations of boredom, by the artist's natural hostility to a void in his work. The root demand of an artistic work for taut lines and economical effects militates against the inclusion of life's everyday slippages and accidents and neutral voids. Just as heroes always find parking spaces when they need them, and never get busy signals on the telephone unless they are to "mean" something, so they are rarely plain bored, because artistic structure seems to call for a tension to be felt, an impetus to be sustained, wherever feasible. Besides, the bored man is of ill omen in a work of imagination which exists ostensibly to combat boredom, as well as an enemy, a snob, who casts doubt on the earnest values of the literary construct itself. Hence the bored within a literary work are usually peripheral figures, and, in the early stages of

2. See the brothers Goncourt, *La Femme au 18e siècle*, II, *passim*.

the topic, if they are not bad or superficial, they are sick. The fault may be mere social shallowness, to be dismissed with a sneer or a gesture of disdain; such is Byron's flip comment in *Don Juan:*

> Society is now one polished horde
> Formed of two mighty tribes, the Bores and Bored.[3]
>
> (XIII, 95)

But, on the other hand, boredom may evince a more radical deficiency in the human being, not only a flaw of social resource but a limitation, as profound as original sin, on the characteristics of human desire and human satisfaction. Basic texts here are numbers 201 and 209 of Pascal's *Pensées,* in which man's restless alternation between unappeased desire and bored satiety is made evidence of his radically incomplete nature:

> Nothing is so unbearable to man as finding himself in complete repose, without passions, without occupation, without amusement, without duty. He feels then his nothingness, his abandonment, his insufficiency, his dependence, his impotence, his void. Immediately there arise from the bottom of his soul boredom, blackness, grief, chagrin, scorn, despair (201).

> So life flows away. One seeks rest at the price of overcoming various obstacles; and if one has overcome them, rest itself becomes intolerable (by the boredom it engenders. We must get out of it and go looking for excitement. No condition is happy without tumult and diversion, and every condition is happy which yields some diversion. But judge for yourself

---

3. Note however that Byron did not consider boredom a full equivalent of ennui:

> For *ennui* is a growth of English root,
> Though nameless in our language: — we retort
> The fact for words, and let the French translate
> That awful yawn which sleep cannot abate. . . .
>
> (XIII, 101)

what sort of happiness it is which consists of being diverted from thinking of oneself.) for we think either of the miseries we have or of those which threaten us. And even when we think ourselves sheltered from every direction, boredom on its own initiative does not hesitate to rise from the bottom of our hearts, where it has its natural roots, and fill the spirit with its venom (209).

Boredom is primarily used, in literature and morality, as a vacuum which the audience can be counted on to abhor. It is satiety with a vindictive edge, a built-in element of instability. One can never tell what the bored man (or woman, e.g. Hedda Gabler) will do, only that he is bound to do something, probably abrupt and violent. His boredom is a lack of any directed intention; it is also a pressure on him to discover an intention. He cannot stay indefinitely where he is; he would not be where he is if a better place were anywhere to hand. Therefore he must be up against some barrier or obstacle which has to be surmounted if he is to escape his boredom. For Pascal, as for most religious apologists, the obvious barrier is faith; bored as a result of the vacuity of this-worldly desires, man can hope for more enduring delights only in the sphere of the heavenly. But any barrier will serve the turn. In *The World as Will and Idea* (1819), Schopenhauer turns to predictable purposes Pascal's alternation of desire and boredom; it is a condition of that insatiable will which drives men interminably on their round of worldly activities. Striving, struggling, and forever deluded, man so long as he is absorbed in the world of will is doomed to pain, desire, and ennui in a never-ending cycle. But through great art or through the direct arduous denial of the will he may rise to the timeless sphere of impersonal contemplation; there all desire and all discontent disappear, and in ecstatic union with a cosmos of which he has become a passive mirror, man achieves the fullest liberation of which he is capable. These doctrines are enough to qualify Schopenhauer as a fellow-traveler if not an agent of Buddhism in the nineteenth century; after releasing a good many clouds of steamy platitude and pedantry, his ethics ultimately boil down to a recommendation of resignation. At the end of the Fourth Book he comes up against the question whether all this resignation is not a recommendation to accept, and commit oneself to, Nothing; and indeed it appears

> that with the free denial, the surrender of the will, all those phenomena are also abolished; that constant strain and effort without end and without rest at all the grades of objectivity, in which and through which the world consists; the multifarious forms succeeding each other in gradation; the whole manifestation of the will; and, finally, also the universal forms of this manifestation, time and space, and also its last fundamental form, subject and object; all are abolished. No will: no idea, no world (tr. Haldane and Kemp, IV, 71).

At first glance, this seems like a good deal to give up; but Schopenhauer assures us that when we have put off the will to live, the phenomena of this world will seem mere appearances, and another world, outside time and space, outside life and matter and change, will appear the only reality.

This verbal gambit is not very easy to question, since it assumes intimate expert knowledge on Schopenhauer's part of a sphere which we can claim to know only by assuming our own sainthood. But Schopenhauer's credentials as a man acquainted with the peace that passeth understanding are far from convincing. When he tells us, with more assurance than discrimination, that the saints and mystics have known how to find absolute peace and that we can do likewise, he is like a bald man selling hair-rejuvenator on the street corner. Every circumstance discredits the substance of his spiel. No doubt, if we become indifferent to enough of the world, we will not suffer from it; but then, the chances are, we will not feel any ecstatic raptures, either. Those eternal, unchanging ideas, the vision of which is supposed to inspire us with supreme bliss, seem just as likely to inspire extreme boredom. And if boredom cannot exist outside of time, how do we know that pleasure can? Some actual saints and contemplatives have testified that they were not exempt from the griefs of ἀκηδεια. But when a philosopher is determined to locate ultimate good somewhere, it will be hard lines if he cannot arrange its advantages and dismiss its difficulties to his own verbal satisfaction. Schopenhauer's arrangement seems particularly specious, and he himself merely conventional, in using *taedium vitae* as a springboard to his chosen Ideal and in placing a facsimile of Nothing at the end of his spiritual trajectory. His Nirvana is simply the Beatific Vision with God made optional. Hegel, though he has little or nothing to say of boredom, is a philosopher much more important than Schopenhauer for the literary history of Nothing, because he encourages men to find it in the texture of this world and the basic structure of things, rather than by withdrawal.

Kierkegaard, on the other hand, as the thinker most concerned with the leap from stage to stage of life, has an obvious exemplary use for boredom. He too treats it as a springboard; and the opening speaker of *Either/Or* (1843), who is already a parody of the hedonistic logic of everyday aesthetic existence, makes boredom the first principle of his existence. "In the beginning there was boredom," he says, and proceeds to reduce the entire Christian story to a fable in which boredom plays the principal role. "In the beginning the gods were bored. Then they created man. Afterwards, Adam was bored, so Eve was given to him. Adam and Eve, Cain and Abel grew bored *en famille*; then humanity *en masse*; and when the Tower of Babel was built, boredom overspread the earth in layers as thick as the tower was high." Since boredom is so deep and powerful, man must exercise all his devices of psychic mobility to escape it. For example, one goes to see just the middle of a certain play — arriving deliberately late and leaving early, so as not to submit to the boring "program" of the author; or one takes a poem in a wholly different sense from that which the poet intended; or again one studies the fine art of breaking off every social relation before satiety threatens. In addition, one cultivates the principle that pleasure is in the mind, and therefore that what one wants is not the exterior stimulus but one's own willful will. If, feeling thirsty, one asked for a glass of water and were served a precious liqueur, one would cast it aside; for no sensual pleasure is so great as that of having one's will precisely obeyed. In short, the aesthetic man who lives in a world where boredom is his primary threat exercises against it the defense of perversity. When thrown into the inevitable company of a bore, he derives exquisite entertainment from ignoring everything he says and concentrating instead on the way sweat forms on the bore's forehead and threatens to drip off his nose.

Thus Kierkegaard uses boredom as a moral diagnostic to point up the paradoxical instability of the "natural" sphere; its function is reductive and ironic. But so agile and dramatic a mind could have no permanent interest in this preliminary condition; and in fact *Either/Or* after this opening ironic exposition quickly leaves the topic behind. I do not find any literary figure before Leopardi who proposes the dignity of boredom as an independent state, nor any in the entire century for whom the "nulla" which one reaches through "noia" is a more important experience.

A pair of famous passages in the *Pensieri* (67 and 68) seem to exalt boredom as a state to which only the spiritual man can aspire. Looking across the world and through the galaxies, Leopardi in the person of this spiritual man finds everywhere nullity, vacancy, and insufficiency by comparison with his own teeming soul and infinite desires. This version of boredom as a kind of cosmic complacency gives it rank among manifestations of the egotistical sublime; but the part which the concept plays in Leopardi's extended thought, and particularly in his poetry, is more various and interesting. It must be prefaced by a few words outlining the psychological-sociological myth which he took for granted.

According to this Leopardian myth, both the individual in his youth and society in pagan days were originally capable of imagination, which filled life with vivid though false imagery, making the world seem alive and sympathetic to its inhabitants.[4] Under these circumstances, man's senses would be quick and unclouded, his passions vigorous. So life was in the age of our primitive ancestors, in the golden age of mankind; so it is for children, and so it may still be in a few surviving wildernesses like California (*quantum mutata*, 1965!). But science and civilization have cut man off from the life of the senses, and so from his own power of imagination; out of this inner, partial death rises *noia*, which is essentially a disease of the civilized, and which, in its early stages, is the simple absence of feeling. So the poem "Ad Angelo Mai" contrasts those fortunate figures of the past who were capable of authentic grief with moderns, who can feel nothing at all:

> Ahi dal dolor comincia e nasce
> L'italo canto. E pur men grava e morde
> Il mal che n'addolora
> Del tedio che n'affoga. Oh te beato
> A cui fu vita il pianto! A noi le fasce
> Cinse il fastidio; a noi presso la culla
> Immoto siede, e su la tomba, il nulla.[5]

4. "Il Sabato del Villaggio" warns the boy to whom it is addressed that his present age is the happiest of all, that the Sunday of his life, like that of the week, will be a weary round of yawning and boredom.

5. Alas, in sorrow begins and ends Italian song. And yet less deep and bitter the pain which stabs than the tedium which smothers. Happy were you whose life was sorrow. About us boredom fastens its bandages; by our cradle and on our tomb sits motionless the Void.

Knowledge has shrunk the world, not expanded it, and made evident its uniformity, not its variety — has rendered it dead:

> Ecco svaniro a un punto
> E figurato è il mondo in breve carta;
> Ecco tutto è simile, e discoprendo,
> Solo il nulla s'accresce.[6]

Thus man is necessarily isolated within the universe; whether he travels, struggles, or socializes with his own kind (as the poem "To Count Carlo Pepoli" declares), he inevitably carries within him the adamantine pillar of boredom:

> ahi, ma nel petto,
> Nell'imo petto, grave, salda, immota
> Come colonna adamantina, siede
> Noia immortale, incontro a cui non puote
> Vigor di giovanezza, e non la crolla
> Dolce parola di rosato labbro,
> E non lo sguardo tenero, tremante,
> Di due nere pupille, il caro sguardo,
> La più degna del ciel cosa mortale.[7]

So heightened and sharpened, boredom passes beyond apathy; it is metaphysical anguish and pure desire, abstracted from this or that particular object, not directly frustrated, yet knowing itself incapable of fulfillment. When other passions and distractions leave the mind, the ground-bass of *noia* rises to fill it. Perhaps a cause and certainly a result of this *noia* is the posture

6. Here, reduced to a point, the world is represented on a bit of paper; see, everything is the same, and from our discoveries only Nothing is increased.

7. Alas, but within the breast, in the depths of the breast, heavy, massive, motionless, like an adamantine column sits immortal boredom, against which even the vigor of youth is helpless; nor will it be shaken by sweet words from rosy lips, or the tender, tremulous glance of two black eyes, the beloved glance, among all mortal things most worthy of heaven.

of hallucinated immobility and total self-abandonment which Leopardi repeatedly describes:

> Talor m'assido in solitaria parte
> Sovra un rialto, al margine d'un lago
> Di taciturne piante incoronato.
> Ivi, quando il meriggio in ciel si volve,
> La sua tranquilla imago il Sol dipinge,
> E erba o foglia non si crolla al vento,
> E non onda incresparsi, e non cicala
> Strider, nè batter penna augello in ramo,
> Nè farfalla ronzar, nè voce o moto
> Da presso nè da lunge odi nè vedi.
> Tien quelle rive altissima quiete;
> Ond'io quasi me stesso e il mondo obblio
> Sedendo immoto; e già mi par che sciolte
> Giaccian le membra mie, nè spirto o senso
> Più le commova, e lor quiete antica
> Co' silenzi del loco si confonda.[8]

We note in this passage from "La Vita Solitaria" (lines 23–38) how a soft, deep phrase like "lor quiete antica" invites the imagination back to an original repose underlying the restless motion of the limbs — as if in this new quiet of the place they were merely regaining a stillness which was their immemorial right. "L'Infinito" too describes a recovery of quiet at the heart of the self, a withdrawing into interior distance. Only when the hedge turns back his gaze from the horizon does the poet's mind go adventuring beyond it:

8. Then I sit solitary on a mound by a lake crowned with quiet plants. There, when noon rises in the skies the sun paints its quiet portrait, and neither grass nor leaf bends to the wind, nor does wave ripple nor cricket call nor bird flutter wing on bough nor butterfly flit; neither sound nor motion from near or far do I hear or see. Deepest quiet covers the bank; so that, sitting motionless, I almost forget myself and the world, and now it seems that my limbs lie still, neither spirit nor sense moves them any more, and their ancient quiet mingles with the silence of the place.

                    interminati
Spazi di là da quella, e sovrumani
Silenzi, e profondissima quiete
Io nel pensier mi fingo.[9]

The wind rustling through the hedge becomes the noise of the
world; and by contrast with the poet's physical immobility, the
comparison of time's rattling noise with the infinite silence of
space is a steadily deepening, advancing experience, as the
strong verbal form underlines:

                    io quello
Infinito silenzio a questa voce
Vo comparando.[10]

The mind is lost in its own contemplations, drowns or is shipwrecked; yet its fate is, for unspecified reasons, "dolce":

             Così tra questa
Immensità s'annega il pensier mio:
E il naufragar m'è dolce in questo mare.[11]

The adjective implies that he has regained or rediscovered
something, and in fact the imagery of drowning is rich in tacit
implications of regeneration, cyclical return, erotic surrender,
mortal abandon, and new counterpart-worlds — all of which are
left to cluster, if they will, around the magnetic, because unexplained, word "dolce."

   In the last of the *Canti*, "La Ginestra" poses the fragile
flower of human life against the hot lava overflowing from
Vesuvius, under the infinite perspectives of interstellar space,
assures us that under these circumstances death and only death
is inevitable, and yet invokes too a chilly, almost astral vision of

9. interminable spaces beyond this one and superhuman silences and deepest
quiet I form in my thoughts.
10. and I go my way comparing that infinite silence with this noise.
11. Thus my thought drowns in this immensity, and shipwreck in this sea is
sweet to me.

love. The flower, which can only be love, grows on the edge of the abyss, in defiance of its own Nothingness, pretending to be only the creature of an instant; yet it returns in the teeth of defeats, pushing continually forward

> Per sì lungo cammino,
> Che sembra star.[12]

The huge cyclical indifference of which Leopardi elsewhere accuses Nature seems here allied to an equally large impersonal force in man — as if, for the first time, love were not a refuge from Nature or an opponent of Nature, so much as an expression of it. Leopardi thus suggests in his last poem a Nothing within or beneath the illusion of love, as well as at either end of it. That this poem should be taken as an affirmative expression seems particularly wrong, since it summarizes the case for a human love which it has already toned down to *caritas* in terms of clear-eyed cynicism:

> Così star suole in piede
> Quale star può quel ch'ha in error la sede. . . .[13]

Startled by Leopardi's bitter, unbelieving pessimism, a good many otherwise-perceptive contemporaries tried to dismiss him as a man who because he was a hunchback denied God. The superficiality of this cruel and rather Latin logic is apparent; but it seems to have been important not to let oneself look into Leopardi's universe or admit that it might be one's own. There is no reason to doubt that the peculiarities of Leopardi's wretched youth and the influence of his classically misguided parents confirmed in him a whole range of idiosyncratic attitudes. Yet in many respects his cosmos is closer to our own than is, say, that of his respectable contemporary Manzoni;[14] eccen-

12. By so long a journey that it seems to stand still.
13. Thus it will stand on its feet as anything stands which has its seat in error.
14. The conversion of the Nameless One, the story of the Nun of Monza,

tric in his own day, he is far less so today. He first drew in the
thin, bitterly cold air of absolute Nothing with the sense that
it was both deadly and inevitable; he proclaimed *noia* the disease of modern man and *nulla* his destiny, and did so in terms
transcending the Rousseauistic primitivism which represented
the rationale of his outlook if not its real roots. By the hardness
of his style and the purity of his perceptions, he gave evidence
of a sort that man could after a fashion survive in the empty
spaces of imaginative non-existence and unbelief. Indeed, we
now know that his experience of *nulla* was more profound and
terrifying than contemporaries could have estimated from his
public writings. The correspondence and the immense *Zibal-
done* or commonplace-book became public property only at the
turn of the century, and in them we find passages like these:

> I was terrified to find myself in the midst of nothing, and
> myself nothing. I felt as if I were suffocating, believing and
> feeling that everything is nothing, solid nothing (*Zibaldone*,
> I, 195).

Or, from a letter to Giordani (19 November 1819):

> If at this moment I were to go mad, my madness I believe
> would consist in remaining seated with eyes staring, mouth
> open, hands upon my knees, not laughing or weeping or
> moving, unless compelled, from the place where I found
> myself. . . . This is the first time in my life when *noia* has
> not only oppressed and wearied me, but suffocates and tears
> at me like an intolerable pain, and I am so terrified by the
> vanity of everything and of man's condition when, as with
> me, every passion in his soul has been extinguished, that I am
> beside myself and have come to believe that my very despera-
> tion too is nothing (*Epist.* I, 240).

and a certain clucking, parochial editorializing tone in the conduct of the
narrative are crying instances where the method of *I Promessi Sposi* makes
its author a little more comfortable in the prefabricated responses than I
think we usually like to see a novelist, or a moralist.

These are the accents, not of spite or pose, but of extreme, direct necessity. Leopardi's triumph is to have recognized in this condition a permanent aspect of man's earthly state, and made it serve major ends in his art. As with Mallarmé, the pure simplicity of his finest lyrics is outlined against the black of void; they do not push because there is nothing for them to push against; the self-contained poise of their carriage is reflected in pools of motionless despair which lie beneath them, liquid and glittering and permanent.

But though relatively adaptable to the contemplative lyric, the immobility and fathomless disinterest of the bored man made him too refractory a topic for narrative to handle. This point is clearly illustrated by the general poverty of fiction dealing with the dandy. At the last moment before the nineteenth century descended into stovepipe hats, tube-like trousers, funereal coats, and grotesque crinolines, this enigmatic creature appeared. Ridiculed in his own day as a degenerate eccentric, he began to seem full of interest and significance a few generations later, and there is now a whole library of dandy-analysis. But the dandies made no move to explain themselves, poetry touched them only lightly, and the representations of them in fiction are laughably inadequate. They are a curious instance of figures too prophetic and significant in their own nature for the literature of their day to use.

There seems no doubt that the root of the dandy-attitude is to be sought in boredom — in a boredom with society's rules and existence-in-the-sight-of-others which takes the peculiar form of parodying it. But the parody is not to be open — indeed, nothing about the dandy is open. Society is a closed corporation, the dandies compose a private little anti-corporation, like Stendhal's little group of men who have decided that they, and only they, know Mexican. The dandy's natural habitat is upstage. He is by definition a hard-shelled, exoskeletal human being, no more likely to be unequivocal in his relation to society than to explain or apologize for himself. He is an individual in command of his appearance in the eyes of others — i.e. of his existence; that is his paradox, the paradox of life imbued with the formality and coldness of a work of art.

It is a token of the spontaneity of the movement that its Moses, Beau Brummell, produced no tablets and left no commandments. He did not even say anything worth repeating; he simply appeared at the appropriate moment and made his stunning, overpowering effect. That essential dandy effect is primarily to be defined as aesthetic. Brummell does not accumulate that immense pile of discarded neckcloths in the search for the perfect crease with the aim of seducing women or arousing desire. Dandies are not bucks; they live in front of a mirror. Desire, which is untidy and natural, would muss the neckcloth's painstakingly achieved perfection and blur the image in the mirror. Interpreted in his own way, the dandy's first principles are *claritas, integritas,* and *consonantia;* the effect he aims at is admiration, not love, nor even liking, but distance and superiority. Flawless dress, being at once social, artificial, and self-regarding neither invites nor expresses desire; it exposes to the world a hard surface, a polished exterior. The one thing the dandy deigns to do surpassingly well is the commonest thing of all — and even here he allows no labor to show, no arduous intent to be sensed. Two fundamental dandy principles are: "To be well dressed one must not be remarked"; and "However elaborate the costume, once completed it must be worn with absolute indifference." The first rule precludes all striving for broad effect. Flash, puff, and swank are out; the dandy's art is severe, for like the artist he is intent to make the least distinguishing gesture. The second rule aims at securing for him the position of unmoved mover. His is to be the art of first appearances. So far as he can seem exempt from desire altogether, he does not betray to the world any of the vulgar mechanisms which lie beneath his surface, or any of the cords by which he achieves that apparent levitation called *poise*. Unlike the romantic, who desires more than ordinary people and desires it more deeply, the dandy desires less and desires it less deeply. If he could manage it, he would desire nothing at all, for every desire revealed is an advantage betrayed. Thus the boredom of the dandy is fathomless, and his interest lies not in concealing it, but in aggravating and exaggerating it; [15] he asserts it as a principle of existence, uses it as a defensive and offensive weapon. Yet his relation to society is never anything but ambiguous; he accepts its rules while turning them to his own interest. He is among us but never of us. And so with boredom; he exposes brutally the boredom of a society in and for which he exists, but always reveals with a minimal gesture that he is outside and above it. As a man dead to his own humanity, he adds a metaphysical overtone to social boredom; he is the poet of scarcely animated and arbitrary exteriors barely concealing an avowal of Nothing. His great refusal is to be understood, for the source of his superiority must always be mysterious — probably it is a mystification. He is "dandy" not because of the clothes he wears but because of the air with which he wears them, not through the sarcasms he drops but the distance from which he drops them. It was a very *dandy* touch which Barbey d'Aurevilly reports, to have one year a vogue for threadbare clothes. Not just any threadbare clothes would do, of course. . . .

15. His posture is most beautifully caught in the last lines of Baudelaire's "Don Juan aux Enfers." Don Juan is being carried off in Charon's boat to his eternal punishment, surrounded by gesticulating screamers, groaners, and threateners:

> Mais le calme héros, courbé sur sa rapière,
> Regardait le sillage et ne daignait rien voir.

This closing of the inner eye, combined with passive exterior conformity in the face of an ultimate threat is the perfection of dandyism.

Not only does the dandy live before a mirror, he also *is* a mirror, a self-made man set up before his fellow men to reveal their condition, an entertainer whose act consists of parodic disdain of the audience. The posture is particularly effective because it monopolizes all the available roles and forces any possible critic into the position of gratuitous, and perhaps envious, outsider. No doubt it was for this reason, which contributes so largely to his immobility, that the dandy proved impossible to adapt to the demands of prose fiction. He appears, badly corrupted, in the pages of Bulwer–Lytton's *Pelham* (1828), as a mixture of fop, intriguer and hypocrite — and so ill-sustained by his own actions that he has to intervene editorially from time to time with explanations of his strategies. He is not, actually, very much of a dandy, but he would play his assigned part in the melodrama much better if he did not attempt the character at all. T. H. Lister's *Granby* (1826) is equally inept at involving the dandy-character in the tissue of a fiction; and the dandy does not assume his rightful place as a hero of modern life till Barbey d'Aurevilly's nostalgic essay of 1845 reinstated him. Dandy influence on Baudelaire and the French symbolists, particularly Mallarmé, has been much discussed, and could easily be extended into a consideration of Yeats, Eliot, Wallace Stevens. But this influence did not involve representing the dandy as a picturesque exterior; rather it led the artist to assume a dandy mask and work dandy games of his own, from the inside out as it were.

A special and very interesting study of a condition verging on boredom but in many ways distinct from it is Goncharov's great isolated novel *Oblomov* (1857), the apathetic hero of which hardly ever rises from his favorite recumbent posture. Energetic friends and even a potential wife do their best to rouse Oblomov to action: but he prefers to dream off into a world where he is perfectly at home, perfectly happy, the world of Oblomovka. This restful countryside evidently has a valid exterior existence: some of the activists go there, rents and letters of complaint come from there, by the novel's end it even appears that railway service may be established. But it also has a mythical existence; it is immemorial Russian manor-life, in which today is just like yesterday and everyone's dream is that tomorrow will be just like today. And finally (for it is no accident that this world goes by his name and is interpenetrated with his mind and spirit), it is Oblomov's private world, the landscape of his mind. There is one side of the book which preaches energetically against this daydreaming; Stoltz and Olga, not to mention most of his other callers, tell Oblomov vehemently enough that his languor is disgraceful, and he must take himself in hand; odious consequences are threatened if he fails to take certain sensible, forward-looking steps. And he agrees; yes indeed, everyone is quite right. But then he drifts off privately, irresistibly, into his own world which corresponds to his own nature. He really has no other. And nobody can show him, or the reader, that the world of anxiety and responsibility is any better, in itself or for some ulterior purpose, than Oblomovka. For though all the predicted misfortunes *do* overtake him, they somehow do not touch him, off in Oblomovka where he exists, and from the reader's point of view it is a good thing they do not. The dream of Oblomov is richer and more enchanting than any dream of which, say, the sturdy usurping parvenu Stoltz is capable. (Oblomov is a fat passive Don Quixote, Stoltz a lean energetic Sancho Panza.) Olga, become Mrs. Stoltz, and swathed in domestic bliss, still has moments when she undergoes the deep attraction of Oblomovism. But it is hard to say whether, in Oblomov's terms, the lifelong fantasy which swallows him can fairly be described as involving either boredom or void. Boredom is properly an active sense of something not happening or not relating, a tension which blossoms ultimately into something like anguish; what Oblomov undergoes is the very reverse of tension. His languor is not boredom

to him, it is more absorbing than anything else. He is not restless or unstable, he is firmly rooted to his couch. There is even
less room for Nothing, since Oblomov's dream is precisely a
denial of Faustian man, whose grasping is the scale against
which all routine is measured and found void. Expecting little
that is new or exciting, Oblomov will never be so radically dis-
appointed as to call a day in which he has merely yawned an
empty day.

And yet, though *Oblomov* is not in the strict sense about
Nothing, it is certainly bold in taking as its hero a man who
does Nothing. However rich Oblomov's inner life, during most
of the book we see him (as Stoltz does) from the outside; his
dream cannot and does not suffuse the whole book, and for
large parts of it he is simply a lazy man on a couch. Moreover,
his position in the novel is central; he is a lazy man on a couch
around whom all sorts of lesser characters gyrate anxiously. Yet
with all this positioning and all these spotlights playing on him,
Oblomov triumphantly continues to do Nothing At All —
which, under the circumstances, proves to be the most force-
ful thing any character could do. Oblomov takes his place in a
line of unheroic, inactive nineteenth-century heroes (among
whom we number offhand Stendhal's Octave de Malivert,
Byron's Don Juan, Flaubert's Frederic Moreau, Turgenev's
Bazarov, and James's unnumbered helpless, sensitive registers);
but he is bolder than most in the privacy of his dream and the
absolute lassitude of his devotion to it. Without representing
absolute Nothing himself, or even harboring it, he belongs
among the precursors by virtue of his talent for doing so much
less than we expect a hero to do.

The usual function of boredom in nineteenth-century fiction,
we have said, is as a compressed spring out of whose torsion
rises an explosive gesture or a radical instability. Though conventional in this respect, Des Esseintes, the great Quixotic hero of

A *Rebours* (1884), represents a genuine genius of modern boredom, whose entire achievement is engendered by one phrase: "Whatever he attempted, an immense boredom [*ennui*] oppressed him" (Notice), and unbalanced by another: "He lived out of himself, nourished himself on his own substance" (Section VII). The novel is a testing of how far an inventive mind can create an artificial world in order to escape the boredom of the natural. "Human nature" is the pre-ordained limitation of the enterprise, and it takes mostly the form of the body's protests. Des Esseintes's elaborate machineries are all fastened to the back of a dying animal, and after the death of that bejewelled tortoise which is so artfully woven in with the nightmare of a ghastly tooth-extraction (Section IV), there can be no real question of his success.

Since there is only one real conflict in the book, and it is essentially pre-judged (almost every chapter ends with the cadence of anti-climax), an odd sense of irrelevance haunts those encyclopedic lists which swell through the pages of *A Rebours* with almost Rabelaisian exuberance. Not only are they static catalogues of material objects; the stockpile effect is augmented by the author, who seems to take his immobile hero almost as a challenge. His chapter divisions are like so many fences, thrown up to ensure that the hero will never move. Thus, from one point of view, there is no room for void in the book because Huysmans is continually stuffing things into it — furnishings, colors, odors, plants, perversities, juice-extractors, taste-organs, late Latin literature, enema bags, an unending list of time- and space-filling machinery. But none of these catalogues serve to fill the gaping void of Des Esseintes's existence; they are arranged in a declining order which exhausts not only the chosen subject but the reader. Only when horror is involved, as in the dream of syphilis, does the catalogue increase in intensity. A favorite word of criticism is "vide," empty — it is applied in various contexts to Virgil, Lucan, and Victor Hugo; and in fact most of the objects with which Des Esseintes is concerned are empty, in relation to his inner life. His books are presented, not as discoveries which alter his spiritual state, but as physical facts; all he can do is have the servant rearrange them, or order them printed in fancy editions, or at most turn listlessly through them. The taste-organ must have been great fun to think up, but it is not the sort of instrument on which one could pass an idle hour improvising, least of all if one were afflicted with the delicate stomach of Des Esseintes. The women whose caresses he can summon up with his elegant pastilles bring back memories chiefly of anxiety and disappointment; even the momentary appetite he gets from watching the gluttony of disgusting little boys fades quickly away, and in revulsion he sets aside the mess he has ordered in imitation of them. As the book advances, we learn more and more about the possibilities for pleasure, or at least interest, in Des Esseintes's dream-house, but the actual experiences of the hero, with one or two possible exceptions, become more and more anguished, more and more frustrating. The book ends with Des Esseintes poised for a leap into the dark; having exhausted nature and the unnatural, he is clearly ready for the supernatural. A Rebours is in effect Pascal's Pensée Number 201 writ large; it carries the dialogue of boredom and satiety to the point of ultimate impasse. But it makes some difference (all to the credit of his integrity if not of his philosophic sophistication) that Huysmans did not know where his thought was inevitably leading, did not have a landing-place already picked out when he led his hero to the point where one must shut one's eyes and jump. It is of course the discovery of another century that the need to jump is itself only provisional.

Closing

Baron von Humboldt waited till he was seventy-five to start writing a complete account of the cosmos, but anyone who wants to cap Gunther's climax by writing an *Inside Nothing* will have to wait some years longer. Even the history of other men's adventures into non-being defies regularity and method. The progress of a conception through the minds of men can never be traced in a single line, however erratic, like a chip thrown into a stream; it is carried on a thousand backs, dropped, shifted, discarded, rediscovered, fitted to an infinity of uses and pretexts. And this conception of Nothing, more than most others, resists the interpretation of a consecutive history, because it does not deepen or ripen as men mull over it. It is never anything but a flat conception, a sudden blank; one is always a beginner in the study of this topic.

The usual assumption is that Nothing supervenes as a result of some subtraction, the death or disappearance of a cosmic Something, probably God; but this does not make much of a rule. Poe and Gogol, for instance, do not dwell at length on the death of the Deity, and Flaubert takes it very much for granted — yet they are among the most inventive and ingenious manipulators of Nothing. It is perfectly possible, despite their unconsciousness of the fact, that a sense of God's disappearance may have underlain or even caused void's appearance within their minds. But solidities and convictions sufficient to make up a plenum are always disappearing beneath the feet of mankind, and in the absence of specific evidence it seems unreasonable to hold one particular disappearance, even of a personage as important as God, responsible for all voids indiscriminately. Cosmic pessimists like Leopardi are explicit in turning void to the purposes of their cosmic pessimism; but hollows and vacancies develop in human, all-too-human circumstances as well and lend themselves to comic tonalities, quite independently of the Deity. Indeed, it takes a bitter, rebellious spirit like Leopardi's to affront Nothing directly; comedy and burlesque often serve as shields behind which to approach a theme which would be too corrosive if handled openly. The "Snark" had to be a funny poem in order to be as serious as it is.

As it appears in literary work, Nothing is either cause or effect of a reversal in lines of literary force; it implies and implements anti-heroism. Ironic in itself and in its working, it appeals to ironists; in *Oblomov*, to take one example of many, it acts as a magnetic force, stronger and more controlling than all the constructive moralities precisely because it leaves then unanswered. It implies a "must" opposed to our everyday infinitude of practical and social "shoulds." Yet it makes no "Excelsior" gestures; when played against idealisms, its effect is radically deflationary.

Every work of art is a series of graduated representative equivalents for intimate experience; Nothing in literature is a series of possible equivalents for what we all know to be Nothing in nature — an indescribable sense that from the limited quota of our experience everything has been taken away. It is strong light, but inversely, by non-representation, like a deliberate hole in an artistic surface; it may have a *trompe-l'oeil* effect, as when the closed boundary and limited scale of the art-work are deliberately violated, but usually it is conditioned by the other objects being represented, and takes its place in the total scale of representative values. Hence many Nothings, variously colored, depending primarily on what one supposes to have been subtracted in order to reach the circular remainder. Not even a grandiose Nothing is excluded, oxymoron in the grand style (*Tristan, Moby Dick*); yet nineteenth-century evidence suggests that astringent limitation of vocabulary and gesture are more closely associated with Nothing. Anti-Romantics, from Leopardi to Ibsen, are Nothing-knowers, Romantics only exceptionally.

A personal distinction, a personal disaster, a personal test, a personal escape — Nothing relates to the figure of the writer in all these ways, and in multiple combinations. He succumbs to void in shuddering horror, he embraces it ecstatically, he submits reluctantly to it in order to learn something about himself, he reaches out for it as a presumed alternative to the ennui of everyday. More often than not, the perspective of Nothing diminishes; but the author's command over it may add to his stature or to that of his characters — manipulation is all. *Vis à vis* an audience, void may serve to demonstrate supreme distinction in characters who elect it, or to mock the emptiness of characters who bear it helplessly at their hearts. It sterilizes certain emotions by depriving them of interested connotations (rewards, advantages) and enhances certain other objectives by acting as a gap across which desire can leap to a presumed value. It diminishes values by appearing, corrosive and corrupting, at their heart; it exalts them by reminding us that, idle and empty as they are, our desires are the only meaning we will ever have.

Every void in a work of literature has one dimension at least, a beginning if not necessarily an end. But more often than not, it is a strictly limited gesture; Gogol drops into little pockets of void and climbs airily out of them; and the sense of falling endlessly into a void which Poe and Baudelaire use to dramatize their guilt does not diminish or overstep the symmetry of their managed literary form. Full void of course brings all literature to a halt. There is no evident reason why it should involve violent suicide or violent anything; it might well be a long tunnel of gray haze through which fade increasingly vague shapes of memory. It might well be the painfully lucid perception of wholly disjointed particulars. Atrophy combined with hyperscopy, unnatural intensity combined with utter blur, may well be the consequences of indefinite subjection to Nothing. But as it appears in literature, void seems to have the effect of hardening and sharpening the values of experience. Because it is a non-rendering of non-experience, and draws its very potency from that, its effect is to lower the whole scale of representative values — as a painter whose highest tone is raw white need move only halfway down the scale of his palette to get a proper range of expressive colors. Nothing is not just one more topic for an author to touch on if he chooses; by its positioning in the scale of experiential values, it has sooner or later an influence on all the other elements in the literary register. Our assurance that the "modern" style is hard and limited and our distaste for romantic affirmations, are no doubt based in part on an awareness of Nothing and the strict deportment it implies. Or, alternatively, they are themselves a base; who in these matters can distinguish foundation from superstructure?

Historically an impossible but nonetheless interesting question is why the English tradition made, relatively speaking, so few and such tentative approaches to the theme of Nothing, while in America and France (not to mention Italy, Russia, Germany), the topic appeared more congenial and its expression was incorporated more freely in literary work. English pragmatism, English common-sense, the continuity of English social traditions after 1688 may be invoked as partial explanations of an unquestioned fact. Certainly the nineteenth-century Frenchman, with the revolution and the career of Napoleon behind him, must have known bitterly what it is to follow a logical process, a social premise, to the edge of disaster and over the precipice. It is defeat in a sustained enterprise, a prolonged narrowing commitment which seems most likely to bring one into the immediate presence of Nothing; English pragmatism would be poor soil for such a growth. But is American pragmatism any better? One of the curious elements in the history of Nothing is the moral uneasiness, the sense of bad faith, which lingers about American authors who handle it. Poe is an evident trickster, who demands to be seen through, Melville a fabricator of translucent screens and anti-actions for delaying an inevitable confrontation, Mark Twain an always-uneasy jokester. For a Frenchman, recognition of Nothing is often an act of the greatest authenticity (Leconte de Lisle, Mallarmé); it confirms an intellectual rigor of which he is proud. But for an American, it casts doubt on his whole character and imaginative enterprise; it is a collapse, not a discovery, its bitter authenticity is a reproach. The American commits himself to fragile, fraudulent bridges over Nothing, which he tears down himself or invites the reader to tear down, even while he is on them. He is a faker whose act includes exposure of his own faking.

If the English are backward with regard to Nothing, and the Americans idiosyncratic, there can be no question that the French are surpassingly audacious; which one of these three performances most needs explaining is a question for Solomon's wisdom. The French record is most striking in historical context. No combination of social factors or intellectual influences seems adequate to explain the number of respectable and established French men of letters who during the last half of the nineteenth century proclaimed their settled conviction that the cosmos did not exist. Some principle of mass reproduction seemed to have taken over, some principle of spiritual existence to have perished — to feelings like these we get reiterated testimony in the work, otherwise so various, of Flaubert, Villiers, Zola, Barbey d'Aurevilly, Mallarmé. It is not just that God has disappeared behind the screen of His creation — that might leave one with a dead but still substantial material universe. The screen itself is felt not to exist any more; it is penetrable, soluble, it lets one fall through into a void without or a void within. The shell of personal identity collapses, the yolk of individuality is spilt. Even grossness is a form of transparency, even knowledge is a form of complicated and difficult ignorance (Flaubert). To say what produced this devastating cynicism, what principle had perished, why it seemed to have perished in France more shatteringly than elsewhere, and perhaps what killed it — all this calls for more subtle and bolder analysis than a preliminary study can undertake.

A particular quirk of social unrelatedness lies behind the frequently expressed French conviction that the mindless masses of modern society are spawning uncontrollably, thereby calling the very definition of man into question. Something like this did indeed happen in nineteenth-century England, where the years after 1800 saw a dramatic multiplication of a growth-rate that had held steady for many centuries. But in France, where Montesquieu had been much exercised over the prospect of imminent total depopulation, no such abrupt increase occurred; the seething populations under which Zola, Huysmans, Villiers, and Barbey felt themselves being swamped were not much bigger in the aggregate, or reproducing appreciably faster, than those which Montesquieu described as on the verge of extinction. If the definition of man was being called into question in nineteenth-century France, it was by a qualitative, not a quantitative change in Frenchmen. Not only Pasteur and Lister but a money society in general, with its pressures upon the bas-tions and backwaters of privilege, rendered nineteenth-century life oppressive to aristocratically minded writers. They attacked the new world, which made life safer and more prosperous, by declaring that it was also becoming easy, vulgar, and cheap. French defenses of cruelty, danger, pain, and ultimately non-existence as good for the vital character run through the century from Stendhal to Flaubert to Huysmans — with the Marquis de Sade and the Comte de Gobineau as terminal points.

A population explosion is only such — a "population" is only such — when it consists of somehow alien creatures; otherwise it is just people. On these terms, the American's peculiar false position is a function of his finding, as he advances into and overcomes the alien barbarism of the frontier, that he is creating and leaving behind him another, more alien, barbarism of the metropolis. In other words, Nothing may well derive much of its nineteenth-century prominence from dilemmas (old to us now and unspeakably tired) of culture in a mass civilization. To say that most authors who cultivate the topic are snobs and isolates (active and passive outsiders) is not to say very much, for the description applies too widely. But it hints at a reason for the English "exception." In various ways, major nineteenth-century authors of the English tradition — Wordsworth, Tennyson, Browning, Arnold, Austen, Scott, Dickens, Thackeray, Trollope — have, or feel obliged to pretend they have, some solid relation with the social structure. They quarrel with it, question it sometimes, but it is there to lean against in hostility or weariness, and whether anyone listens or not, a man like Arnold feels it is his ultimate job to relate, to criticize, to apportion praise or blame according to a set of values. Under Napoleon III, Victor Hugo played, more grandly and violently, that sort of role. There is very little sense of Nothing in Victor Hugo. For few devoted Nothing-viewers ever appointed themselves "critics of life" because as a class they are too remote and too alien from it. They tend to be artists of a long perspective, and void serves them as a way of getting a long, outside point of view and perhaps of washing clean the sight in darkness, so as to see the familiar anew.

To see things from outside the perspective of mere flesh and blood, to escape the smudge of humanity, is necessary for a certain lofty and perhaps varnished temperament. Roles become exhausted, gestures lose their significance, and the common counters in which experience must be expressed wear down. When all experience is second-hand merchandise, the impulse to withdraw from the market — the sense that everything of authentic value is outside — becomes very strong. Passion for Nothing is often anti-literary for this reason; literary=contrived=falsified. More than that, it expresses a choked, profound hostility to the conscious mind which finds very general expression in the late nineteenth century and becomes a howling chorus in the twentieth. Consciousness comes to seem a glowing band of steel; crowning human development, it constricts and tortures man, limiting his development and cramping his full nature. Some other organ than the brain, or at least than the conscious part of it, some other process than ratiocination, is invoked to take over; and to indicate an alternative to syntax and logic, the terminologies of void, infinity, and dark unconsciousness are sometimes employed. Failure of rationality in the world complements tyranny of rationality in the mind; too much reason here, not enough there. It looks like petulance, but in fact both complaints signal in different ways the playing-out of the middle range of experience, the approach of a terminus for some sort of social representation. An abdication of the whole idea of authorial arrangement and contrived effects is in the air; automatic writing and free fantasy, *objets trouvés*, and art-as-unstructured-violence will all make their appearance before the new century is twenty years old. The art of Joyce, Eliot, and Yeats, though it includes a hard mosaic surface, is in its inner dialectic an art of visionary insight, which requires on the other side of the transparencies a featureless, timeless void. The double perspective of historical or moral irony, as a characteristic mode of modern feeling, makes abundant use of void to back-light or counterpoint a primary pageant — to render reality tangible, illumine it from within or behind, and at the same time to avoid any flat-footed commitments to it.

The solidities, it seems, are gone for good — at least, if they are ever re-established, it will only be provisionally, and what good is a provisional solidity? So much of nineteenth-century drama was devoted to making the audience think that billowing canvas equals stormy ocean, billowing rhetoric equals seething passion. The painters too were committed to rendering textures and exact appearances — even when they waxed heretical, as in pre-Raphaelitism or Impressionism, it was in terms of a more real, more immediate conception of reality. The novels, the architecture, the politics, the morals, the very furniture of the age overwhelmingly took the solidity of their surfaces for granted. That it was rigorously necessary in some abstract logical sense to disintegrate all these solidities would be hard to demonstrate, and one sometimes has, in Ibsen or Flaubert, a sense of pitiful fragilities under fire of siege guns. Destruction was the Beatrice of other nineteenth-century authors besides Mallarmé. But the collapse of one ideology invited the testing of another — they all went down together, and now lie encumbering the earth like dismembered cathedrals. And even though the logic for destroying them was feeble, to reconstitute them after disintegration would be like reconstituting heroism, old-fashioned love, or a splintered bottle; no copy or reconstruction can be quite like the original.

One minor difficulty appears on the current horizon. Now

that void (in the sense, just at the moment, of the earth's outer atmosphere, but before long in the sense of interplanetary or even interstellar space) is being explored and inhabited, it too will surely appear commonplace before long. Even without help from the space-travelers, something like a point of satiety may have been reached in modern literature. After *Madame Bovary*, nineteenth-century novelists who felt obliged to introduce a sudden ghastly touch amid their sentimental amenities sometimes spoke of working on their "Hippolyte's leg." Voids are often introduced into modern novels, plays, or movies, just about as coolly as that. The non-impulse, the non-reaction, the unexplained non-performance is a standard property as ornament, episode, or structural principle. One can scarcely expect this device, any more than another, to remain untouched by the erosion of time.

Where does one go from the absolute? If it can be understood that I make no claim whatever to authority in the matter, perhaps it can be suggested that this question does not mean very much. Wherever one goes, the mark of where one has been is bound to be perceptible; and where one has been, imaginatively, is more a function of what one has been able to make experience mean than what experience one has had. Bigness is nothing — this we know from the history of the epic; far-outness is also nothing — this not everyone has yet learned. In effect, there are no new subjects. But there are ways of seeing old themes in individual ways, usually by compounding afresh some of the old ways. The art of modern life is the art of washing clean in dirty water: this is a reflection that goes far beyond literature, but in literature it has special potent applications. The notion of Nothing is pretty dirty water by now, but it can still be used — like a good many other tired topics when seen from a new direction or handled in a knowing way — to make clean the mind.

After living a long time in intimate contact with a pawky topic like Nothing — even though seen mostly at second hand, through literary stained glasses — one puts it down with a certain reluctance born of conscious insufficiency. The best intellectual pilgrimages are never the easy ones, and sometimes they are not even possible. To rise each day to an O *altitudo!* to fall, inevitably and lamentably, but to be sure always of the next day's climb, cold and steep and with no reward but the exhilaration, is an exercise beyond apology, as beyond real explanation.

Perhaps there never was any real domesticating of a wildness like void; maybe void simply stood still while the world went wild around it.

The strongest impulse to sound one void comes from bitter familiarity with another; to see that the sequence leads to no fixed term is to approach that security which doubts even the value of doubt, denies the value of denial.

If we ever see how we got here, we may know a little better where we are.

Ithaca-Firenze, 1964–65